questions of funding, publishing and distribution/
questions d'édition et de diffusion

HOLIC * HILAC

questions of funding, publishing and distribution/ questions d'édition et de diffusion

Edited by
I.S. MacLAREN and C. POTVIN

Proceedings of a Conference

Towards a History of the Literary Institution in Canada 2
Vers une histoire de l'institution littéraire au Canada 2

Organized by the Research Institute for Comparative Literature at
The University of Alberta
April 9-11, 1987

Research Institute for Comparative Literature

University of Alberta

1989

Published by
The Research Institute for Comparative Literature
University of Alberta
Edmonton, Alberta
Canada T6G 2E1

Copyright © 1989

Canadian Cataloguing in Publication Data
Main entry under title : Questions of funding, publishing and distribution = Questions d'édition et de diffusion
Proceedings of a conference held in Edmonton, Alberta, April 9-11, 1987.
Text in English and French.
ISBN 0-88864-868-5

1. Publishers and publishing - Canada - History - Congresses. 2. Authors and publishers - Canada - Congresses. 3. Literature and state - Canada - Congresses. 4. Literature publishing - Canada - Congresses. 5. Scholarly publishing - Canada - Congresses.
I. MacLaren, I. S., 1951 -   II. Potvin, Claudine, 1947 -   III. University of Alberta. Research Institute for Comparative Literature.   IV. Title: Questions d' édition et de diffusion.
V. Title: Towards a history of the literary institution in Canada 2.   VI. Title: Vers une histoire de l'institution littéraire au Canada 2.
Z483.Q48 1989   070.5'0971   C89-091524-5E

Données de catalogage avant publication (Canada)
Vedette principale au titre: Questions of funding, publishing and distribution = Questions d'édition et de diffusion
Comptes rendus d'une conférence tenue à Edmonton, Alberta, du 9-11 avril, 1987.
Textes en français et en anglais.
ISBN 0-88864-868-5

1. Édition - Canada - Histoire - Congrès. 2. Écrivains et éditeurs - Canada - Histoire - Congrès. 3. Littérature - Politique gouvernementale - Congrès. 4. Littérature - Édition - Canada - Congrès. 5. Édition savante - Canada - Congrès.
I. MacLaren, I. S., 1951 -   II. Potvin, Claudine, 1947 -   III. University of Alberta. Research Institute for Comparative Literature.   IV. Titre: Questions d'édition et de diffusion.   V. Titre: Towards a history of the literary institution in Canada 2.   VI. Titre: Vers une histoire de l'institution littéraire au Canada 2.
Z483.Q48 1989   070.5'0971   C89-091524-5F

Distribution:
The Research Institute for Comparative Literature
University of Alberta
Edmonton, Alberta
Canada T6G 2E1

Printed by Hignell Printing Limited

Acknowledgements

The papers collected here were presented at a conference held at the University of Alberta in April 1987, and organized by E. D. Blodgett, S. C. Neuman, and A. G. Purdy. The editors wish to thank these three colleagues for their extensive planning and realization of the conference. They extend their thanks as well to the university's departments of Romance Languages, Comparative Literature, and English, to Milan Dimic of the Research Institute for Comparative Literature, and to Vice-Presidents Peter Meekison and the late Gordin Kaplan. Funding for the conference was gratefully received from the University of Alberta Conference Fund and the Social Sciences and Humanities Research Council of Canada.

Thanks are hereby extended as well to Anne Dyck, the Research Institute's former Administrative and Editorial Assistant. The editors owe a special debt of gratitude to Fern Ness, Programmer/Analyst with University Computing Systems, for her tireless and cheerful dedication to the manuscript's preparation and typesetting.

Table of Contents/Table des matières

Periodical Publishing/Périodiques et revues littéraires

Scholarly Publishing/L'édition savante

Afterword/Postface

**questions of funding, publishing and distribution/
questions d'édition et de diffusion**

I. S. MacLAREN

Introduction: Entering the Z Zone

It may safely be said that most scholars and critics of Canadian Literature go about their work, often for entire careers, without needing, or feeling the need of a familiarity with, their library's Z zone, where books about books are found. Perhaps some noble point of courtesy has relegated this subject, thought to be somehow para-literary by many of us, to the last section in the Library of Congress' system of classification. 'questions of funding, publishing and distribution/questions d'édition, et de diffusion,' the second conference of the Research Institute for Comparative Literature's History of the Literary Institution in Canada/Histoire de l'institution littéraire au Canada project, attempted, as it were, to query that habitual neglect. As its series of ten projected conferences aim to determine how best to structure and initiate a thorough study of, not the literature but, the literary institution in Canada, the colloquium brought together a diversity of authoritative researchers and spokespersons in order to confer on the numerous aspects of the process that brings words into print in this country; not so much the interpretation of words, then, as their contexts, patterns of subsidization, publication, marketing , and consumption, as well as the interactions of these contexts with social and political changes, both today and in former times, were examined. The programme effectively bridged the gap — at least it spanned it with several cables — between the production of literature and the literary study of it. This book places on view a selection of those papers, some of them only slightly resembling their original forms: post-paper and post-conference discussions were brisk and lively, raising valuable points of consideration for some while strenuously debating the ideas of others.

The essayists would not want it thought that they considered theirs exotic explorations into the Z zone: it is by no means uncharted territory. Indeed, George L. Parker's essay is rather more like a voice from the Z zone than a voyage into it, for his *The Beginnings of the Book Trade in Canada* (1985) and 'A History of a Canadian publishing house: a study of the relation between publishing and the profession of writing 1890-1940' (1978) stand beside James Lorimer's *Book Reading in English Canada* (1983), Maurice Lemire's edition, *l'Institution littér-aire* (1986), Jean–Pierre Chalifoux' *l'Édition au Québec, 1940–1950* (1973), Ig-nace Cau's *l'Édition au Québec de 1960 à 1977* (1981), Pomahac and Richeson's edition, *Publishing in Canada* (1972), H. Pearson Gundy's *Book Publishing and Publishers in Canada before 1900* (1965), and the *Symposium of Scholarly Com-munication* (1981) as forerunners in the exploration. But Frank Davey is not in-accurate in remarking in his paper that the critic of the literary institution is reduced to prospective rather than propositional comments given the dearth of empirical studies of publishing in Canada. Many of the participants echo Davey's remark.

For purists and idealists, this group of essays will seem little more than a drag-ging down of literature into the mire of non–art out of which it so resolutely strives to arise. Be that as it may, because the Research Institute for Compara-tive Literature has been persuaded that polysystemic study of the literary insti-tution in Canada will most clearly delineate the complexity of relations that obtain between a society and its literary productions,[1] the series of ten confer-ences aims to contextualize the areas of study in which literature — far from being a lonely alouette, singing to cheer its own soul — forms a part. 'What fac-tors did, do, or should impinge upon the making of literature?' is the question that each of the following essays raises and addresses in one way or another.

The first paper, André Vanasse's 'Échec référendaire, échec de l'édition: une hypothèse à vérifier,' represents the conference's opening session, on the book market. As he freely admits, Vanasse speculates on something that one cannot verify: the failure of the referendum in Québec had a negative effect on sales of books by Québecois in that province. The hypothesis cannot be proved, but it provides Vanasse with the occasion for discussing how a variety of factors conspired in the early 1980s to strike a devastating blow to the book market in Québec. The economic downturn/recession, the governmental decision to cur-tail its purchase of books for distribution abroad, the failure of teachers at all levels to update their curricula with works by new authors, and the school sys-tem's decision to teach French as much out of magazines and newspapers as out of novels and poems are all contributing factors, in Vanasse's view. Still, the fact remains that with the election of the Parti Québecois and the apparent simul-taneous reassurance that Québec's nationalism was fully enfranchised, all levels and spheres of Québec culture halted their growth and popularity. Vanasse shows from his survey of the book review pages of *le Devoir* that coverage of Québecois literature was at a high in 1970, never to be matched since. With the

---

1 See E. D. Blodgett, 'Afterword' in *problems of literary reception/problèmes de réception littéraire*, ed. by E. D. Blodgett and A. G. Purdy ([Edmonton]:Research Institute for Comparative Literature, University of Alberta, 1988), 168–176.

culmination of the Quiet Revolution, the literature of Québec, one can only conclude from the figures provided, began to experience neglect where it had enjoyed attention and authority as the voice of Québec culture and life.

Four historical perspectives of publishing follow the opening paper. All are surveys, some of broad, some of narrow areas of enquiry. Taking Feltes's study of the production of Victorian novels as a starting point, Frank Davey examines how the English-Canadian literary institution was caught in the mid-nineteenth century between two highly contrasting English-language publishing models: a British model, which preferred the 1000-copy expensive edition that sold mostly to private libraries, and an American model that emphasized the large, inexpensive edition distributed either through bookstores or by post. Davey extends this finding to analyse how English-Canadian authors of today remain in an essentially unchanged relation to publishers while writing for a relatively small, middle-class audience. Meanwhile, Canadian publishers tend themselves to be small, driven by and serving 'ideologically focussed discourse communities,' specializing in some cases even in particular genres of literature. Davey then canvasses the contemporary literary institution for other decisive factors, including the role of government agencies and of universities, the inclination of some authors to emulate the old model of series publication for the same restricted (although in Atwood's case, not small) audience, and so forth. His makes a comprehensive and provocative survey indeed, touching on questions that recur in later papers.

In a stage report of their on-going study of the literary institution in Québec between 1940 and 1960, Richard Giguère and Jacques Michon analyse, from the standpoint of the history of literary publishing in the province, how literature relates to coincidental social and historical events. In a sense, then, Vanasse's paper looks at a specific event — the referendum — along the lines that this team project, GRELQ (Groupe de recherche sur l'édition littéraire au Québec), argues for in an extended way. This is not literary history as we commonly know it in English-Canadian literary criticism, for the project aims to study the relation between a published text and the conditions of the market in which it makes its appearance.

The authors' findings include the fact that genres enjoy development at different times (poetry at times of crisis [1950-1959], on the eve of the Quiet Revolution, for example). So far Giguère and Michon have completed work on poetry in the period: 'Nous avons,' they report, 'constitué des dossiers et rédigé des monographies sur les éditeurs de poésie les plus importants de 1940 à 1960 (histoire, des maisons, catalogue de titres, réception critique, inventaire des archives accessibles et/ou enquête et interviews auprès des éditeurs encore vivants). . . .' This is enlightening for the researcher of English-Canadian literature for, whereas Davey accurately remarks on the infancy of such study of English-Canadian literature and publishing, the work of GRELQ has already achieved splendid results and knows how complex the study of literature in terms of publishing mechanisms can be. Their essay offers a blueprint, then, for procedures that, with slight modification to account for altered circumstances, might with profit be considered for adoption in the study of other periods of the French-language literary institution, and for the literary institution in English Canada. Their ideas of how best to attack general literature, apart from novels and poetry, as well as their appended bibliography of the project's work so far, help to bring into full view in English Canada the direction and results of their valuable work.

Sylvie Bernier, another researcher in Giguère and Michon's project, addresses a different facet of the literary institution that conventional literary history leaves aside. This is the physical properties of books, and the ways in which decisions about them reflect and anticipate the sector of the market for which they are intended. Two editions of *Maria Chapdelaine*, a Québec one, illustrated in black-and-white by Suzor-Coté, and a later, Parisian one, illustrated in colour by Clarence Gagnon, provide a specific study of how books' material qualities determine their readership. In the case of Hémon's novel, the artistic participation perhaps even produced the readership, for, as Bernier points out, Hémon and his work were still unknown when the edition with illustrations by Québec's most celebrated painter appeared. But Bernier goes on to note the different relations between illustration and text in a popular and in an intellectual book, further probing the question of how a book's materiality answers to and creates a readership. To ignore this aspect of literary production is to risk mere literary and, thus, literary-critical idealism. Bernier extends her examination through the first five decades of this century, and to genres as diverse as literature for adolescents and the publication collaborations of the avant-garde.

George L. Parker provides another key component in this collection. Dwelling on the nineteenth century, which Davey uses more as a pretext in his essay, Parker disprizes his reader of the notion that copyright law protected authors: despite its intentions, it all too frequently served to permit foreign entrepreneurs to dump foreign editions of foreign-authored works onto the Canadian market. Meanwhile, publication by a Canadian publisher provided a Canadian author with virtually no copyright control, Canada being a colony. Through the nineteenth century, Parker explains, the alternatives of colonial organization, of independence, and of compromise faced local publishers; entrepreneurial publishers, when they came into being (mainly only after 1880), faced the same alternatives. The responses to them extended to legal and illegal compromises which saw John Lovell, Belford Brothers, John Ross Robertson, and Hunter, Rose all legally selling pirated reprints in an effort to control and supply the Canadian market. In 1891, the elimination of the notion of piracy occurred with the Anglo-American Reciprocal Copyright Agreement; thereafter, Canadian publishers metamorphosed into agents for foreign publishing houses. At worst, these Canadian publishers were, by the turn of the century, reduced to wholesalers; at best to publishers with control over the works of Canadian authors. Never autonomous, argues Parker, the book trade remains just such a compromise today: Macmillan, Oxford, and McGraw-Hill, for example, publish Canadian books, but they can afford to only because they market foreign works from their parent houses. Meanwhile, Canadian publishers handle only Canadian books, and serve only regional interests, for the most part. Such a complex evolution makes English-Canadian publishing an intricate study, as yet far from completed or widely understood. Parker's valuable survey signals the difficulty even of pinpointing what is Canadian about the English-language literary institution in Canada, and, by extension, implies one possible advantage of studying the relatively more autonomous French-language literary institution.

The third session of the conference, whose concern shifted to the contemporary literary institutions, furnished three papers for the collection, representing national and provincial perspectives on the role of government in the funding of writing and book publishing, as well as views on the effects of government policies respecting the translation of books. Naïm Kattan, long a controlling force at the Canada Council, explains his understanding of a federal government's role as vital participant, not merely as arbiter or regulator, in the Arts. He argues, contentiously I think, that such an intensive role nevertheless can still exclude government from the stage at which art is created. Interestingly, as Kattan perceives it, Canada has but two cultures, which government must serve in the manner not only of a dispenser but also of a transmitter and a guardian. The brevity of Kattan's remarks will doubtless be variously interpreted by different readers.

Byrna Barclay provides points of view as a writer and as a member of the Saskatchewan Arts Board, which, created in 1948, was the first of its kind in North America. Barclay's analysis of the board's role does not significantly realign the tripartite function of the government agency that Kattan delineates, although she does advocate government involvement only from an arm's-length distance. Here is the nut of the problem: the literary institution is perceived as desirous of operating apart from, while it remains reliant on, government support. It must define its identity itself, but also continuously respond to the identity foisted on it, however unintentionally, by the implementation of government policy, however arm's-length. In short, it both must not and must know government intimately. This fact of subsidization makes such a paradox inevitable.

Ray Ellenwood begins his essay with just this recognition: that government 'interference' in the literary institution both disturbs it and sustains it. In the case of translations, government 'interference' tends to have the result that many works appear from small publishing houses, but their distribution is weak and their life in print short. Moreover, because a ten-cents-per-word granting formula is deployed, translators understandably shy away from lyric or minimal-ist poetry (and there isn't much epic poetry going around these days). Finally, the role of government extends even to the choice of which prose works are to be translated, in so far as government policy dictates that both the author being translated and the publisher be Canadian in order for the project to qualify for support. Ellenwood provides perhaps the most graphic study of the prominent role being played in the literary institutions by arm's-length government agen-cies. Nor does Ellenwood underestimate 'how difficult it can be to reconcile the perceived need of writers and writers' groups for government assistance, with their determination to be as independent as possible from government policy and indeed to influence it.'

The conference's fourth and fifth sessions turned to studies of specific sec-tors of publishing in the literary institution: periodicals and scholarly publish-ing. Ken Norris' essay argues for a clear distinction between a little magazine and a literary periodical; the latter represents the literary establishment or or-thodoxy while the former is experimental, having a heretical, subversive disposi-tion towards the establishment in the literary arts. Norris' point is that this distinction could once be made more clearly than it now can, for many of the magazines that began in opposition to the prevailing literary scene have evolved to a point where they represent it today, effectively ending the dissemination of an avant-garde aesthetic. (Could the same be said for a generation of small pub-lishing houses?) The government funding that sustains the periodical publish-ing industry effectively renders it, in Norris' view, a collective organ for the age's orthodoxies.

For her part as the editor of a literary periodical – of the establishment, Nor-ris would say – Constance Rooke depicts her avocation as necessarily a labour of love. Not only generating the funding of literary periodicals, but arranging payments to contributors, and acting as an intermediary between writers and book publishers impose duties on an editor which ineluctably detract from the attention that s/he can give to soliciting, evaluating, and improving manuscripts. Moreover, because it rarely provides an income, such a multi-faceted career must be worked around the demands of an occupation that does provide one. Her real concerns leave little time for consideration of Norris' ideological ones. Rooke goes on both to anatomize the toll taken of volunteer manpower and of talent by gross underfunding, and to decry failures by government agencies – ostensibly the dispenser, transmitter, and guardian, in Kattan's words – to be in any adequate sense responsive to the needs of literary periodicals.

A self-confessed newcomer on the block of journal editing, David Staines bemoans what he perceives as the lack in the English-Canadian literary institu-tions of objective criticism of literature. He vows to regain it in his own journal. Aligning himself with older critics in Canada, he esteems the Arnoldian model as the correct one for critics. That the literary institution in English Canada remains the poorer for not having followed Arnold, is self-evident for Staines in this polemic, which readers who have considered the preceding essays will want to contemplate. Certainly, to take one example, Canadian literature's extensive government involvement, a dimension that impinged in no way on Arnold's notion of the role of criticism, but a fact which Staines says that he encountered when determining the frequency of his journal's appearance, makes the adoption of the Arnoldian model anything but straightforward. Both Sherry Simon's and Lorraine Weir's essays suggest obliquely another reason why the Arnoldian model cannot be as universally embraced as Staines would wish.

Simon's essay traces the fitful ways in which feminism occupies a place in the periodical publications of the French-language literary institution. *That* feminism must find its place in the discourse, goes without saying for Simon, but *how* this occurs is problematical because the literary institution into which feminism seeks entry simultaneously defines, by its structure, what feminism is. Thus, the *politics* of periodical publication for a feminist occupy Simon extensively. Noting the demise of *La Vie en Rose*, she states that feminism has found a place only among other interests and ideologies, not a locale of its own. Militant reviews that harboured feminism on its own have not lasted long. For the most part, the periodicals of Québec have provided very little voice to feminism: it is almost non-existent in the university periodicals, *Voix et Images* providing odd exceptions; there is little at all, and that only in a diffused way, in the literary-political reviews; of the critical reviews, only *Spirale*, for which Simon serves as editor, has, since 1979, given feminist concerns and perspectives consistent and committed airing; and in the periodicals of creative literature it may be said that feminism *has* found fundamental expression. Among eight journals, two— *Herbes rouges* and *nbj*—have provided places for reflection and dialogue.

Because Simon can refer to other discussions of the relation between feminism and 'modernité'[2] in *Herbes rouges* and *nbj*, she proceeds to speak of *Spriale* and its liaison of literary critical feminism with broader feminist concerns. In particular, *Spirale* has evolved to a point where it not only sustains feminism's voice, but calls divergent aspects of its praxis into question, and extends it to consider generally such questions as the relation of language to power, and of marginalized discourse to authority. Still, *Spirale* is exceptional in this regard, and feminism remains paradoxical, central as a concern but diffuse and margi-

---

2   For readers unaccustomed to the use of this term in Québecois literature, it may be useful to note that it does not mean what Modernism means in English literature; Québecois writers of the seventies who were preoccupied with theories of writing, who worked against the grain of realism, and who were influenced by the latest literary-theoretical and psychoanalytical discussions, espoused what was called 'modernité.' At that time, but no longer, feminism and 'modernité' were virtually unquestioned as aligned ideologies and discourses.

nal as a published expression. Simon concludes by speculating on what the future may hold for any discourse if it does not find an acknowledged place within a literary institution's periodical publications. Can it survive in an unacknowledged place? If so, one cannot help but wonder how historians of the literary institution will take account of it.

Francess G. Halpenny's paper opens the discussion of scholarly publishing's place in the literary institution. She provides a valuable, thorough overview of scholarly publishing, and her profound knowledge of the book trade, amassed over the course of a distinguished career, also discovers what, in her opinion, remains to be done: 'Badly needed are histories and analyses, long or short, of individual publishing houses and of players in them (directors, editors, promotion planners, designers), of the authors they have presented and the lists they have developed.... we lack the careful exploration of what literary careers have meant in Canada that will take us beyond the sketchiness of interview, preface, and anecdote.' Halpenny also pleads for studies of the history of government involvement; the fact that this topic arises repeatedly in this volume suggests that the area of enquiry has been badly neglected. (Do we blench when it comes to dissecting the hand that feeds us?) As yet, the Z zone, Halpenny might be said to imply, is far too slim to house much more than the darkness of our collective ignorance.

Jacques Pelletier offers a report on a unique, grass roots project of scholarly publishing, *Cahiers d'études littéraires*, at l'université du Québec à Montréal. His essay explains how the administrative, technical, and editorial procedures of the series were designed, successfully, to avoid the economic problems encountered previously by larger university presses. Taking as its premise a social function rather than a business entity because the notions of a scholarly publication and profitability have virtually nothing in common, the group of researchers at l'UQAM struck on a plan to produce moderately-priced scholarly works, intended for classroom use as well as for research, in short periods of time (two months), authored only by members and graduate students of the university's Département d'études littéraries following their own pedagogical interests, and distributed by already existing university services.

The project has now achieved a level of professionalism without any government subsidies or the constrictions that their conditions impose. Not only in terms of many of the foregoing essays, but also in light of the ways in which such projects as, to name one, The Centre for the Editing of Early Canadian Texts, have depended upon massive government support, this information makes one pause. *Cahiers* does not lose money, staying marginally in the black after the first seven titles, which sell within the university and by mail to individuals and libraries across Canada and abroad for between $8 and $15. Bookstores are not used, thus precluding the problem of discounted sales. The success of this novel reshaping of scholarly publishing suggests alternative ways for this sector to relate to the rest of the literary institution. Now that *Cahiers* has found a firm base, it has enlarged; its eighth and ninth volumes have come from authors outside l'UQAM and as the series attracts attention, more 'outsider' manuscripts are being submitted and considered. Here is a healthy alternative to the sometimes unwieldy models of traditional university presses in Canada.

Canvassing the critical perspectives of the two editors – George Woodcock and W. H. New – who have set out the ideological conditions of production for *Canadian Literature*, Lorraine Weir concludes the conference's examination of scholarly publishing. It may be said, in terms of an earlier essay, that Weir examines in periodical literature one of the 'ideologically focussed discourse communities' that Davey considers typical of the Canadian publishing industry. Weir finds Woodcock's point of view in his editorials difficult to locate, rather to be inferred than distilled. What is clear is his salute to the values of the 'curious reader' whom *Canadian Literature* was initiated to serve. Weir maintains that although New presents himself differently, as an academic critic rather than as a widely-read common reader, his views can be readily aligned with Woodcock's, and so can his literary values. But, according to Weir, their views are not as innocent, self-evident, or universally shared as the two men think: 'the "complex heritage" studied in the pages of *Canadian Literature* since its inception has been, for the most part, the patriarchal heritage of Anglo-Canada with its subtle, gender-biased assumptions about "moral understanding, custom, ceremony" and other tag phrases of a group long enough in power that the lexicon of their own comfort and status seems innocent.' Weir proceeds to clarify through graphs the actual breakdown of the involvement of men and women in the journal and in the content studied in it. Her findings are provocative.

The papers of this collection work independently and collectively to shed some light on the dark corners of the Z zone. The volume poses a series of questions, but they are posed by informed researchers and participants in the literary institution. Some questions beg others, while some receive answers or at least direction towards possible answers. It is hoped that the reader will find the papers stimulating and new, and will be prompted to reconsider the 'para-literary' notion of these aspects of the literary institutions in Canada.

The University of Alberta

ANDRÉ VANASSE

Échec référendaire, échec de l'édition: une hypothèse à vérifier

Préambule

Ma communication se divisera en deux parties: une première consacrée à la vérification de l'hypothèse 'échec référendaire, échec de l'édition au Québec'; la deuxième tentera d'élaborer une deuxième hypothèse qui consiste à établir une corrélation entre le processus de légitimisation d'une littérature donnée (en l'occurrence la littérature québécoise) et le phénomène de démobilisation qui l'accompagne parfois.

On aura compris que ma première hypothèse s'est révélée plus ou moins vérifiée dans les faits. Voilà pourquoi j'ai ajouté à mon titre initial *une hypothèse à vérifer*.

* * *

Le titre de ma communication peut paraître provocateur voire un tantinet racoleur compte tenu que ce texte est d'abord destiné à un auditoire en grande partie canadien-anglais. À vrai dire, l'idée que l'échec référendaire ait pu avoir des effets négatifs sur le flux de la circulation des livres 'made in Québec' relève de la pure spéculation. Elle n'a jamais été vérifiée.

Cette hypothèse est d'autant plus fragile qu'on peut difficilement isoler l'événement politique (le référendum) du phénomène économique (la crise économique des années 80) qui l'accompagnait. Car au moment où se déroulait la campagne du référendum, les décisions de l'OPEP décrétant les hausses spectaculaires des prix du pétrole, jugulées en 1973, mais dont les effets furent catastrophiques lorsqu'elles furent promulguées à nouveau en 1978, secouaient effectivement l'économie mondiale. La crise allait, de fait, connaître le maximum de son amplitude en 1981-1982. Au point qu'on redouta pendant un certain temps que la machine ne craque. Les taux d'intérêt atteignirent alors des sommets jamais imaginés (22% au Canada) et d'aucuns, les plus pessimistes il va de soi, prédirent qu'ils continueraient encore de grimper. On vit, à cette époque, l'édifice trembler sur ses assises. La perspective d'un crash fut perçue comme imminente. On se réfugia dans l'or. On craignit l'éclatement du système économique mondial...

Au moment où se déroule le référendum en mai 1980, nous n'en sommes qu'aux signes annonciateurs d'une grave récession. Les plus prudents surveillent leur capital tandis que les plus optimistes augmentent inconsidérément leurs emprunts. Les premiers sortiront indemnes de la tourmente. Les autres y laisseront leur chemise.

C'est donc dans ces conditions assez confuses qu'a lieu le référendum. On connaît la réponse du peuple québécois: malgré une proportion suffisamment importante pour confirmer que la menace de séparation était sérieuse, les tenants du non, ceux qui voulaient demeurer dans la Confédération canadienne, l'emporteront dans une proportion de 55%. Pour les perdants, ce sera la fin d'un rêve, pour les gagnants, apparemment l'aube d'une ère nouvelle...

Le peuple s'étant prononcé, on assistera alors à une diminution d'intérêt pour les productions nationales. Dans ce contexte, la littérature québécoise sera durement touchée. Comme je l'ai dit, il est difficile de juger la situation avec objectivité compte tenu de l'interrelation entre l'événement politique et la crise économique. Chose certaine, pour la première fois depuis que les statistiques sur l'édition québécoise sont compilées, c'est-à-dire depuis la mise en vigueur du dépôt légal en 1968, l'édition littéraire québécoise accuse un fléchissement significatif de près de 15%. Ainsi si en 1981, il s'était publié 791 titres littéraires, il ne s'en publiera que 681 en 1982[1]. La chute s'accentuera en 1983, le nombre de titres produits tombant à 601 (-24%) pour remonter légèrement en 1984 à 701 titres (+ 14% par rapport à l'année 83, mais -11,5% par rapport à 1981[2]).

---

1 Sources: Pierre Allard, *Statistiques de l'édition au Québec en 1982*, Montréal, Bibliothèque nationale du Québec, ministère des Affaires culturelles, 1983, 15.
2 Sources: Claude Fournier, *Statistiques de l'édition au Québec en 1984*, Montréal, Bibliothèque nationale du Québec, ministère des Affaires culturelles, 1985, 15.

Nous ne disposons malheureusement pas de statistiques concernant les tirages moyens des titres littéraires. Seules les statistiques pour l'ensemble de l'édition sont disponibles. Or là encore, les résultats sont significatifs: pour la première fois depuis 1968 (à l'exception de l'année 1975, année où les statistiques ne sont pas fiables[3]) les tirages toutes catégories diminuent, en 1982, au-dessous du seuil des 3,000 exemplaires. De 3,353 qu'ils étaient en 1981, ils tombent à 2,733 en 1982, à 2,732 en 1983 et à 2,746 en 1984.

Faute de statistiques spécifiques sur la littérature, j'ai cru nécessaire de consulter quelques éditeurs. Ces derniers sont catégoriques: la chute des tirages a été encore plus brutale pour ce qui concerne le secteur littéraire. Les tirages qui oscillaient autour des 3,000 exemplaires en 70 tombent à 1,200 en 1986. C'est le cas pour la maison VLB (où j'ai enquêté en 1984), chez HMH où j'ai travaillé jusqu'à tout récemment comme directeur de la collection 'Littérature' (les Cahiers du Québec/HMH) et chez Québec/Amérique où j'agis actuellement comme directeur littéraire de la collection 'Littérature d'Amérique'.

L'écart est tellement important que les anciens, c'est-à-dire les romanciers qui ont publié au cours de la décennie soixante-dix, sont quasi incrédules quand je leur dis qu'ils ne pourront quère vendre plus de huit cents exemplaires de leur dernier-né. Ils sont d'autant plus sceptiques qu'ils ne peuvent concevoir que, ayant acquis du métier, ils vendent moins d'exemplaires qu'au début de leur carrière. C'est pourtant la pure vérité. Hélène Rioux, pour ne nommer qu'elle, avec *Yes Monsieur* (La Presse, 1973) et *Un sens à ma vie* (La Presse, 1975) avait, dans les deux cas, vendu près de 4,000 exemplaires de ses récits. Mais les ventes d'*Une histoire gitane* (Québec/Amérique, 1982) publié en 1982 n'ont même pas dépassé les 300 exemplaires. Faut-il, dans son cas, redouter le même sort pour *L'Homme de Hong Kong* (Q/A, 1986), son dernier recueil de nouvelles d'une qualité bien supérieure à ses productions antérieures? Je crains bien que oui.

La cas d'Hélène Rioux n'est pas unique. J'aurais pu citer beaucoup d'autres noms. Celui d'André Major par exemple qui a vendu des dizaines de milliers d'exemplaires de son *Cabochon* (Parti pris, 1964) et qui, pourtant, n'a pas réussi à écouler plus de 1,500 exemplaires de son recueil de nouvelles *La Folle d'Elvis* (Q/A, 1981).

Ces chiffres sont si déprimants qu'on hésite à les croire. Pour m'assurer de leur authenticité, j'ai fait sortir la feuille de droits d'auteurs remis aux auteurs

---

3　Voir au sujet des baisses des années 75 et 80, les remarques explicatives (feu et problèmes de l'Éditeur officiel avec le gouvernement) dans: Pierre Allard, Pierre Lépine, Louise Tessier, *Statistiques de l'édition au Québec, 1968-1982*, Montréal, Bibliothèque nationale du Québec, ministère des Affaires culturelles, 1984, 12.

de Québec/Amérique. À cause de difficultés techniques (Québec/Amérique vient de déménager), je n'ai pu obtenir la liste complète des oeuvres littéraires publiées par la maison. Ainsi sur un total de 55 oeuvres répertoriées en date du ler mai 1986, je n'ai pu obtenir que les chiffres de 35 d'entre elles. Ceci étant dit, le pourcentage (63.5%) des oeuvres compilées me paraît suffisamment élevé pour me laisser croire que les moyennes obtenues ne pourraient être modifiées de façon significative même si je disposais de l'ensemble des dossiers.

Pour éviter toute confusion ou biaisement des chiffres,

1. j'ai éliminé tous les auteurs qui ne sont pas québécois, mais qui figurent dans la liste des 'littéraires' (Jack Kerouac, Joyce Carol Oates, Marilú Mallet, etc.);

2. j'ai aussi éliminé les auteurs qui, à cause de leur chiffre de vente exceptionnel, auraient modifié totalement la moyenne et l'auraient rendue quasi absurde à cause de l'incommensurable écart qui les sépare des autres auteurs. Ce sont: Yves Beauchemin qui, avec *Le Matou*, a vendu plus d' un million d'exemplaires en diverses langues dont 105,000 chez Québec/Amérique et Pierre Billon qui a vendu chez Québec/Amérique 58,068 exemplaires de *L'Enfant du cinquième nord*.

3. Ces critères étant connus, il faut signaler que les oeuvres retenues pour fins de compilation ont été produites à la fois par des auteurs chevronnés et éminemment connus, comme par exemple Gérard Bessette, Gilbert LaRocque, André Major, Jacques Poulin, Madeleine Quellette-Michalska, etc. et des auteurs qui le sont moins comme Marc Gendron, Pierre Goulet, Agnès Guitard, etc. Chose certaine la liste me paraît suffisamment variée pour être considérée comme un échantillonnage satisfaisant.

Les résultats obtenus sont les suivants:

Les 35 oeuvres indexées totalisent 37,037 livres écoulés. Cela signifie des ventes moyennes par oeuvre de 1,058 exemplaires. Ce chiffre, il faut bien le dire, ne me paraît pas indicatif à cause des trois ou quatre best-sellers qui en augmentent indûment la moyenne (*Volkswagen blues* de Jacques Poulin s'est vendu à 8,273 exemplaires; il équivaut, par rapport à la moyenne obtenue, à l'équivalent 8 oeuvres!) Ainsi en retranchant les trois oeuvres les plus vendues et les trois oeuvres les moins vendues, la moyenne chute brutalement à 770 exemplaires [4] au lieu de 1,058. Cette moyenne reflète, me semble-t-il, beaucoup mieux la situation réelle des ventes du livre 'littéraire' pour la période concernée.

Si nous pouvions disposer d'un échantillonnage semblable pour ce qui concerne la période des années 70, ce serait le rêve. Malheureusement, à cause

---

4   C'est-à-dire: 37,037 - (520) + (-14,169) divisé par 29 = 770 ex.

des multiples changements de direction et des faillites qui ont frappé en série les maisons d'édition, il est extrêmement difficile d'obtenir des chiffres précis pour cette période. À titre d'information, signalons que les Éditions du jour, les éditions de l'Aurore, les éditions Leméac, les éditions La Presse, VLB éditeur, Quinze éditeur, HMH ont soit fait faillite soit changé de bureau de direction au cours des quinze dernières années. Ainsi, faute de temps — mais aussi, je dois l'admettre de patience — je n'ai pu aller aux sources et compiler les chiffres de vente pour les années 70.

Pourtant, si je me fie aux ex-directeurs littéraires, les Victor Lévy Beaulieu, Pierre Turgeon et Yves Dubé, les ventes étaient autrement plus élevées qu'elles ne le sont actuellement. Tous parlent d'âge d'or pour cette période. De fait, on était assuré, en autant que le contenu était valable, d'un bassin constant (quoique variable) de 1,000 lecteurs. Ces inconditionnels de la littérature québécoise (ils faisaient partie du noyau dur des 50,000 Québécois considérés comme de forts lecteurs) achetaient massivement 'québécois' et jouaient à la fois un rôle de supporteurs financiers et de défenseurs de la littérature québécoise.

Mais comment expliquer un écart aussi grand en l'espace d'une quinzaine d'années. On peut avancer quelques explications. Il faut, dans un premier temps, noter que la production du roman québécois n'a pas cessé d'augmenter au cours des ans. Dans un article publié ailleurs, j'écrivais: 'En 1961, il s'était publié 21 romans et 14 recueils de poésie. En 1970, les chiffres sont multipliés par trois (et même plus): 68 romans (dont 14 rééditions) et 51 recueils de poésie. Évidemment, nous sommes loin des 180 romans (dont 52 rééditions) et des 74 recueils publiés en 1980.'[5] Ainsi, le nombre des romans publiés actuellement est dix fois plus élevé qu'il ne l'était en 1960. En soi, cela ne serait pas si grave (comme toute entreprise, l'industrie du livre progresse en fonction de la croissance économique) si le bassin de lecteurs avait suivi le même rythme. Ce n'est malheureusement pas le cas (comme nous le verrons plus loin à propos des jeunes et de la lecture) avec le résultat que le nombre des lecteurs n'a à peu près pas augmenté au cours des vingt dernières années. Les livres ont eu de moins en moins de preneurs.

À cette stagnation des lecteurs potentiels, s'ajoutent les coupures budgétaires décrétées par le gouvernement au cours de la période 1980-1986. Celles-ci se sont faites cruellement sentir particulièrement dans les budgets consentis

5   André Vanasse, 'D'emblée la rupture,' *Écrits du Canada français*, no 52, 1984, 100.

aux bibliothèques (de même qu'à la culture en général[6]).Ces coupures étaient d'autant moins souhaitables que les 111 bibliothèques publiques réparties à travers le Québec recevaient déjà des subventions nettement inférieures à celles consenties aux bibliothèques de l'Ontario: 5,51 $ par habitant au Québec contre 14,79$ par habitant en Ontario.[7] Ainsi les bibliothèques québécoises n'avaient d'autre choix, faute d'argent, que d'alimenter leurs tablettes des derniers best-sellers français ou américains (en traduction bien sûr) au détriment des livres québécois.

Il faut en outre signaler que c'est à partir du début des années 80 que les gouvernements fédéral et provincial (je parle pour le Québec) ont diminué puis cessé leurs achats de livres en vrac destinés à être distribués dans les ambassades, dans les bibliothèques éloignées des centres urbains ou dans les centres d'études canadiennes et québécoises situées à l'extérieur du pays. Dans certains cas, cela pouvait signifier pour un seul roman des achats s'élevant à mille exemplaires. L'interruption de cette politique généreuse s'est traduite par une diminituon des ventes qui a eu pour effet de mettre en danger la bonne santé financière de certaines maisons d'édition.

D'autre part, ces mêmes coupures ont eu des effets catastrophiques sur les budgets de l'éducation. Si tous les niveaux ont été touchés, les niveaux supérieurs (collégial et universitaire), où devraient se recruter les lecteurs potentiels de la littérature, ont été encore plus affectés.

Ainsi, les coupures budgétaires ont obligé les écoles à diminuer leurs achats scolaires. Par ailleurs, on ne pouvait obliger les étudiants à acheter des livres dont les prix ne cessaient d'augmenter. En outre on n'a pas su trouver une solution de rechange aux récriminations des étudiants qui se disaient 'écoeurés' de toujours lire les mêmes livres.

Car, par manque d'imagination ou d'intérêt réel, le fort contingent de professeurs formés au cours des années 60 et 70 n'a pas su renouveler sa banque de lectures. Au menu donc, toujours les mêmes noms et les mêmes oeuvres de la même période: Anne Hébert, Yves Thériault , Marie-Claire Blais, Jacques Godbout...

---

6   Le cri d'alarme à propos de la diminution des budgets consacrés aux arts (en dollars constants) était lancé dès le début de la décennie (voir à ce sujet le 23e rapport annuel du Conseil des Arts du Canada pour l'année 1979-1980 dans lequel le président Mavor Moore s'inquiète de la stagnation du budget qui lui est consenti au point, dit-il, qu'il a fallu 'hypothéquer notre avenir' Depuis lors, les artistes et écrivains, autant du Québec que d'ailleurs, n'ont pas cessé de réclamer 'leur juste part').

7   Il y en a 514 en Ontario! Le Québec, de ce point de vue, est nettement en retard sur l'Ontario. Voir, pour plus de détails à ce sujet, l'article de Maurice Lemire, *op. cit.*, 35-36.

Ainsi par démission devant une population étudiante de plus en plus hostile aux auteurs québécois, les professeurs décidèrent-ils de modifier leurs programmes jusque-là axés sur l'enseignement de la littérature québécoise, pour les repenser plutôt en fonction du 'savoir parler'. Mais l'insistance accordée à la maîtrise de la parole devait avoir des conséquences néfastes sur la lecture. Car en plus de diminuer le temps imparti à la lecture obligatoire, on avait jugé préférable de favoriser, en utilisant les journaux du matin, une lecture de la quotidienneté. En clair, cela a signifié qu'aux niveaux secondaire et collégial, il y a eu désertion de la fréquentation du livre québécois au profit de nouvelles méthodes qui ont donné les résultats que l'on sait: les Québécois, lors d'un concours réunissant les élèves de la francophonie occidentale (France, Suisse, Belgique, Luxembourg) qui fut diffusé dans *la Presse*, se sont classés bon derniers à peu près dans toutes les matières et particulièrement dans celle de la maîtrise du français. On peut toujours se consoler en considérant que les élèves américains n'ont pas fait mieux dans des conditions similaires (ce qui a fait bondir le président des USA), mais ce ne serait là qu'une mince consolation. À vrai dire, la situation est assez alarmante pour que le gouvernement du Québec s'en inquiète et propose des mesures susceptibles de la corriger. Le ministre de l'Education, Claude Ryan, a décidé d'accorder toute priorité à la maîtrise du français en favorisant, dans un premier temps, le recyclage des professeurs! La situation est un peu absurde si l'on songe que ce sont les membres de la génération des 35-44 ans qui détiennent le plus haut taux de lecture (27% disent qu'ils lisent très souvent[8])alors que les étudiants eux ne lisent à peu près pas (14% qui disent lire très souvent contre 60,4% en France!)

Il y a a donc un énorme travail de rattrapage à faire. À preuve: si 44% des Français lisent 'souvent', seulement 21% des Québécois lisent très souvent[9]. L'écart va du simple au double. Et s'il nous prenait l'envie d'accuser les Français d'être des incorrigibles intellectuels, nous n'aurions qu'à nous retourner vers le Canada pour baisser pavillon: l'enquête menée par le Secrétariat d'État en 1978 sur les habitudes de lecture des Canadiens a révélé que 'ce sont les Québécois qui ont consacré le moins d'heures à la lecture dans la semaine ayant précédé l'enquête, soit 2,3 heures comparativement aux Colombiens britanniques qui se classent au sommet avec 4 heures.'[10]

Mais nous nous éloignons de la question nationale.

---

8 cf. Maurice Lemire, 'L'écrivain et son public lecteur, *Les Pratiques culturelles des Québécois Une autre image de nous-mêmes*, sous la direction de Jean-Paul Baillargeon, Québec, Institut québécois de recherche sur la culture, Québec, 1986, 37.

9 *Ibid*, 37 (chiffres tirés de l'enquête menée en vue de la 'Rencontre franco-québécoise sur la culture' tenue en 1984).

10 *Ibid*, 34.

En fait, les commentaires qui précèdent avaient pour but de dresser un tableau de la situation du livre au Québec, tableau qui tiendrait compte à la fois des conditions politiques et économiques de la situation du Québec au cours de la dernière décennie. Ces réflexions laissent entendre, du moins je l'espère, qu'il était peut-être présomptueux d'établir une corrélation entre le référendum et la baisse d'intérêt pour notre littérature nationale. Ayant proposé ce titre dans le cadre de ce colloque, je n'avais d'autre choix que de le vérifier. À la réflexion, je crois que le référendum représente plutôt la pointe du iceberg car ce qu'il faut plutôt constater c'est que, à partir des années 75-80, c'est-à-dire au moment de l'élection du parti québécois en 1976 jusqu'au référendum de 1980, s'amorce le déclin de l'engouement pour la littérature québécoise, lequel déclin culminera dans la période 80-85.

À ce titre, peut-être faut-il prendre au sérieux l'hypothèse du linguiste Jean-Claude Corbeil selon laquelle les législations dans le domaine culturel ont parfois pour effet de démobiliser les gens qui avaient pourtant fait front commun autour de l'une ou l'autre des questions culturelles. En promulguant la loi 101, le Parti québécois, selon Corbeil, aurait creusé sa propre tombe. Car rassurés sur la 'légitimité' de leur langue, les Québécois se seraient sentis dorénavant en sécurité et n'auraient plus vu l'utilité de se séparer du Canada.

On peut émettre une hypothèse analogue pour ce qui concerne la littérature: tant et aussi longtemps qu'elle ne s'est pas imposée comme littérature 'légitime', elle a bénéficié du support inconditionnel des nationalistes. Mais dès l'instant où on a été rassuré sur son existence future, on a commencé à la déserter.

Pour vérifier cette nouvelle hypothèse, j'ai fait une mini enquête dans *le Devoir*. N'étant pas un spécialiste des statistiques, j'ai procédé au mieux de ma connaissance en adoptant la méthode suivante:

1. j'ai selectionné des exemplaires du *Devoir* en pratiquant une coupe dans les années suivantes: 1970, 1976, 1980, 1986.

À noter que les années choisies correspondent à des périodes privilégiées soit: la crise d'octobre en 1970; l'élection du Parti québécois en 1976; le référendum en 1980; l'élection du Parti libéral en 1986.

2. pour éviter toute distorsion et malgré que les événements se soient déroulés soit antérieurement soit postérieurement, j'ai choisi d'indexer le mois d'octobre et lui seul pour toutes les années concernées. La raison? Le mois d'octobre correspond en gros à la rentrée d'automne. Il est donc très actif tant du côté français et étranger que du côté québécois.

3. dans mon travail de sélection, je n'ai retenu que les articles, et eux seuls, qui traitaient de la littérature. J'ai même exclu le théâtre puisque cette inclusion aurait désavantagé le théâtre français ou étranger qui peut difficilement faire l'objet d'un compte rendu (il est difficile d'inciter les lecteurs à aller voir une pièce jouée à Paris ou à New York!).

4. j'ai classé les articles en quatre catégories: littérature québécoise [Q], littérature canadienne [C], littérature française [F], littérature étrangère [É].

5. la place qu'occupe l'article dans la page a été indiquée en pourcentage selon les barèmes suivants: un sixième de page = 16%; un quart = 25%; un tiers = 33%; une demi-page = 50%.

Les résultats obtenus confirment de façon éclatante l'hypothèse selon laquelle la littérature québécoise occupait dans les années 70 une place privilégiée. De fait la compilation pour les quatre semaines du mois d'octobre donne les résultats suivants: 5,25 pages ont été consacrées à l'analyse de la littérature québécoise contre 1,27 page en littérature française, canadienne ou étrangère. Cela signifie que 77% des commentaires étaient consacrés à notre littérature nationale.

Ce chiffre de 5,25 pages ne sera plus jamais atteint par la suite. Le nombre de pages se situera plutôt entre 4,28 p. et 4,93 p. alors que les commentaires consacrés à la littérature française, canadienne ou étrangère augmenteront considérablement (de 1,27 en 70 à 4,98 p. en 1980 pour redescendre à 2,87 en 86).

Voici donc les résultats obtenus pour les années 1970, 1976, 1980 et 1986:

1970: 5,25 p. consacrées à la litt. québécoise contre 1,57 p. pour les autres littératures.

En proportion: 77% en litt. québécoise contre 33% pour les autres littératures.

1976: 4,28 p. consacrées à la litt. québécoise contre 4,61 pour les autres littératures.

En proportion: 48% en litt. québécoise contre 52% pour les autres littératures.

1980: 4,93 p. consacrées à la litt. québécoise contre 4,98 pour les autres littératures.

En proportion: 49,7% en litt. québécoise contre 50,3% pour les autres littératures.

1986: 4,45 p. consacrées à la litt. québécoise contre 2,87 pour les autres littératures.

En proportion: 61% en litt. québécoise contre 39% pour les autres littératures.

De ces résultats, on peut tirer un certain nombre de conclusions. D'abord que ce n'est pas tant la littérature québécoise qui diminue en importance dans les pages littéraires que les littératures étrangères qui occupent de plus en plus d'espace. La question qui peut se poser concerne précisément la 'visibilité' de l'une et de l'autre. Avant le remaniement récent du *Devoir* (sur lequel je reviendrai), la chronique 'Les lettres québécoises' était coiffée d'un titre égal en nombre de points à celui des 'Lettres allemandes'. Il y avait là une disproportion choquante puisqu'il est ridicule de considérer que la littérature allemande puisse avoir autant d'importance au Québec que la littérature québécoise. On peut faire le même type de réflexion pour ce qui concerne la première page du cahier culturel. Qu'une vedette étrangère y occupe tout l'espace, cela est tout à fait concevable. Mais que ce soit toujours le cas, cela ne paraît pas normal. Or durant le mois d'octobre 1980, ce sont les vedettes étrangères qui assiègent la première page trois semaines sur quatre.

La crédibilité d'un produit repose en grande partie sur sa visibilité. Coke l'a compris depuis longtemps. Il devrait en être de même pour la littérature québécoise. Plus on la voit, plus on devrait l'aimer, un peu à la manière de la saucisse Hygrade. Il y a donc un risque à la confiner à l'arrière -page. C'est en lui accordant la place d'honneur qu'on lui rendra son panache.

Tout ceci pour dire qu'on doit se féliciter d'une couverture de plus en plus internationale de la littérature en autant que cette couverture 'n'abrille' pas complètement la littérature québécoise. S'ouvrir au monde n'a jamais fait de tort à qui que ce soit. Se dévaloriser au profit des autres, oui.

Je suis donc pour une ouverture sur le monde mais une ouverture qui ne repousse pas notre littérature sur les tablettes poussiéreuses. Dans ce sens, je me félicite que *le Devoir* ait décidé de publier un cahier spécial consacré uniquement aux livres (il s'intitule: 'Des livres').

Car depuis quelques mois, on vient de découvrir que les industries culturelles occupent une place de premier choix dans l'économie du pays. 'La culture est plus importante que le sport' clamait récemment la ministre Lise Bacon[11]. En fait, elle reprenait à son compte les analyses faites par son ministère lequel en arrivait au constat suivant:

[...] selon les données fournies par la Conférence canadienne des arts [...] la contribution directe des industries culturelles au produit intérieur brut en 1980 était supérieure à 6,3 milliards de dollars, soit environ 2,4% du produit intérieur brut. Cela dépasse les industries du textile, du meuble, de la chimie et correspond à peu près à la contribution des mines, de la métallurgie, de l'électricité et de l'alimentation au produit intérieur brut. Si l'on y ajoute la contribution indirecte des industries de la culture, on y obtient un total de 16,8 milliards de dollars.[12]

11 '[...]au chapitre de la vente au détail, en 1985, les produits culturels ($616 millions) ont déclassé d'aussi vénérables industries que celle du meuble ($609 millions) ou celles du sport ($474 millions).' Lise Bacon *la Presse*, Montréal, Samedi, 3 janvier 1987, E10.
12 'De la propriété intellectuelle et du statut de l'artiste', *Bulletin d'information*, Vol. 5, no 3, Québec, ministère des Affaires culturelles (Service gouvernemental), 1986, 17-18.

Voilà pour les chiffres au Canada. Au Québec, ils sont à peu près du même ordre:

> L'importance des industries culturelles au Québec, peut, entre autres, être perçue par le volume de l'emploi, des salaires versés et des revenus. Le tableau 2 permet de constater, que les industries étudiées comprennent plus de 3,200 entreprises, procurent près de 50,000 emplois, versent plus d'un milliard en salaires et totalisent plus de 2 milliards de revenus. En 1984, cela représentait 2,3% du PIB québécois.[13]

Il ne tient qu'à nous de découper dans cet immense gâteau la part qui nous revient de droit... ou continuer à fermer les yeux et laisser les multinationales du livre envahir impunément notre territoire (quelle catastrophe s'il fallait que les accords sur le libre échange soient signés sans qu'une clause spéciale protège les industries culturelles!) et tuer à grands coups de best-sellers nos littératures nationales.

À nous de jouer...et de bien jouer!

Université du Québec à Montréal

---

13 cf. Jean-Guy Lacroix et Benoît Lévesque, 'Les industries culturelles, un enjeu vital', *Cahiers de recherche sociologique*, Vol. 4, no 2, Automne 1986, 149.

FRANK DAVEY

Writers and Publishing in English-Canada

My invitation to participate in this conference asked me to contribute to a panel on 'Mainstream Publishing'—a panel that now seems to have vanished from the programme. I wish it hadn't, not merely because I had initially expected to take part in it but because 'mainstream,' at least in a Canadian context, is a wonderfully problematical term, the problematics of which illuminate many of the persistent issues in Canadian publishing. Canada currently has no 'national' publishers, merely regional ones which serve various geographically, generically, or ideologically focussed discourse communities. One question, certainly, which 'mainstream' raises is 'mainstream where? mainstream within Canada or mainstream in world or multi-national terms?' Another is 'mainstream Canada?' — that is, can such a culturally diverse and decentralized country as Canada have a mainstream that is not merely the hegemony of one region — usually Ontario — over the others. Yet another is 'mainstream how?' — does 'mainstream' refer to ideological or cultural criteria, as my first two questions appear to assume, or perhaps to narrowly economic ones? That is, are 'mainstream' books understood to be culturally significant books or to be trade books?

A possible fourth question here is one that concerns covert meaning or privilege — 'mainstream' as opposed to 'by-channel.' The use of 'mainstream' invokes or constructs a number of dialectical pairs: major and minor, professional and amateur, commercial and non-commercial, big press and small press, centre and margin, cultural industries and literary presses. These pairs have much to tell us about the politics of Canadian publishing, even about the dialectics of Canadian publishing, although little about its day-to-day practice. 'Mainstream' here is an assertion of importance, an attribution of value, a claim made in the course of ongoing ideological conflict. My activity is mainstream, as Ronald Sutherland (*passim*) has argued; yours is backwater.

If this were indeed a session on 'mainstream publishing,' my paper would have focussed on the 'mainstream' claims of the trade book, on the impact of such claims over the last two centuries on what kinds of English-Canadian texts have been produced, and on what presently constitutes an English-Canadian trade title. The two things that would have most interested me are how various ideological issues (mostly disguised as 'cultural') presently conflict in the Canadian trade-book market, and how various English-Canadian writers and publishers have struggled in the nineteenth and twentieth centuries to possess the illusion of being 'mainstream'—struggled while usually assuming 'mainstream' to be marked by 'trade' success. Now perhaps I have a paper in search of a session.

However, instead of examining the implications of 'mainstream,' I propose today to look at the history of English-Canadian publishing, and to do this partly in terms recently developed by Norman Feltes in his book *Modes of Production of Victorian Novels*. Feltes argues that in the nineteenth-century British book publishing moved from the 'petty-commodity' production mode to the much more efficient one of 'capitalist production'—a change that took publishing from the production and marketing of *books* to the production and marketing of *texts*. Feltes observes that the new mode was marked by some of the classical features of the capitalist organization of production: (1) the separation of production into distinct and progressive stages, so that publishers, who had previously been printers, publishers, and booksellers, eventually became publishers who contract the printing of their books and wholesale their books to independent booksellers; (2) series production, as in Victorian part-publishing, serial publishing, or in book series or genre-novels; and (3) the commoditization of labour, so that writers who had previously produced text-objects to be sold become workers whose labour can be alienated by contract for the creation of texts of a size and character specified by the publisher. This second change was valorized by the invention of the concept of a 'professional' writer who contributes to what some might call 'mainstream' book production, but whose 'professionalism' in actuality lies in being willing to write to the specifications of others (Feltes [41] notes that the first use of 'professional' as the antonym of 'amateur' is recorded by the *OED* as occurring in 1805).

In Britain this transformation was marked, Feltes argues, by the 1852 struggle for control of pricing between the Booksellers' Association (a conservative association of booksellers and publishers) and various independent price-cutting booksellers, by the growing practice after Dickens's *Pickwick Papers* of the first publication of fiction being by serial rather than book, and by the controversy over 'cheap books,' which saw by the end of the century the replacement of the limited edition leather-bound 31-shilling triple-decker (the standard vehicle for Victorian fiction which was marketed primarily to lending libraries like Mudie's) with the cloth-bound single-volume edition marketed through bookstores to the general public. We might add that in ideological terms this transformation was from an indulgence of excess and eccentricity in the restricted eighteenth- and early nineteenth-century book markets to a privileging of efficiencies both of signification and of text production.

Although Feltes deals only with the nineteenth-century British book trade, his approach to it, particularly his insistence, taken from Terry Eagleton (xii), that the material conditions of a text's production leave their marks within the text itself, can be quite helpful in the interpreting and understanding of the development of the English-Canadian book trade. This trade began in the nineteenth century, situated almost midway between the conditions Feltes describes and a quite differently constructed U.S. book industry. To some extent the U.S. industry in the nineteenth century was the inverse of the British, concerned more to protect its home market than to exploit it, more interested in adopting the 'capitalist' production forms required by the technology of long press-runs than in resisting it. The separation between printer, publisher and bookseller became evident in Boston in the second half of the seventeenth century, and became dominant by the second quarter of the nineteenth. Private lending libraries played a much lesser role in determining the market and press-run of books; at the middle of the nineteenth century, Lawrence Wroth and Rollo Silver report, 'novels were sold in editions of thirty, forty and fifty thousand' (Lehmann-Haupt, 124). Serialization of new fiction in weekly papers resulted in 1841 in complete novels being printed and distributed as newspaper supplements and priced as low as twenty-five cents. When powerful publishers such as Harpers contested this market with inexpensive editions of their own, the concept of cheap books in large press runs became firmly established (130). Until the passage of the Chace act in 1891 a large and profitable component of U.S. publishing consisted of pirated single-volume editions, often in 'cheap' formats, of recently published British titles.

English-Canadian writers and publishers in the mid-nineteenth century were thus positioned between two highly contrasting English-language publishing models, a British model which preferred the 1000-copy expensive edition, which sold mostly to private libraries, and a U.S. model that emphasized the large inexpensive edition distributed either through bookstores or by post. Aided by copyright acts (in Britain notably the statute '8 Anne, Chapter 19,' 1710, and its 1842 revision; in the U.S. the 1790 'Act for the encouragement of learning') that paradoxically gave authors the illusion of being autonomous subjects while allowing their labour-power to be sold and re-sold, publishers in both countries were rapidly 'professionalizing' their writers, the British often as producers of fictional texts of a length and continuity suitable for publication as the triple-decker novel preferred by the libraries, and the Americans as writers of the short fiction and serial fiction preferred by the weeklies or as writers of popular book series, among the best examples of which are Cooper's Leather-stocking novels and the five romances with which Melville began his career.

English-Canadian writing and publishing was also positioned throughout the nineteenth and twentieth centuries in a marketplace dominated by books written in Britain and the United States. As H. Pearson Gundy remarked to the 1971 Ontario Royal Commission on Book Publishing, 'Canada is unique in attempting to provide readers with all the books in the English language. Our bookstores carry more American titles than do British bookstores, and more British titles than are found in the average American bookstore' (*Background Papers*, 32). Some of the material causes of these contrasts have been the long period of protectionism in the U.S. book industry (the *New York Times Book Review* still has a policy of reviewing only books that have a U.S. imprimatur), the failure of nineteenth-century Canadian protectionist measures in the face of British copyright legislation, the much lower unit cost of book production in the American and British markets, and the still unexamined assumption that books should be distributed in Canada by freemarket bookstores rather than (as are the things Canadian society truly values — telephone service, railways, highways, postal service, electricity, natural gas) by publicly owned or regulated utilities. The result has been that, unlike in other countries where national publishers operate on a similar scale to that of the countries' bookstores, and supply roughly 90% of the titles stocked by those stores, in English Canada national publishers have usually had access to only 20% or less of bookstores' sales. In order to operate at a similar scale to that of the Canadian bookmarket, and to expand their 'participation' in English-Canadian book sales to more than 20%, Canadian publishers over the years have had two strategies. One has been to attempt to become manufacturers of the American and British titles that occupy most Canadian bookstores' space. This was the strategy of publishers like John Lovell and George Rose in the 1850s and 60s. This strategy, when frustrated by the reluctance of British publishers to jeopardize their potential U.S. market by licensing Canadian publishers to produce Canadian editions, and by the importation from the U.S. of inexpensive pirate-editions of British books on payment of the 12 $\frac{1}{2}$% duty allowed by the Foreign Reprints Act of 1847, led to the 1872 Canada Copyright Act, 'which licenced the Canadian printer to produce a foreign copyright work not registered in Canada' (Parker, 173). This act resembles recent ones that license Canadian pharmaceutical companies to produce patented drugs. The 1872 act was quickly disallowed by the Colonial Office, at which point Lovell ingeniously established a printing plant just south of the Canadian border to produce his own pirate-editions of British books for legal import under the Foreign Reprints Act. After Britain ratified the Berne Copyright Convention in 1885, lobbying by Canadian publishers resulted in the 1889 'Act to Amend "The Copyright Act",' which granted copyright protection in Canada only to work 'printed and published and produced in

Canada, or reprinted and republished and reproduced in Canada, within one month after publication or production elsewhere. . .' (qtd. in Parker, 221). This act (although its insistence on local manufacture was roughly the same as that of the U.S. Copyright Law of 1890) was also disallowed by the Colonial Office, but defiantly re-passed by Parliament in 1890, 1891 and 1895.

The other strategy attempted by English-Canadian publishers to participate in the British and American share of the Canadian bookstore market has been agency publishing, a strategy which became the main one after the failure to obtain the manufacturing clause. With this strategy the Canadian publisher attempts to become the exclusive source in Canada for the books published by a number of foreign presses, and in some cases to use the profits from agency sales to finance original publications. Despite significant 'buying around' by libraries and some bookstores, this was the standard publishing strategy in English Canada in the first half of this century, and despite some indications in the early 1960s that this situation might change, recent increases in the numbers of branch-plant publishers suggest that it may be dominant for a while longer — most likely for as long as bookselling is allowed to remain exclusively in the free-market.

While the interests of booksellers historically have been to have access to the cheapest editions of the most publicized titles — invariably those of the British and American presses — and the interests of trade publishers have been to find ways to participate in the distribution of such titles, the interests of English-Canadian authors have undergone significant changes. One thing which is clear in the nineteenth-century is that the writers who succeeded in inscribing themselves quickly into the canon of English-Canadian literature, and who succeeded in obtaining some earnings from their writing — Haliburton, Parker, Leprohon, Moodie, Traill, Roberts, Carman, Lampman — were mostly ones who succeeded in obtaining British or U.S. publishers. (Not surprisingly, writers with such publishers lobbied against the licensing and manufacturing clauses and favoured unrestricted importation of British and U.S. books.) The nineteenth-century writers who had the most severe disappointments in obtaining both financial and critical recognition — Richardson, Kirby and Crawford — were writers who relied on Canadian publishers. One factor here was copyright: under the British copyright acts of 1846 and 1890, works first published in Britain enjoyed protection throughout the empire, but work first published in the colonies was protected only in that colony. But a larger factor was the credibility constructed for the foreign publishing house by its access to the larger markets. One of the ideological assumptions of the emerging capitalist mode of production was that the quantity produced correlated with the 'success' of the product. So that for the nineteenth-century writer the number of books published and number of copies sold were important indicators; in 1894 Lampman reflects this quantitative view when he writes of Sara Jeannette Duncan, 'Her success has been phenomenal, and her name meets the eye in almost every newspaper' (qtd. in Fowler, 216). Only the British or American markets could provide the scale necessary for such success; only British or American publishers had the resources to undertake the sort of consecutive publication of one author's books (Duncan averaged a book a year between 1891 and 1914; Susanna Moodie published 6 novels between 1852 and 1856; Gilbert Parker published 22 between 1892 and 1902 [cf. Watters]) that 'success' required.

Most Canadian authors who published with British and American publishers in the nineteenth and early twentieth centuries were influenced by the growing emphasis on serial publication, and by the way serial publication creates an audience for itself as its sections unfold. Such writing, however, also creates, to a large extent, its own future as well as its own audience, establishing a range of character and setting, and a kind of action. It is perhaps notable that the first 'success' of English-Canadian writing was Haliburton's *The Clockmaker* (1836), serialized in Howe's *The Novascotian*, and becoming itself the beginning of a series of Sam Slick books which recapitulated the serial form of the original newspaper presentation. It was also an ironic success, since the new capitalist mode of production of which both the newspaper and book series are examples, was part of the new Yankee ethos which Sam Slick praised and about which the Deacon expressed reservation. Moodie's successes in the early 1850s comprised a series of parlour romances. Many of Parker's 22 novels of the 1890s were North American historical romances or northern romances; Watters describes his *Romany of the North* (1896) as the 'Second Series of *An Adventurer of the North* [1895]. [Itself] Being a continuation of *Pierre and his People* [1892].' In the early twentieth century such series publications as Roberts's and Seton's animal stories, Ralph Connor's Christian northern adventure novels, Arthur Stringer's *The Prairie Child, The Prairie Mother, The Prairie Wife*, and Mazo de la Roche's *Jalna* novels continued to characterize the most 'successful' publications by English-Canadian writers who chose trade publication outside of Canada, now mainly by U.S. publishers.

Except for Westminster Press's publication of five of Connor's early novels and a few Stephen Leacock titles, Canadian literary books published by English-Canadian publishers in the nineteenth and early twentieth centuries were nearly all what Feltes terms 'petty commodity productions' rather than capitalist productions. That is, they were one-of-a-kind events, produced in small numbers at relatively high prices for a closely defined market. Unlike in the case of the capitalist mode, there is no participation by the publisher in determinations of what kind of text the author will produce, and no attempt to create a larger readership by serial presentation in less expensive formats. In the nineteenth century the market was often defined by educational orders, or by advance subscription; in the twentieth century it began to be defined, as it often is now, in terms of library standing orders and the order patterns of various booksellers.

The empirical study of twentieth-century English-Canadian publishing is extremely scant. Autobiographies by bookmen like John Gray and Lorne Pierce offer little detail about relations between author and publisher, or about publishing and marketing practices; the few biographies of twentieth-century authors often have had surprisingly little to say about how a book came to published, on what contractual terms, with what influence by the publisher, or about what sales ensued. So my comments that follow do not enjoy the factual ground I would wish, and should be regarded as prospective rather than propositional.

My first proposal is that the petty commodity mode remains the dominant form of literary publication in English Canada. Texts are written, even by experienced authors, with little conscious thought for the marketplace and with little input by publishers, whose staffs generally lack the manpower or talent to give such input. The audience inscribed in such texts, however, is a small, middle-class, educated one, and very often with a regional or specifically ideological character.

My second is that the distinction often assumed between English-Canadian trade publishers such as General Publishing or McClelland & Stewart and 'mall presses' such as Oberon or Talonbooks is simultaneously slight and substantial. Both groups are involved, at least in most of their publications of poetry and fiction, in petty-commodity production. The few available sales figures suggest that the 'average' fiction or poetry title is published in small press runs of relatively expensive paperbacks to pre-defined markets. Where the trade publishers differ from the small presses is in publishing a few authors, such as Farley Mowat or Pierre Berton, whose texts are produced according to the capitalist mode. A Berton text typically involves a specialization of labour early in its production, with researchers being employed to produce facts and anecdotes which Berton himself can process into the working text. It is written to an audience which has been progressively constructed by his earlier texts to be excited by Canadian history and nationalist issues. In recent English-Canadian fiction only Margaret Atwood has engaged successfully in this kind of audience creation, by publishing a series of novels with similar female narrators, nearly identical narrative voices, and similar uses of irony and symbolism. Each novel has inscribed a similar audience: female, white, North American, university educated, middle-class (i.e. the 'you' that the narrator could address, trust, and confide in); each has also 'educated' additional readers in how to read other Atwood novels. Matt Cohen is noteworthy here as a writer who consciously engages in both the petty-commodity modes (with books like *Too Bad Galahad*, *Peach Melba* and *In Search of Leonardo*) and the capitalist mode (with his series of Salem novels and recently with two Jewish history novels *The Spanish Doctor* and *Nadine*).

In poetry books, although the petty-commodity mode is general, a number of the most 'successful' poets are ones who have published a series of similar titles with McClelland and Stewart — Irving Layton, Al Purdy, and Leonard Cohen. Again we can see the marks of capitalist production on these texts — each one an extension rather than a departure from the last, each one potentially creating an audience for the others, each one decisively inscribed with the 'trade-marks' (some critics might say 'personality' or 'voice') of its author and thereby reaffirming the major capitalist myth of the unified and coherent subject, each text, in the case of Layton, participating in a regular rhythm of production. To the extent that such publication has been valorized in English-Canada as the mark of a canonical contemporary poet, and has become the goal of writers still restricted to small press publication, its effects can be seen in petty-commodity texts also. That is, in aspiring to become a successful 'McClelland & Stewart poet,' a writer tries to inscribe a distinctive and consistent subject position for herself within her texts — to develop a distinctive style, a continuity of theme and language from book to book, a visible 'personality,' all things which are market-creating and marketable within commercial publishing. Some examples of this are Pat Lane's dead animals, Susan Musgrave's recurrent lexis of witchcraft and death, Tom Wayman's persistence with the 'work' theme.

The capitalist device that occasionally appears in both trade and small press publishing in English-Canada is what Feltes terms 'branded goods'(83). In a sense this device is always present in series publication, since author and publisher create a monopoly on 'genuine' continuation, a monoply secured by the publisher through the option clause in the standard book contract. The name of a widely known author operates as a brand-name, offering the reader a text that is presumably producible by no other writer. In Canada a few small publishing houses have established themselves as quasi brand-names in specific genres — Oberon in the short story, Talonbooks in plays. In each case, although there is no genuine monopoly (short story collections and plays can be published by other publishers), the press's unchallenged concentration on the genre enables the press name to stand for genuine goods, and attribute 'credibility' or value to the particular texts published. Certainly, it is not unreasonable to propose that the policies of Oberon have encouraged the writing of short fiction in English-Canada, much like the CBC's broadcasting of short stories appears to have encouraged it in the 1940s and 50s. One might also propose, however, that Oberon has encouraged a particular kind of fiction — predominantly realistic, arranged in books that have a similarity of diction and syntax among the stories — that is marketable in the small towns and cities in which many Oberon authors live and which Oberon owner Michael Maclem visits in his summer cross-country sales trips.

My third proposal is that the market I have attempted to represent above is anything but a stable one. In fact, the ideological conflicts within the English-Canadian book market have grown in severity over the last three decades; these conflicts have also been increasingly exacerbated by contradictions within industrial capitalism. The late capitalist economy of Western Europe and North America claims to embody ideologies of 'public demand' and obedience to 'free market forces,' but acts continuously through advertising and close control of design to construct additional markets and 'free' consumers for its products — thereby to increase the efficiency of their scale of production and extract surplus value from them. At times the society itself, perhaps spurred by a competing ideology, will intervene through its government, or through an agency like the Canada Council, to become a 'market force' within its own economy, preserving the myth of a 'free market' while acting to add value to military hardware, wheat, textiles, automobiles, petroleum or art, to make production of these more efficient and profitable than it would otherwise be. Many businesses in such a society must alternate between profiting because of the ostensibly 'market-driven' economy and profiting because of government intervention (although in reality both the government and to some extent the market forces are creations of the society, which can, theoretically at least, construe itself and its economy as it wishes).

In English-Canadian publishing today this paradoxical construction of the market causes small presses like Talonbooks and Coach House schizophrenic lives. The same federal government which through subsidy adds value to 'inefficient' short-press-run texts that, because of their plurality or excess of significations, resist easy consumption and commoditization will often tell publishers that they are 'cultural industries' and should seek whenever possible to produce long press-runs of easily consumed texts which embody utilitarian and representational ideologies and from which, through advertising, packaging, and close control of the writing and publication process, surplus-value can be extracted. The government that subsidizes writers and publishers expects their numerous short press-run books to be sold in unsubsidized bookstores which depend for their revenue on efficiencies that can best be achieved by large sales of a few titles. Writers who produce texts in 'inefficient' discourses that resist commoditization blame small presses for not successfully distributing them in commodity-oriented freemarket bookstores. The present ongoing transformation of NeWest Press and Coach House Press from small presses to trade publishers may tell a little bit of this story in some detail.

* * *

What I have been arguing here are that the material conditions of book production act as determinants of the kind of texts authors create, the kinds of publishers that can be available to consider them, and the kinds of text that these publishers will favour, and that these conditions leave their marks within the texts themselves. Too often literary criticism treats such matters psychologically or sentimentally, as if the writer has a simple choice between 'selling out' to commercial values and writing enduring texts, or as if 'great' writers have such a choice and lesser ones naively follow commercial fashion. The first kind of analysis has sometimes been applied to the contrast between Melville's *Moby Dick* and his popular romances or between Stead's *Grain* and his other fiction. The second, the idealization of genius, has been commonplace in the criticism of major figures, and only in the last few decades has received the kinds of antidotes Eagleton has offered in his materialist readings of George Eliot, Conrad, James, Lawrence and Joyce (*Criticism and Ideology*) or which Feltes suggests of Dickens's *Pickwick*. As Feltes argues, literary historians have been similarly negligent in implying that changes in audience and book production 'simply happen' or that they occur as responses to a changing audience or marketplace. Various economic interests in society which have no direct interest in literature or culture play major roles in determining what a society views its culture to be and what kind of cultural works its members produce, and in constructing the audience for these works. A cursory look at the cultural consequences in Canada of the policies of cable-TV operators and of private radio and TV broadcasters should convince us of this.

The policies of these and similar economic interests are ideologically grounded and leave ideological marks on the audiences they create and on most of the cultural acts produced within the society. (Changes are indeed also produced by individuals – but only when they attend to the contradictions among their own discourses, and by writers only when they attend – like Godfrey, Kroetsch, or Marlatt – to the potential for disjunction rather than for coherence within their texts.)

Before I conclude, however, I want to point to two other major determiners of contemporary English-Canadian literary texts – the Canada Council's 'block-grant' programme, and Canadian universities. Two policies of the Council in its 'block-grant' support to Canadian publishers have been of decisive consequence. One is its policy that titles that qualify under the program must meet the UNESCO definition of a 'book' – that is, be of at least 49 pages. This policy has effectively made it impossible for block grant recipients to publish books like George Bowering's pennant-shaped *Baseball* (Coach House 1972), my *King of Swords* (Talonbooks, 1972) or *The Clallam* (Talonbooks 1971), or Livesay's *Plainsongs* (Fiddlehead 1971) or required them to supplement such texts with additional poems (as in various editions of Kroetsch's Seed Catalogue) or with artwork. The chapbook has thus in the last decade become a medium for beginning writers and for unsubsidized presses.

Another significant element in the block-grant subsidy is its inability to respond to the size of books. It is normally tied to a fixed number of titles rather than to a fixed number of pages, with the Council apparently believing the publisher able to assign the grant to individual titles in proportion to their size and cost. In practice, this policy discourages long books. Publication of a long book does not enable a publisher to publish fewer books and fulfill block-grant obligations, it forces it to underfund shorter ones, which themselves cannot be cut below 49 pages. One publisher has on at least two occasions published books longer than 250 pages in initial editions of three or four volumes, thus enabling a $6,000 or $8,000 subsidy for a book that could otherwise have received little more than $2,000. The result for authors has been the privileging of the 100-200-page novel as the standard of English-Canadian publishers. The longer novel is further disadvantaged by the understaffing of most Canadian publishers, which can rarely afford to assign anyone to read an unsolicited text that takes more than a few hours to read. In contrast, in the U.S. the 300-page or longer novel is a publishing standard, both because of the larger scale of the U.S. market and because of its consequent ability to assert size as an indicator of quality.

The role of Canadian universities in English-Canadian literary publishing, however, is perhaps the most interesting of all. Terry Eagleton in his *Criticism and Ideology* outlines a history of literary modes of production according to audience, kind of recompense, characteristic genres and style, and means of reproduction and circulation. His outline proceeds from the bard, who recounts for kings and warriors, is paid a stipend, composes in stylized language and genres, and who relies on oral distribution, through the eighteenth-century petty-commodity writer who writes for a patron, receives a fee, works in traditional genres, and relies on short press-run distribution, to the nineteenth- and twentieth-century capitalist novelists who work for a publisher, receive payment for their copyright, write in accessible language, and rely on long press-run distribution. The universities, through their tenure and promotion policies, have in this century created another possibility: the writer who writes for a small, educated audience, is rewarded not by royalties or stipends but by university position, who writes in relatively complex combinations of genres, and who relies on short-run distribution by literary or academic presses. Because of the difficulties of trade publishers in the English-Canadian book market, this kind of writer plays a much larger role in Canadian writing than it does in countries in which national publishers enjoy a majority share of book sales. Critics often mistakenly think of these writers as merely other poets or novelists who happen to 'support' themselves by non-literary work much like Eliot or Souster did by their bank employment. But here the employer is not merely 'support' — it is audience, and leaves its generic, thematic and stylistic marks on the writer's text just as did the patron who paid and sheltered the medieval court poet. It is the presence of the university as audience, together with its associated university and little magazines, that allows most petty-commodity book publishing in Canada to flourish despite the general entrenchment of capitalist modes of book production.

The university audience is also that of most literary criticism, including that of Eagleton. In English-Canadian publishing, however, at least until recently, this audience was defined by academic publishers not as university scholars but as the larger one of university students, high school and college students and teachers. This allowed only two kinds of critical books to be commonly written and published — the monograph or casebook on a well-known author with its inevitable valorizing of personality and subjectivity (as in the Copp Clark, Forum House or New Canadian Library series) and the thematic survey of Canadian literature. Such a narrow choice of format discouraged the discussion of critical issues, and invited unitary theories and the biographical and thematic reading of texts.

None of my characterizations here should be construed as 'criticisms' of nineteenth- or twentieth-century English-Canadian publishing. What kind of publishing, to what audience, to whose advantage, with what kind of remuneration — all these are questions to be answered differently by different interests within our culture. We become capable of changing these answers only by becoming aware of how they have been constructed until now and how some of them have come to prevail. English Canadians have produced a book-distribution system which privileges the products of multi-national late capitalist publishers. This system serves the interests of the shareholders in those multi-national companies and of booksellers; it serves the interest of a few Canadian writers who are able to produce the kinds of texts this system requires; it does not serve the writers of the petty-commodity texts which form the bulk of English-Canadian writing and confines most of these to regional distribution. It encourages those who choose not to write or publish such texts to focus their work to narrowly defined audiences that can be easily reached outside of a national distribution system, and thus contributes to maintaining the regionalization and fragmentation of audience and literature that have become characteristic of Canada. Except under the influence of Ontario hubris, few English-Canadian writers can conceive of having a 'national' audience. The question of whether such a situation would prevail if bookselling were not in the freemarket but were regulated much like Canadian radio remains unasked and unanswered.

Texts Cited

Eagleton, Terry. *Criticism and Ideology: A Study in Marxist Literary Theory*. London: New Left Books, 1976.

Feltes, N. N. *Modes of Production of Victorian Novels*. Chicago and London: University of Chicago Press, 1986.

Fowler, Marian. *Redney: A Life of Sara Jeannette Duncan.* Toronto: Anansi, 1983.

Lehmann-Haupt, Hellmutt. *The Book in America.* New York: Bowker, 1952.

Parker, George L. *The Beginnings of the Book Trade in Canada.* Toronto: University of Toronto Press, 1985.

Royal Commission on Book Publishing. *Background Papers.* Toronto: Queen's Printer and Publisher, 1972.

Sutherland, Ronald. *Second Image: Comparative Studies in Québec/Canadian Literature.* Toronto: New Press, 1971.

Watters, Reginald Eyre. *A Check List of Canadian Literature and Background Materials 1628-1960.* Toronto: University of Toronto Press, 1972.

York University

RICHARD GIGUÈRE ET JACQUES MICHON

Pour une histoire de l'édition littéraire moderne au Québec

La réflexion sur la théorie et la sociologie de la littérature nous a appris à concevoir la littérature comme une entité inséparable du processus social et historique qui consacre les textes et les institutionnalise. Que l'on observe le texte dans ses structures internes, pour repérer les marques du processus de socialisation ou d'institutionnalisation de la littérature, comme le fait une certaine approche sociosémiotique (voir l'approche bakhtinienne appliquée au Québec par André Belleau), ou que l'on s'arrête à la description des institutions et des appareils qui produisent, sélectionnent, diffusent les textes, ne fait que confirmer cette constatation. Pour notre part, nous considérons ces deux approches comme complémentaires.

L'étude de l'édition nous apparaît être un lieu privilégié d'observation des stratégies, des rites et des règles qui président à l'instauration et à l'intronisation de l'écrit en texte littéraire. Les analyses historiques détaillées, que nous nous proposons de poursuivre, devraient permettre de reconstituer une pratique sociale restée relativement méconnue et obscure et de nourrir notre réflexion sur la spécificité de cette fonction dans le champ littéraire. On pourra voir dans notre approche une préoccupation théorique complémentaire des recherches qui se poursuivent ailleurs au Québec dans les domaines de la théorie de la réception, de la socio-sémiotique et de la sociologie des milieux intellectuels.

Avant de préciser les objectifs de notre projet de recherche et de tracer un bilan des travaux déjà accomplis portant sur l'édition du roman et de la poésie au Québec de 1940 à 1960, il importe de dire un mot sur la période que nous avons choisi d'étudier, soit 1940 à 1960. Pourquoi ces deux décennies? Lorsque nous avons lancé notre projet, en 1982, Ignace Cau venait de publier son livre sur l'*Édition au Québec de 1960 à 1977* (Québec, ministère des Affaires culturelles, 1981, 229p.), où il signalait que tout était à faire sur l'histoire de l'édition au Québec. Comme nous connaissions déjà le mémoire de maîtrise de Jean-Pierre Chalifoux qui rappelait l'extraordinaire boom de *l'Édition au Québec, 1940-1950* (École de bibliothéconomie de l'Université de Montréal, 1973, 105 f.), boom qui coïncide avec la Deuxième Guerre mondiale, nous avons décidé de concentrer nos efforts sur cette période qui nous semblait représenter la naissance de l'édition littéraire moderne au Canada français.

Depuis cinq ans que nous étudions cette période, nous nous sommes rendu compte que l'édition au Québec avait une histoire de deux siècles (voir l'ouvrage collectif publié sous la direction de Yvan Lamonde, *l'Imprimé au Québec. Aspects historiques (18e - 20e siècles)*, Québec, IQRC, 1983, 368 p.) et que l'édition littéraire en particulier a une tradition d'à peine un siècle. A partir de quels critères peut-on préciser où commence la période moderne et que faut-il entendre par un éditeur littéraire moderne? Lors d'une réunion de travail du Groupe de recherche en histoire de l'imprimé au Québec tenue à l'Université McGill (20 mars 1987), l'historien Yvan Lamonde a suggéré que la période 1880-1920, qui a vu naître la concentration verticale dans le domaine de l'édition (un libraire qui est à la fois éditeur, distributeur, et même imprimeur) chez des éditeurs comme Beauchemin ou Granger & Frères par exemple, marque les débuts de l'édition moderne au Québec. L'historien Claude Galarneau, de l'Université Laval, est plutôt d'avis que c'est en 1920 précisément, avec l'apparition d'un éditeur indépendant, sans lien avec le clergé, un journal ou l'édition scolaire, qu'il faut voir les véritables débuts de l'édition littéraire moderne. De ce point de vue, des éditeurs comme Louis Carrier ou Édouard Garand dans les années vingt, les éditions Albert Lévesque ou les éditions du Totem d'Albert Pelletier dans les années trente semblent lui donner raison.

Si on accepte l'hypothèse que la période de l'entre-deux-guerres voit l'apparition des premiers éditeurs indépendants au Québec, c'est vraiment pendant la Deuxième Guerre mondiale, alors que l'édition française est muselée par l'Occupation nazie, que l'édition littéraire québécoise connaît son essor. Qu'est-ce qui se produit exactement? Le Canada accepte que les éditeurs d'ici rééditent des titres français épuisés, devenus introuvables sur le marché, à condition toutefois qu'une demande formelle soit adressée au Registraire du droit d'auteur, à Ottawa, pour chaque titre qui fait l'objet d'une réédition. Une fois le livre imprimé, les éditeurs sont tenus de verser des droits d'auteur de 10% au Bureau du Sequestre des biens ennemis, droits d'auteur qui seront remis aux auteurs et aux éditeurs français une fois la Guerre terminée.

Étant donné une forte demande de livres français au Canada et à l'étranger à partir de l'automne 1940, de nouvelles maisons sont fondées presque du jour au lendemain, si bien que Jean-Pierre Chalifoux rapporte qu'en 1946 la Société des éditeurs canadiens du livre français (fondée en 1943) compte 27 maisons d'édition alors qu'il y en avait à peine une demi-douzaine au Québec avant la Guerre. Au total ces nouveaux éditeurs publient près de 3,000 titres (environ vingt millions d'exemplaires) de 1940 à 1949, surtout de 1942 à 1946.Il s'agit surtout de rééditions de livres d'auteurs français. Des éditeurs comme Beauchemin, Fides, Granger, Pony, Variétés publient en majorité des rééditions de titres français alors que quelques maisons, Parizeau, Bernard Valiquette, Pilon, publient un certain pourcentage de nouveaux titres d'auteurs québécois. C'est donc cette période 1940-1950, à laquelle nous avons ajouté la décennie cinquante — juste avant la Révolution tranquille —, que notre groupe de recherche a d'abord étudiée.

L'édition littéraire 1940-1960: bilan et objectifs

L'année 1986 a marqué la fin d'une étape importante de nos travaux qui avaient comme objectif de retracer l'évolution de l'édition du roman et de la poésie. Nous avons dans l'ensemble réalisé cet objectif général grâce aux appuis soutenus du FCAR (1982-86) et du CRSHC (1984-86). Les résultats de la recherche ont été publiés en partie sous forme d'articles dans des revues (québécoises et française), des ouvrages collectifs (québécois et belge) et dans une publication de groupe qui a été très bien reçue par la communauté universitaire et par certains éditeurs. Plusieurs autres articles vont paraître sous peu et nous avons actuellement en chantier trois ouvrages collectifs qui feront le bilan de la recherche effectuée depuis 1982. Pour plus de détails sur les publications de l'équipe, nous vous prions de consulter la bibliographie qui figure à la fin de notre texte.

Les études que nous avons publiées ou qui sont en cours de publication se divisent en deux séries:

1) les monographies consacrées à un éditeur particulier et à sa production littéraire;

1) les articles qui rendent compte de l'évolution générale du champ de l'édition au Québec de 1940 à 1960 dans deux genres particuliers: le roman et la poésie.

Les premières servent de point d'appui et d'illustration aux seconds, alors que ceux-ci permettent de situer les études particulières dans le contexte général des productions romanesque (cf. J. Michon) et poétique (cf. R. Giguère) et dans leurs rapports au champ littéraire et au marché. Sur ces deux plans, le roman et la poésie sont d'ailleurs apparus comme des pratiques symboliques relativement distinctes et autonomes.

Les études générales sur la production littéraire nous ont permis d'établir dans leurs grandes lignes les rapports étroits qui existent entre littérature et marché, de constater des stratégies spécifiques aux éditeurs et aux écrivains, de signaler le développement du roman dans la période de croissance de l'édition (1940-47) et sa régression au profit de la poésie en temps de crise (1950-59).

Les monographies d'éditeurs nous ont permis de donner des exemples plus spécifiques et concrets, de montrer les moyens particuliers développés par certains
d'entre eux pour profiter de la croissance ou pour contrer les effets négatifs de
la crise. Il s'agissait aussi dans certains cas de rendre compte de l'activité générale de l'éditeur. Nous avons pu constater que les collections littéraires d'un
éditeur et ses politiques éditoriales ne pouvaient être définies et saisies sans
cette mise en perspective, c'est-à-dire sans être situées dans l'ensemble de sa
production et de ses pratiques. Cette analyse, qui devait être appliquée surtout
aux éditeurs de littérature générale — la question ne se pose pas pour les petits
éditeurs de poésie dont le corpus restreint fait partie au départ du corpus ana-
lysé —, exigeait une recherche plus longue et plus approfondie compte tenu de
l'importance du catalogue (entre 200 et 1,000 titres), de la longévité de la maison et de la diversité de ses activités. Étant donné l'ampleur de la tâche et les
moyens modestes mis à notre disposition, il va sans dire que nous n'avons pu
effectuer ce travail pour chacune des maisons littéraires importantes (de 100 titres et plus) qui étaient en activité durant la période 1940-1960. En ce qui a trait
aux maisons de poésie, la tâche s'est avérée plus facile. Dans ce secteur, le programme tracé dès 1982 a pu être complété sans trop de difficultés.

Dans le domaine de la poésie, nous avons accompli depuis 1982, grâce à la
collaboration de plusieurs assistant-e-s de recherche (Silvie Bernier, Liette
Gaudreau, Hélène Lafrance, François Landry, Dominique Garand, Carole Ha-
melin, André Marquis), à peu près l'ensemble du programme que nous nous
étions fixé. Nous avons constitué des dossiers et rédigé des monographies sur
les éditeurs de poésie les plus importants de 1940 à 1960 (histoire des maisons,
catalogue de titres, réception critique, inventaire des archives accessibles et/ou
enquête et interviews auprès des éditeurs encore vivants), soit Beauchemin, les
Éditions du Bien public (1932-1982), les Cahiers de la file indienne (1946-1948),
Erta (1949-1968), l'Hexagone (1953-, première version), Nocturne (1955-
1966), Orphée (1953-), Cascade (éditions du Collège Sainte-Marie, 1955-
1957), Atys (1957-1963), Quartz (1958-1960), sans parler des éditeurs de
littérature générale comme Fides, Parizeau, Pony, Valiquette qui publient oc-
casionnellement de la poésie. Nous avons publié ou publierons bientôt une
grande partie de ces travaux. De plus, pas moins de cinq de nos assistant-e-s
sont à rédiger des mémoires de maîtrise ou des thèses de doctorat reliés directement à notre recherche.

La pratique et l'expérience nous ont amenés à formuler l'objectif d'une description globale de l'activité éditoriale des 'gros' éditeurs et à établir les démarches à suivre pour atteindre cet objectif, c'est-à-dire:

1. établir le catalogue complet de l'éditeur à l'aide des différentes sources
imprimées mises à notre disposition (Canadiana, Catalogue rétrospectif du
Québec, Catalogues de libraires et d'éditeurs, publicité dans les revues et les
journaux, etc.);

2. décrire chaque titre, autant que possible 'livre en main', en tenant compte des différentes éditions. Cette étape est nécessaire à cause de l'insuffisance des sources officielles et des nombreuses erreurs qui se sont glissées dans les bibliographies qui n'ont pas été contrôlées par les deux Bibliothèques nationales;

3. consulter les fonds d'archives des écrivains qui contiennent de précieux renseignements sur leurs rapports avec les éditeurs (cette source peut suppléer à l'absence d'archives d'éditeurs);

4. rencontrer les éditeurs ou des témoins de l'époque pour compléter nos renseignements et cerner, entre autres, les pratiques éditoriales et commerciales de l'éditeur, reconstituer les réseaux d'influence et de sympathie qui se trouvent souvent à l'origine d'une collection ou d'un regroupement d'écrivains, saisir également la perception que l'éditeur lui-même pouvait avoir de son rôle et de sa fonction dans le champ littéraire ou intellectuel.

Nous avons appliqué ces démarches de façon systématique dans le cas des petites maisons de poésie et de quelques gros éditeurs comme le Bien public, Beauchemin, Valiquette, Parizeau. Par ailleurs plusieurs maisons littéraires importantes comme les Éditions Albert Lévesque, les Éditions du Totem, les Éditions de l'Arbre, le Cercle du Livre de France et l'Institut littéraire du Québec n'ont pas encore été analysés.

Au cours de nos recherches, nous avons compris la complexité de l'activité éditoriale et conçu la nécessité de procéder à des analyses approfondies, maison par maison, pour rendre compte de manière objective et précise de l'activité éditoriale d'un éditeur et documenter l'histoire de l'édition au Québec. Il ne s'agit pas de décrire toute les activités impliquées dans la fabrication et la diffusion du livre, étude qui demanderait des moyens et des compétences multiples, qui devrait d'ailleurs être menée de front avec d'autres recherches sur l'histoire de l'imprimerie et de ses techniques, de l'illustration et du design, sur l'histoire économique de la librairie et de l'importation du livre, sur l'évolution de la lecture et de la scolarisation, etc. Mais nous voulons offrir une vue d'ensemble du marché de l'édition littéraire au sens large. Que la littérature constitue une partie seulement des activités d'un éditeur nous a semblé suffisant pour faire entrer ce dernier dans notre corpus. Par ailleurs, nous voulons concentrer nos recherches sur des maisons qui ont marqué l'évolution de la notion de littérature et qui ont été identifiées au champ littéraire de manière plus étroite. Parmi celles qui méritent une étude approfondie et nécessitent un examen détaillé, nous retenons celles qui ont marqué la littérature québécoise depuis les années 1920.

L'édition de littérature générale[*]

En étudiant par le détail le mode de fonctionnement de ces éditeurs nous pourrons reconstituer, à l'aide de la documentation et des analyses déjà faites, l'histoire de l'édition littéraire moderne au Québec. En retraçant l'évolution de chaque éditeur, nous aurons un bon exemple du processus par lequel certaines positions littéraires s'élaborent, se développent et finalement s'institutionnalisent. Il s'agit de voir d'abord comment le projet littéraire d'un éditeur s'inscrit dans son programme général de sélection, de production et de diffusion du livre, ce qui sous-entend que l'on tienne compte de ses collections (littéraires et non-littéraires), de ses publications périodiques (revues, almanachs, journaux), de ses activités de distribution et de diffusion, de son fonctionnement commercial et de son marché.

Les renseignements sur les tirages et les différentes éditions d'un même titre devraient nous donner des indications sur le marché et ses réactions aux initiatives de l'éditeur. En ce qui concerne l'analyse des publications périodiques, elle nous permettra de cerner les stratégies de diffusion. La revue, le journal, l'almanach servent souvent de rampe de lancement ou de banc d'essai pour les écrivains qui vont plus tard se retrouver au catalogue de l'éditeur, ils offrent également une tribune qui permet de prolonger l'action du livre sous la forme de comptes rendus, de commentaires, d'articles connexes d'accompagnement ou de publicité directe ou indirecte.

Ce sont toutes ces activités qu'il s'agit d'étudier pour dégager les rapports, les relations qui se tissent entre toutes ces instances du processus éditorial. Cette approche devrait nous montrer que l'éditeur n'est pas tant une personne ou un personnage (bien que la personnalité de l'éditeur compte pour beaucoup dans la fabrication de son image de marque) qu'un réseau, un noeud de relations et de complicités. L'éditeur se conçoit d'abord comme un intermédiaire, un médiateur, un relais. Entre l'auteur et son lecteur, l'éditeur cherche à se constituer un espace propre qui devient à la longue un lieu d'identification, de rassemblement et de reconnaissance. Et il s'agit ici moins d'un expace réel que d'un lieu imaginaire où se trouve rassemblée dans une collection ou une série, une collectivité d'auteurs et de textes placés sous un même nom. La maison d'édition est investie de valeurs qui dépassent la personnalité de son directeur littéraire, elle implique aussi la participation active d'un groupe d'écrivains qui vont s'y reconnaître. Le nom de la maison devient ainsi un lieu de rencontre. Explorer les conditions de l'institutionnalisation de l'éditeur littéraire, c'est aussi rendre compte de cette alliance objective entre une génération d'écrivains et un éditeur pour la conquête du pouvoir symbolique.

---

[*]   Cette section reprend les propos de Jacques Michon publiés dans 'L'édition littéraire pour grand public de 1940 à 1960,' *l'Institution littéraire*, 1986, 166-168.

On sait que des éditeurs réussiront souvent à s'imposer sur le marché en s'associant à la montée d'un groupe, d'une école, d'une écriture ou d'un mouvement esthétique. On connaît les rapports étroits entre le groupe de *la Relève* et les Éditions de l'Arbre dans les années quarante, entre les jeunes poètes des années cinquante et les Éditions de l'Hegagone animées par Gaston Miron ou la nouvelle génération de romanciers psychologues et le Cercle du livre de France de Pierre Tisseyre.

Même si l'éditeur survit au mouvement avec lequel il a été associé, il peut difficilement se départir de cette première image de marque. Une fois que le public visé s'actualise en public réel autour de certains auteurs et de quelques titres, l'éditeur a tendance à reproduire le même livre et à créer une collection qui répond à l'attente de ce public. Il s'agit d'un moyen, pour celui qui pratique un commerce qui comporte des risques, d'introduire dans son mode de fonctionnement une forme de programmation. Ainsi le nom d'un éditeur devient à la longue le symbole d'une série ou d'une tradition qui constitue à la fois un appel d'offre et un critère de sélection.

L'alliance objective d'un groupe d'écrivains autour d'une maison et des positions idéologiques et esthétiques qu'elle représente, constitue un aspect important des données que l'on peut dégager des analyses mentionnées plus haut (étude des catalogues, des correspondances d'écrivains, etc.). Elle fait partie de ce qu'on pourrait appeler l'action 'éducative' de l'éditeur. D'un autre côté, l'éditeur doit tenir compte de la demande sociale et du marché que, dans une certaine mesure, il représente auprès des écrivains et qu'il essaie par une traduction appropriée de faire coïncider avec l'offre. Cette dimension 'réceptive' de l'édition, qui a trait à l'horizon d'attente du public lecteur, peut être saisie par le biais des tirages, des rééditions, des réimpressions et des bilans financiers et nous renseigner sur les effets et les résultats de l'action idéologique de l'éditeur et des intérêts qu'il représente.

L'éditeur en tant qu'acteur du jeu institutionnel se trouve donc au carrefour de plusieurs lieux de détermination. Diachroniquement, il est tributaire d'une tradition de lecture et d'un fonds littéraire. Synchroniquement, il s'interpose entre les intérêts des auteurs et ceux des lecteurs pour les ajuster les uns aux autres et en tirer des bénéfices. On ne peut cerner la spécificité de son rôle qu'en le situant à l'intersection de ces deux axes de légitimation. L'éditeur est d'abord un personnage collectif, inséparable de ce réseau auquel il prête son nom. À cause de cela sans doute, c'est souvent après coup que peut se dégager une tendance, une cohérence ou une politique éditoriale explicite. C'est lorsqu'un réseau de relations objectives se cristallise dans un catalogue, autour de certaines idées et d'un groupe d'écrivains (qui a réussi à faire prévaloir son droit à faire, refaire ou défaire la littérature), que peut s'imposer une image de marque qui, avec le temps, devient à la fois un appel d'offre et un critère de sélection.

Mais plusieurs petites maisons ne vivent pas assez longtemps pour atteindre ce degré de maturation ou cette masse critique nécessaire pour se distinguer sur le marché des valeurs littéraires. Si on dénombre plus de 170 maisons de littérature pour la période 1940-1960, seulement une dizaine d'entre elles réussissent à se faire un nom, à se constituer un marché et à trouver des lecteurs fidèles. Ainsi, malgré un grand nombre d'éditeurs, rares sont ceux qui réussissent à durer et à imposer leur conception de la littérature.

Si on définit à la suite de Jacques Dubois 'l'institution littéraire' comme un système doté de rationalité qui assure la socialisation des individus par l'imposition de normes, de valeurs ou de catégories esthétiques ou idéologiques, on définira l'édition comme un appareil qui participe à cette action éducative et législative. L'édition représente bien l'une des bases matérielles qui permet au système de se perpétuer (Dubois, p. 31-33). L'institution n'est pas localisée ou concentrée en un lieu précis que l'on pourrait désigner par un nom propre, mais elle est diffuse, elle est immanente au système et aux relations qui s'établissent entre les agents qui participent à sa reproduction. On pourra saisir la dynamique propre au champ littéraire dans la mesure où l'on s'arrêtera non pas à un auteur, à un éditeur ou à un critique en particulier, mais aux relations ou aux rapports qui s'articulent entre eux. L'éditeur est l'un de ces intermédiaires qui, tout en occupant une place précise dans la production et la diffusion du livre, participent à l'institutionnalisation et la constitution de la littérature.

L'édition de poésie

Dans le domaine de la poésie nous nous sommes rendu compte qu'il faudrait étudier de plus près le phénomène de l'auto-édition et du compte d'auteur qui représente le mode de publication de plus de 25% des recueils de poèmes parus de 1940 à 1959. Il faudrait aussi, étant donné son rôle capital d'éditeur, d'animateur et de liaison entre différentes maisons d'édition de l'époque, réaliser une série d'interviews avec Gaston Miron. Nous ne parlons pas de Miron le poète et le personnage public, étudié et célébré par la critique et les médias depuis une quinzaine d'années, mais de l'éditeur qui a travaillé chez Beauchemin, à l'Hegagone, chez Fomac, chez HMH et qui a été un acteur de premier plan et un témoin privilégié de l'édition de poésie des années 50, 60 et 70 au Québec. À la lumière de ces interviews (avec Miron et quelques poètes de l'Hexagone), nous en profiterons pour récrire une version plus substantielle de notre monographie sur les Éditions de l'Hexagaone.

Nous constatons, par le biais des travaux que Richard Giguère mène présentement en vue de la publication d'une édition critique d'*À l'ombre de l'Orford* d'Alfred DesRochers (dans le cadre du projet 'Corpus d'éditions critiques') que les années 20 et 30, et particulièrement les années 1925-1939, constituent la première période active de l'histoire de l'édition littéraire moderne au Québec. Mon collègue Jacques Michon étudiera de près les Éditions Albert Lévesque qu'il a déjà abordées dans un article à paraître. Grâce à une correspondance très riche de renseignements entre DesRochers et le critique et éditeur Albert Pelletier (une centaine de lettres dans le fonds DesRochers, Archives nationales du Québec, centre régional de l'Estrie à Sherbrooke), Richard Giguére se propose d'étudier les Éditions du Totem (dirigées par Pelletier de 1932 à 1936) et les rapports étroits avec la revue *les Idées* (dirigée par Pelletier de 1935 à 1939 et à laquelle DesRochers collabora).

Non moins intéressant est le rôle que joua Alfred DesRochers comme éditeur de ses propres recueils — *l'Offrande aux vierges folles* (1928) et *À l'ombre de l'Orford* (1929) réédités par Lévesque en 1930 — et éditeur également de deux livres de poésie de son ami, le critique et poète Louis Dantin (voir la correspondance DesRochers-Dantin qui comprend quelque 230 lettres, de 1928 à 1939, dans le fonds DesRochers des ANQ à Sherbrooke). DesRochers a aussi une correspondance très intéressante avec Albert Lévesque dans les années 30, les Éditions Fides et Gérard Dagenais de la Société des éditions Pascal dans les années 40 et 50. Notre recherche sur les Éditions du Totem d'une part et sur le rôle de DesRochers éditeur d'autre part tiendra compte du contexte général de l'édition littéraire des années 20 et 30 au Québec (Édouard Garand, Albert Lévesque, Déom, les Éditions du Mercure, entre autres).

Par ailleurs, la série d'interviews que nous nous proposons de faire avec Gaston Miron au sujet de son travail d'éditeur (à l'Hexagone et ailleurs) nous amènera à déborder la période 1930-1960 pour progresser vers le présent. Nous entreprendrons une recherche sur la revue *les Herbes rouges*, fondée par François et Marcel Hébert en 1968 (150 numéros à ce jour), devenue aussi maison d'édition en 1978 grâce à la collaboration de Gaston Miron et d'Alain Horic des Éditions de l'Hexagone. Essentiellement les frères Hébert reprennent les titres parus dans la collection 'Lecture en vélocipède' qu'ils dirigeaient aux Éditions de l'Aurore (1973-1976), où se trouvait aussi à cette époque un auteur maison des *Herbes rouges*, Roger Des Roches. Les Herbes rouges n'est pas la seule revue de poésie et maison d'édition des années 60 et 70 au Québec, mais étant donné le cheminement particulier du périodique qui devient aussi maison d'édition grâce à l'aide de deux autres éditeurs de poésie (Miron et Horic), étant donné aussi que les frères Hébert ont publié des auteurs et des oeuvres qui ont marqué fortement l'écriture québécoise des années 70, il s'agit sans aucun doute d'un des éditeurs de poésie les plus importants de cette période.

En plongeant d'un côté dans les années 20 et 30 et en explorant de l'autre les années 60 et 70, nous élargissons la période privilégiée jusqu'ici, toujours dans le but d'analyser et de mieux comprendre les mécanismes d'établissement, de fonctionnement et d'évolution de l'édition littéraire moderne au Québec.

Nous vous proposons donc de poursuivre le projet inauguré en 1982, en l'orientant de la manière suivante:

1. élargir la période d'observation de 1920 à 1960 et au delà;

2. élargir le corpus observé, en ne nous limitant plus aux deux genres (roman et poésie) jusqu'ici étudiés, et rendre compte de la production globale de l'éditeur (collections littéraires et non littéraires, publications périodiques, etc.);

3. retracer l'histoire et l'évolution de l'édition moderne au Québec depuis 1920, en procédant à l'analyse des éditeurs les plus importants dans la constitution du champ littéraire.

Publications de l'équipe: 1984-1986

Bernier, Silvie, 'Bernard Valiquette, la nouvelle image de l'éditeur québécois,' *Bernard Valiquette*, Montréal, Publi-Liaison/AEC, 1985, 110 p.

—, 'Literary Prizes in French,' *The Canadian Encyclopedia*, Edmonton, Hurtig, 1985, 1016.

—, 'A la croisée des champs artistique et littéraire, le livre d'artiste,' *Voix et images*, 33, 1986, 528-536.

Gaudreau, Liette, 'Les prix littéraires québécois, 1940-1960,' *l'Institution littéraire*, sous la direction de Maurice Lemire avec l'assistance de Michel Lord, actes du colloque organisé conjointement par l'Institut québécois de recherche sur la culture et le Centre de recherche en littérature québécoise, Québec, IQRC-CRELIQ, 1986.

Giguère, Richard, 'La revue Amérique française (1941-1955),' *Revue d'Histoire littéraire du Québec et du Canada français*, 6, 1984, 53-63.

—, 'L'édition de la poésie, 1940-1960,' *l'Institution littéraire*, sous la direction de Maurice Lemire avec l'assistance de Michel Lord, actes du colloque organisé conjointement par l'Institut québécois de recherche sur la culture et le Centre de recherche en littérature québécoise, Québec, IQRC-CRELIQ, 1986.

GRELQ, *L'Edition littéraire au Québec de 1940 à 1960*, par le Groupe de recherche sur l'édition littéraire au Québec, 'Cahiers d'études littéraires et culturelles,' no 9, Université de Sherbrooke, 1985, 215 p.

Sommaire:

- *L'édition littéraire au Québec,1940-1960* (J. Michon)
- *Variétés, premier éditeur québécois des années quarante* (Silvie Bernier)
- *Bernard Valiquette, la nouvelle image de l'éditeur québécois* (Silvie Bernier)
- *Fides, oeuvre de propagande catholique* (Hélène Lafrance)
- *Notes sur deux petites maisons d'édition surréalistes: 1946-1959* (Robert Yergeau)
- *Les éditions Erta: un surréalisme sans frontière* (Richard Giguère)
- *Bibliographie de l'édition au Québec, 1940-1960.* (+ index)

GRELQ, *L'Édition du livre populaire*, Sherbrooke, les éditions Ex Libris, 1988, coll 'Etudes sur l'édition,' 204 p.

Sommaire:

- *Introduction: L'édition du roman populaire* (Jacques Michon)
- *Les Éditions Édouard Garand et les années 20* (François Landry)
- *L'Illustration du 'Roman canadien'* (Silvie Bernier)
- *Le Roman sentimental et la biographie romancée: les Éditions de l'Étoile* (Sylvia Faure)
- *Un imprimeur régional: les Éditions Marquis* (François Landry)
- *La Librairie et la distribution: Granger Frères* (Dominique Garand)
- Annexe: Publications des chercheurs du GRELQ. (+ Index)

Comptes Rendus:

- R. Martel, *La Presse*, 18 mars 1985, cahier C.
- A. Thério, *Lettres québécoises*, 38, 1985, 68-69.
- *Livre d'ici*, avril 1985, 17.

Lafrance, Hélène, *Yves Thériault et l'Institution littéraire québécoise*, Québec, IQRC, 1984, coll, 'Prix edmond de Nevers,' 169 p.

Landry, François, 'La Librarie Beachemin, doyenne de l'édition au Québec,' *Présence francophone*, 28, 1986.

Michon, Jacques, 'Esthétique et réception du roman conforme, 1939-1957,' *le Québécois et sa littérature*, sous la direction de René Dionne, Sherbrooke,

Editions Naaman/Agence de Coopération culturelle et technique, 1984, 99-106.

—, 'Les revues d'avant-garde au Québec de 1940 à 1979,' *Trajectoires: littérature et institutions au Québec et en Belgigue francophone*, travaux publiés par Lise Gauvin et Jean-Marie Klinkenberg, Bruxelles, Editions Labor/Presses de l'Université de Montréal, 1985, coll. 'Dossiers Media,' 117-127.

—, 'L'édition littéraire au Québec, 1940-1960,' *Itinéraires et contacts de cultures*, publication du Centre d'études francophones de l'Université de Paris XIII, Paris, l'Harmattan, vol. 6('Paris-Québec'), 1985, 59-70.

—, 'Edition littéraire et autonomie culturelle, le cas du Québec', *Présence francophone*, 26, 1985, 57-66.

—, 'L'édition littéraire pour grand public de 1940 à 1960,' *l'Insitution littéraire*, sous la direction de Maurice Lemire avec l'assistance de Michel Lord, actes du colloque organisé conjointement par l'Institut québécois de recherche sur la culture et le Centre de recherche en littérature québécoise, Québec, IQRC-CRELIQ, 1986, 161-168.

—, responsable du numéro spécial sur 'L'édition littéraire,' *Présence francophone*, 28, 1986.

—, 'Croissance et crise de l'édition littéraire au Québec (1940-1959),' *Littérature*, 66, mai 1987, 115-126.

A Paraître:

Bernier, Silvie, *Prix littéraire et champ du pouvoir: le prix David, 1923-1970*, mémoire de mâitrise, DEF, Université de Sherbrooke, 1983, 166 p. Présenté *dans* la *Revue d'histoire littéraire du Québec et du Canada français*,11, 1986, 159-164.

Giguère, Richard, 'La réception critique de l'Hexagone dans les revues (1954-1970),' Actes du colloque de l'Université de Toronto sur les '25 ans de l'Hexagone' A paraître aux éditions de l'Hexagone.

—, 'La réception critique d'Alain Grandbois publié à l'Hexagone, 1955-1965,' Actes du colloque de l'Université de Toronto sur 'Alain Grandbois,' avril 1985.

—, 'Le déplacement de l'horizon d'attente de la série littéraire du terroir: la réception critique de *A l'ombre de l'Orford*, 1929-1965,' Actes du colloque sur 'les Problèmes de réception,' Université d'Alberta, Edmonton, octobre 1986.

GRELQ, *Etudes sur l'édition littéraire au Québec*.

Michon, Jacques, 'L'édition littéraire durant la crise: Albert Lévesque, 1926-1937,'*Actes du Congrès international d'études canadiennes sur la Culture et la Société au Canada en période de crise économique,* juin 1985, 12 p.

Université de Sherbrooke

SILVIE BERNIER

Fonction de l'illustration dans la diffusion et la légitimation de la littérature

Aujourd'hui, et depuis longtemps, parler de littérature se résume le plus souvent à parler des textes. Combien d'histoires littéraires prennent la peine de mentionner l'édition (ou les éditions) des ouvrages dont elles traitent? Dans l'esprit de bien des critiques, ou des simples lecteurs, le sens d'un texte demeure le même, qu'il soit lu en poche ou en édition courante, avec ou sans illustrations. L'identification du livre aux valeurs de l'esprit a pour conséquence de refouler ses bases matérielles, de dénier sa nature d'objet. Mais tenir compte de l'objet-livre,[1] c'est déjà le rendre palpable et démystifier son statut en l'insérant dans le réseau culturel, en mettant en lumière son inscription dans la logique du marché, comme produit d'échange et de consommation.

Le livre, c'est avant tout un certain medium qui, malgré les transformations encourrues avec le temps, ou selon les différents genres, garde une très grande stabilité d'apparence. Les atteintes au fameux rectangle demeurent rares et sans véritable portée.[2] C'est précisément cette stabilité du format du livre qui finit par le rendre si 'naturel' et nous fait oublier sa matérialité et son arbitraire. Pourtant, bien avant de lire le texte, le lecteur est interpellé par un objet, et dès ce premier contact visuel et tactile prennent place des éléments de signification. De grand ou de petit format, mince ou épais, le livre donne des indications de lecture. Qui ne connaît pas de ces lecteurs qui choissisent leurs livres à l'épaisseur? La couverture, qui synthétise soit le contenu du livre, soit l'image de la maison d'édition, la présence ou l'absence de photographie de l'auteur, le

---

1 Yves Reuter, 'L'objet-livre,' *Pratiques*, no 32, décembre 1981, 30-38.
2 Yvonne Johannot, *Quand le livre devient poche, une sémiologie du livre au format de poche*, Grenoble, Presses universitaires de Grenoble, 1978, coll.'Actualités-Recherches/ Sociologie,' 199(1)p.

sigle de l'éditeur ou de la collection, la qualité du papier, les caractères typographiques, tous ces indices 'parlent' au lecteur et orientent sa lecture.

Ainsi, une version illustrée d'un texte proposera une signification différente d'une édition strictement limitée à l'écrit. Elle le ponctuera de façon particulière. De la même façon, deux éditions d'un même texte illustré par des artistes différents peuvent produire des significations radicalement divergentes. Quels liens existent-ils, par exemple, entre le *Maria Chapdelaine* de Suzor-Côté, paru chez J.-A. Lefebvre en 1916, et celui de Clarence Gagnon, édité à Paris par la maison Mornay en 1933? Le caractère luxueux de la seconde contraste avec la sobriété de l'édition princeps. Les illustrations en noir et blanc de Suzor-Côté, de petite dimension, mettent en scène un univers où l'austérité domine et tient lieu de valeur positive. Au contraire, chez Clarence Gagnon, la couleur, combinée aux effets décoratifs, vient renforcer l'euphorie générale des compositions et ne laisse entrevoir que la douceur de la vie paysanne. Ici, l'évolution de l'imagerie suit pas à pas l'évolution de l'archi-texte, c'est-à-dire de la lecture institutionnelle du texte. On trouverait sans aucun doute un écart aussi important entre les éditions ultérieures de ce célèbre récit du terroir.

Une fois admise l'importance de la politique éditoriale (et plus particulièrement des illustrations) dans le procès de lecture de l'ouvrage, on peut s'interroger sur les motivations d'un écrivain ou d'un éditeur à produire un livre illustré plutôt qu'une édition courante. Quelle(s) fonction(s) précise(s) accorde-t-on à l'illustration dans le processus de diffusion et de légitimation du livre? De toute évidence, cette fonction varie selon le type d'ouvrage et le réseau culturel dans lequel il s'inscrit. En reprenant les classifications déjà effectuées par Robert Escarpit[3] et de façon un peu différente par Pierre Bourdieu,[4] on peut distinguer d'une part un circuit populaire, celui de la littérature de masse ou pour grand public, et d'autre part, un circuit 'lettré,' limité à la classe intellectuelle et 'cultivée.' Utilisée par les éditeurs des deux réseaux, l'illustration y joue cependant un rôle différent. Bourdieu, dans 'Production de la croyance; contribution à une économie des biens symboliques,'[5] a bien circonscrit les logiques économiques divergentes qui alimentent ces deux types de production. Le réseau populaire demeure soumis aux impératifs qui régissent l'ensemble des rapports de production capitaliste: accroissement de la demande et maximisation des profits. Le but premier des éditions pour public élargi sera donc de réaliser le plus grand nombre de ventes possibles en allant

3   Robert Escarpit, *Le Littéraire et le social*, Paris, Flammarion, 1970, coll. 'Champs,' 245(1)p.
4   Pierre Bourdieu, 'Le marché des biens symboliques,' *l'Année sociologique*, no 22, 1971, 49-126.
5   Pierre Bourdieu, 'La production de la croyance, contribution à une économie des biens symboliques,' *Actes de la recherche en sciences sociales*, no 13, février 1977, 4-43.

chercher de plus en plus de lecteurs. Dans cette perspective, l'illustration aura pour fonction de rapprocher l'ouvrage du lecteur, de le lui rendre accessible. À cet effet, l'illustration de page couverture joue un rôle de premier ordre. Puisque, selon les enquêtes, 40% des livres se vendent en vitrine,[6] l'éditeur se doit d'éveiller, au premier coup d'oeil, l'attention du lecteur éventuel. D'où le recours à des couvertures voyantes, où les scènes représentées évoquent une surcharge d'émotions et de sentiments, amour, sexe ou violence. Les illustrations insérées dans le corps du texte répondent à des principes de composition similaires. On y retrouve généralement des personnages en action, ce qui favorise l'identification du lecteur. Dans les ouvrages qui s'adressent à un public peu familiarisé avec la lecture, l'image a aussi pour fonction de faciliter la compréhension du texte, en permettant un décodage plus rapide et moins complexe. C'est la raison pour laquelle, en France, les éditeurs commencent, au 19e siècle, à rééditer les grands romans en versions illustrées, de façon à répondre aux exigences d'un nouveau public peu scolarisé.[7]

Puisque la meilleure façon d'augmenter les profits consite à minimiser les coûts de production, le choix des composantes matérielles du livre respectera ce critère premier. Le papier est généralement de qualité médiocre, les caractères typographiques sans variété, les illustrations peu nombreuses ou reproduites grossièrement. Le rythme rapide de production et de mise en marché conduit les illustrateurs à travailler à l'intérieur de laps de temps très courts, ce qui n'est pas sans influencer leurs dessins, qui répètent souvent des formules stéréotypées: physionomie codée selon que le personnage est bon ou méchant, imagerie folklorique, etc. Ces illustrations, issues d'un travail en série, favorisent cependant chez le lecteur un sentiment de familiarité avec les personnages qui, d'un livre à l'autre, conservent un air de parenté. Le style adopté par ces illustrateurs est généralement réaliste et d'une facture plutôt conventionnelle. Même au 20e siècle, les images demeurent figuratives, avec à l'occasion une stylisation discrète. Il va sans dire que ces choix stylistiques correspondent au goût du public généralement peu friand des tendances esthétiques d'avant-garde. Encore aujourd'hui, le grand public apprécie un art 'vrai,' qui reproduit fidèlement la réalité. La stylisation n'est acceptable que si elle ne remet pas en cause la vision du réel et n'apparaît que comme un 'effet d'art,' une sur-value de l'image.[8]

Dans les productions réservées à l'élite cultivée, l'illustration adopte des fonctions différentes. Il faut rappeler, à la suite de Bourdieu, que le principe

6   Yves Reuter, *op cit.*, 32.
7   Michel Melot, 'Le texte et l'image,' *Histoire de l'édition française, le temps des éditeurs, du romantisme à la belle époque*, tome III, Paris, Promodis, 1985, 287-311.
8   Voir Pierre Bourdieu, *La Distinction, critique sociale du jugement*, Paris, Éditions de Minuit, 1979, coll. 'le sens commun,' 670 p.

organisateur du réseau cultivé consiste à dénier ses propres fondements économiques. Plutôt que d'afficher des visées financières, l'éditeur d'élite prétend oeuvrer pour le seul plaisir de l'art et de la littérature. Sa préoccupation première sera la conquête du prestige et de la légitimité culturelle. C'est à cette fin qu'il utilisera l'image. Dans le livre de luxe ou le livre d'artiste, l'illustration sert au départ de marque de distinction. L'ajout d'illustrations, tout comme l'utilisation de papier de qualité, d'une reliure riche, et parfois même d'un étui, permet au livre de se démarquer des productions courantes. L'emphase sur la matérialité de l'objet sert à accréditer la plus-value symbolique de l'oeuvre. Si les illustrations sont des estampes originales, le livre se dote d'un surcroît de valeur et accède au marché de l'art, au même titre qu'une gravure isolée. On lui reconnaît non seulement un statut d'objet, mais d'objet *d'art*, ce qui l'élève et le rapproche d'une certaine sacralité.

Mais même s'il ne s'agit pas d'estampes originales, l'illustration favorise la légitimation de l'oeuvre. Le prestige d'un illustrateur connu rejaillit sur le livre et augmente sa valeur, grâce à un phénomène de transfert de capital symbolique. C'est le cas de Suzor-Côté, l'un des plus importants peintres québécois, qui illustre *Maria Chapdelaine*, oeuvre d'un auteur encore inconnu, Louis Hémon. Souvent l'illustration sert à légitimer, non pas un texte mais un genre marginal, ou une écriture innovatrice. C'est ce qui explique que de nombreux textes poétiques se présentent accompagnés d'illustrations. La beauté du livre et des images donne de la crédibilité à un ouvrage peu conventionnel. C'était la politique de petites maisons de poésie comme les Cahiers de la file indienne, Quartz, Malte, Orphée, dans les années 40 et 50. Nous y reviendrons.

Mais malgré les allégations des éditeurs, le livre de luxe est aussi un produit rentable, grâce à une reconversion du capital symbolique en capital économique. Le livre d'artiste, qui s'insère dans le marché de l'art, acquiert sa valeur marchande selon les cotes de l'artiste-illustrateur. Ainsi, bien que les tirages soient limités, chaque exemplaire peut acquérir une valeur jusqu'à 50 fois supérieure à celle d'un ouvrage courant. De plus, le tirage limité crée une situation de rareté qui participe à la surenchère de l'oeuvre. Et même lorsque les estampes ne sont pas originales, la seule collaboration d'artistes importants, ou en voie de le devenir, donne au livre une valeur qui augmente avec les années, selon la reconnaissance de l'artiste, de l'écrivain et de l'oeuvre.

Dans ces productions pour public restreint, l'iconographie et la facture des illustrations diffèrent de celles des ouvrages populaires. La stylisation y est beaucoup plus fréquente, de même que l'abstraction. Le rôle des illustrations n'est pas tant de reproduire le référent que d'afficher leur propre valeur artistique. La transformation de la réalité par le regard de l'artiste est donc souhaitable et concourt à la réception de l'oeuvre comme 'originale.' La représentation de personnages n'a pas non plus la même importance que dans les ouvrages populaires, puisque la fonction référentielle n'est pas dominante.

L'image vaut pour ses qualités décoratives et esthétiques, ce qui convient bien à la représentation de paysages ou de compositions abstraites. L'utilisation de la couleur, fréquente dans les livres d'artiste, contribue elle aussi à l'effet esthétisant en séduisant le lecteur au premier coup d'oeil.

Aperçu historique

Voyons maintenant de quelle façon, ces deux réseaux, populaire et lettré, se développent et tirent profit de l'illustration. Au Québec, on le sait, l'édition, et surtout l'édition littéraire, commence véritablement avec le 20e siècle. Les quelques éditeurs importants au siècle précédent, Beauchemin, Granger, se spécialisent dans les ouvrages religieux et les manuels scolaires. La majorité des publications demeurent l'oeuvre d'imprimeurs, de journaux, de communautés religieuses ou de particuliers. Il faudra donc attendre le 20e siècle et même les années vingt, avant de parler d'une politique éditoriale soutenue en faveur du livre illustré. Au 19e siècle, le livre illustré privilégie le récit historique, qui constitue l'un des genres dominants. Ces ouvrages s'apparentent en outre à des traités de géographie quand ils cherchent à valoriser les diverses régions du Canada. On y trouve des images gravées ou photographiées des coins pittoresques du pays. Puisqu'au 19e siècle, l'histoire est abordée avant tout par l'intermédiaire de ceux qui la font, la biographie devient rapidement la formule la plus courante. On y raconte alors la vie de personnages célèbres, ou celle de héros moins connus mais que l'on cherche à populariser. La coutume veut que l'on ajoute à la biographie un portrait du héros ou de l'auteur, généralement placé en frontispice.

Ces ouvrages s'adressent dans l'ensemble à un public moyen. Même s'ils ne sont diffusés que localement (les livres d'histoire régionale, par exemple), ils ne visent pas strictement l'élite intellectuelle, mais bien toute la population qu'ils cherchent à éduquer aux valeurs nationales. Ces publications revêtent donc les caractéristiques des productions populaires. Les tirages sont élevés et la qualité des livres modeste. Pour diminuer les coûts de production, on évite de payer un illustrateur et au lieu d'un dessin, on utilise une simple photographie noir et blanc. Le contenu et la forme des images sont également typiques des productions pour grand public: représentation de personnages qui facilite l'identification au héros ou à l'auteur, traitement réaliste renforcé par l'utilisation de la photographie.

Du côté de la fiction, on trouve au plus une quinzaine de titres en version illustrée, qui se répartissent à peu près également entre le récit et la poésie. Parmi les plus connus, on peut signaler *Mélodies poétiques* (1893) d'Albert Ferland, avec en frontispice un portrait du poète et *Femmes rêvées* (1899) du même auteur, illustrés par Georges Delfosse et A. Morissette, édités aux frais de l'auteur.

Plus tard, Albert Ferland reprendra la formule du livre illustré avec sa série du
Canada chanté en quatre volumes qu'il accompagnera de ses propres dessins.
Mentionnons aussi le roman *Claude Paysan* (1899) du Dr Ernest Choquette, illustré en noir et blanc par Ozias Leduc et publié par la Cie d'imprimerie de gravures Bishop. Ozias Leduc va réaliser d'autres livres illustrés, dont *Mignonne
allons voir si la rose...* (1912) de Guy Delahaye. C'est également lui qui dessi-
nera le sigle de la revue d'art *le Nigog*. En 1900, paraît un ouvrage qui se démar-
que nettement des autres publications: *la Chasse-galerie* d'Honoré Beaugrand,
illustré par Henri Julien et Raoul Barré. Ce livre, inspiré de l'art nouveau, renoue avec la tradition des manuscrits médiévaux. Les marges y sont généreuses,
la typographie variée, les lettres ornées abondent ainsi que les bandeaux décoratifs et les culs-de-lampe. En plus, neuf planches hors-texte illustrent chacune
des légendes. Il s'agit là sans aucun doute de l'un des premiers livres de luxe paru au Québec.

De 1920 à 1940

Mais malgré l'intérêt de ces quelques publications, elles demeurent peu
nombreuses et sont le résultat de pratiques isolées. Seul l'éditeur Beauchemin
entreprend la publication suivie de livres illustrés, pratique qui recevra une
orientation définitive dans les années 20 et 30. Nous en reparlerons plus loin
lorsqu'il sera question de la littérature de jeunesse.

L'édition au Québec, et à fortiori l'édition de livres illustrés, débute vérita-
blement dans les années 20. C'est à cette époque que naissent les Éditions de
l'Action canadienne-française, qui deviendront en 1926 la propriété d'Albert
Lévesque. On assiste alors à l'avènement d'éditeurs indépendants: outre Albert
Lévesque, on retrouve Louis Carrier (Éditions du Mercure), Edouard Garand,
Albert Pelletier (Éditions du Totem), puis un peu plus tard, Bernard Valiquette,
Lucien Parizeau et quelques autres. Les années 20 et 30 marquent un développement considérable du livre illustré. Près de 200 titres sont publiés au cours
de ces deux décennies, qui laissent une place à l'image. Sur ce nombre, presque
la moitié sont attribuables à l'éditeur Edouard Garand. Cette maison, presque
oubliée aujourd'hui, représente un cas unique dans l'édition québécoise. Entre
1923 et 1931, elle fait paraître dans la collection 'Le roman canadien' plus de
70 livres illustrés, ce qui représente un rythme de huit romans par année. Ces
publications typiquement populaires se rapprochent de la presse à grand tirage
et en adoptent plusieurs caractéristiques: le papier-journal, la disposition du
texte en colonnes, le lettrage extrêmement serré (facteur d'économie), et surtout, l'insertion de pages publicitaires à l'intérieur même du livre. La présence
tout à fait inusitée d'annonces commerciales trahit on ne peut plus clairement
la visée lucrative de l'édition populaire: on ne publie jamais à perte. Ici, le livre

affiche son insertion dans la vie économique et franchit le tabou qui veut que la culture et le commerce soient deux univers incompatibles.

Dans ce type de productions orientées avant tout vers la demande du public, l'éditeur commande aux auteurs des manuscrits et leur assigne lui-même un illustrateur. Edouard Garand, par exemple, pour sa collection 'Le roman canadien,' a toujours recours au même artiste, Albert Fournier, qui signe 74 des 75 volumes de la série. Mis à part la couverture, imprimée en deux ou trois couleurs, les figures sont en noir et blanc et généralement peu nombreuses. L'iconographie privilégie les personnages, présentés en relation les uns avec les autres, ce qui produit une impression de vitalité et d'activité. Quant aux écrivains, ils sont généralement peu connus et cachent parfois leur identité derrière des pseudonymes, phénomène fréquent dans les littératures non légitimées. Ceux dont le nom revient le plus souvent sont: Jean Féron (pseudonyme de Joseph Lebel), Ubald Paquin, Jean Nel, Alexandre Huot, Mme Alcide Lacerte. Les titres des ouvrages sont plutôt racoleurs et garantissent des sensations fortes: *La Mort qu'on venge* (1926), *le Mystérieux inconnu* (1929), *le Spectre du ravin* (1924), *le Lys de sang* (1923). Aux dires d'un écrivain-maison, Alexandre Huot, le tirage des romans atteignait les 10,000 exemplaires, ce qui représentait (et représenterait toujours) un véritable exploit.[9]

Voilà le cas d'un éditeur populaire, ignoré par l'institution. Mais celui qui tient le haut du pavé à cette époque, d'un point de vue symbolique tout au moins, c'est Albert Lévesque, qui en 1926 rachète le fonds de la Bibliothèque de l'Action canadienne-française. Chez Lévesque, l'illustration des livres répond à deux tendances: l'une rattachée au marché scolaire et au circuit des bibliothèques et des écoles (livres pour la jeunesse); l'autre, dirigée vers un public beaucoup plus restreint, plus particulièrement les poètes de la 'jeune génération.' Lévesque fut toujours partagé entre deux publics assez différents pour être parfois contradictoires: le premier, plus traditionnel, était formé des premiers abonnés de l'Action canadienne-française et le second, plus jeune et anticonformiste, d'intellectuels et de nouveaux écrivains rassemblés autour de quelques grandes figures comme Alfred DesRochers et Albert Pelletier.[10] C'est d'ailleurs à l'aide des revenus assurés par le marché scolaire que Lévesque pouvait se permettre de lancer de jeunes auteurs qui, bien que prometteurs et parfois même réputés, s'avéraient peu rentables à court terme.

La littérature pour la jeunesse se concentre autour de quelques écrivains majoritairement féminins: Marie-Claire Daveluy, Maxine, Marjolaine, Marie-Louise d'Auteuil. James McIsaac illustre la plupart des ouvrages que ces

9 Claude-Marie Gagnon, 'Les éditions Édouard Garand et la culture populaire québécoise,' *Voix et Images*, vol. X, no 1, automne 1984, 128.
10 Jacques Michon, 'L'Édition littéraire durant la crise: Albert Lévesque, 1926-1937,' communication présentée au colloque de l'ALCQ, Montréal, le 5 juin 1985.

auteures publient chez Lévesque. Quand ce dernier fermera ses portes, en 1937, McIsaac poursuivra son travail pour le compte des éditions Granger, qui rééditeront d'ailleurs plusieurs volumes publiés chez Lévesque. Le style de McIsaac caractérise l'illustration des ouvrages pour la jeunesse de toute une époque. Ses dessins, contrairement aux images des livres de jeunesse actuels, relèvent de la tradition académique et s'inspirent des grands maîtres romantiques. Les illustrations sont plutôt nombreuses, environ une dizaine par livre, et sont présentées en hors-texte. Les scènes représentées entretiennent des liens très étroits avec le contenu du texte comme en témoigne la présence de légendes. Ce sont généralement des épisodes historiques, puisque la littérature de jeunesse à cette époque se plaît à relater aux enfants les hauts faits de l'histoire canadienne, dans une perspective morale et éducative. Comme pour la littérature populaire, l'illustrateur opte pour la représentation de personnages en action, qui sert fidèlement la narration des péripéties des héros canadiens. Parmi les livres de jeunesse qui se distinguent, il faut mentionner *le Petit page de Frontenac* (1930), de Maxine, illustré par Jean-Paul Lemieux (à l'époque encore jeune artiste fraîchement sorti de l'école des Beaux-Arts) et *l'Épopée canadienne* (1934) de Jean Bruchési, également illustré par Lemieux, assisté cette fois de René Chicoine. Contrairement à la facture réaliste des dessins de McIsaac, ceux de Lemieux développent une plus grande stylisation. L'artiste, beaucoup moins soumis au contenu à représenter, met l'accent avant tout sur la composition et annonce l'ordonnance caractéristique de son oeuvre ultérieure.

La deuxième tendance, celle des poètes de la jeune génération, s'affirme au début des années 30, où quatre livres de poésies paraissent, agrémentés d'illustrations. *Les masques déchirés* de Jovette Bernier paraît en 1932, avec des dessins de Robert Lapalme. Il s'agit à notre connaissance du premier livre illustré par Lapalme, qui deviendra par la suite, comme nous le verrons plus loin, l'illustrateur attitré des Éditions Lucien Parizeau. L'année suivante, Lévesque publie *Dominantes* de René Chopin, accompagné de dessins d'Adrien Hébert; puis, *Du soleil sur l'étang noir*, d'Ulric Gingras, imagé par Rodolphe Duguay. En 1936, vient enfin le recueil de Jacqueline Francoeur *Aux sources claires*, illustré par Simone Hudon, professeur de gravure à l'École des Beaux-Arts de Montréal. Bien qu'il ne s'agisse pas d'un recueil de poésie, le roman *Dans les ombres* d'Eva Sénécal, orné de gravures sur bois de J.-P. Audet, s'inspire d'une même conception, esthétisante et raffinée, du livre.

L'importance de ces quelques publications tient au fait qu'elles manifestent ce que l'on pourrait appeler une 'coalition des avant-gardes,' phénomène qui se développera plus tard avec les éditeurs de poésie, dont la maison Erta demeure la plus significative. Cette coalition, non-exclusive au Québec, a vu le jour en Europe à la fin du XIXe siècle avec le développement des avants-gardes et l'autonomisation des champs artistique et littéraire. Manet illustre Mallarmé (*l'Après-midi d'un faune*), plus tard Apollinaire fait accompagner *l'Enchan-*

teur pourissant de bois gravés de Derain, tandis que Gide et Maurice Denis s'associent pour la conception du *Voyage d'Urien*. Cette collaboration entre artistes et écrivains a pour origine une même position dans l'institution littéraire, généralement une position d'avant-garde en bute aux pratiques dominantes. On sait que l'amitié entre Manet et Mallarmé repose sur un certain rejet institutionnel subi par chacun des deux artistes dans leur champ respectif. Ainsi, en 1874, Manet prend la défense de son ami suite au refus que le jury du Salon signifia à deux de ses tableaux: *Paysage en Normandie* et *le Foyer du bal de l'Opéra*. C'est de cette solidarité que naît leur premier ouvrage collectif: la traduction du *Corbeau* d'Edgar Allan Poe.[11]

Dans le Québec des années trente commence à se développer une même sympathie entre producteurs artistiques et littéraires de la jeune génération. D'un côté comme de l'autre, on prône l'autonomie des pratiques, c'est-à-dire la prise de distance vis-à-vis le discours idéologique dominant et l'importance du travail formel axé sur l'expérimentation des matériaux propres à chaque discipline, la langue d'un côté, la peinture de l'autre. La fonction de l'illustration se modifie. Plutôt que de donner un rendu servile du texte, l'image est conçue comme une oeuvre d'art, à la limite viable sans le support de l'écrit. Les légendes disparaissent, la représentation de personnages ou de scènes explicites diminuent, la stylisation domine et frôle par moment l'abstraction. De cette élévation du travail de l'illustration, le livre acquiert une valeur supplémentaire. La qualité artistique ne se limite plus à l'écrit, elle concerne également l'image. On ne peut encore parler de véritables livres de luxe: les formats demeurent petits, le papier est d'une qualité moyenne. Pourtant, le souci de créer un beau livre est présent selon la tradition mise de l'avant par l'art nouveau en Europe. La mise en page est aérée, les caractères typographiques assez grands et l'impression bien contrastée.

Toujours dans les années vingt, Louis Carrier, propriétaire des Éditions du Mercure, se montre lui aussi soucieux de la qualité matérielle de son produit. Entre 1927 et 1929, il publie 7 livres illustrés, dont deux accompagnés de dessins originaux de Jean-Paul Lemieux: *la Pension Leblanc* (1927) de Robert Choquette et le *le Manoir hanté* (1928) de Régis Roy. On doit mentionner également *l'Homme qui va* (1929) de Jean-Charles Harvey, illustré par Simone Routier. Du côté de la critique d'art, *Ateliers* (1928) de Jean Chauvin prend la forme d'un essai sur vingt-deux artistes. Chaque étude est étayée de nombreuses reproductions noir et blanc des oeuvres des artistes. Par ailleurs, la page couverture présente une estampe originale et en couleur de Robert Pilot. Mais ce que l'on retient surtout des Éditions du Mercure, c'est d'avoir publié le premier livre d'artiste entièrement conçu au Québec, bien que paru en version anglaise:

11 François Chapon, 'Grands illustrés modernes,' *Bulletin du bibliophile*, 1978-1, 48.

Other Days, Other Ways (1928) est la traduction de *Vieilles choses, vieilles gens* de Georges Bouchard dont l'édition originale, réalisée par Beauchemin, date de 1926. Ce livre tiré à 100 exemplaires comporte 22 bois gravés en noir et blanc et un bois gravé en brun et noir de l'artiste Edwin Holgate.[12]

Ainsi, *Other Days, Other Ways* marque les débuts du livre d'artiste au Québec. Trois ans plus tard, Edwin Holgate renoue avec cette formule et conçoit *Metropolitan Museum* sur un texte de Robert Choquette. Grâce à son papier de qualité, son grand format et l'intérêt de ses illustrations, cet ouvrage constitue l'une des publications locales les mieux réussies. *Courriers des villages* (1940) de Clément Marchand, d'une édition plus modeste, se distingue également pour la qualité des bois gravés de Rodolphe Duguay. En 1939, Cécile Chabot publie *Vitrail*, un livre unique pour l'époque que l'on peut ranger aujourd'hui parmi les précurseurs du livre-objet. Sur un tirage total de 100 exemplaires, les 20 premiers contiennent tous six aquarelles originales, les 20 suivants, 6 eaux-fortes et les 60 derniers, une aquarelle chacun et six hors-textes.[13] L'aquarelle ne permettant pas la reproduction en multiples, Cécile Chabot a dû exécuter en tout 180 aquarelles, en plus des six eaux-fortes. Ce travail inouï et tout à fait exceptionnel inaugure le concept de livre unique où chaque exemplaire se distingue des autres.

Ces couvrages tirés à très peu d'exemplaires et garnis d'estampes originales, s'adressent à un public limité, amateur d'art autant que de littérature. Dans ces livres, l'importance de l'image dépasse de beaucoup celle des productions courantes. Dans *Metropolitan Museum*, les 29 feuillets doubles réunissent 13 bois gravés que l'on retrouve dès la couverture, sur la page titre et à la suite de chacun des poèmes. Le format du livre, l'originalité des illustrations et la réputation de l'artiste invitent à une lecture lente et comtemplative. La préciosité des matériaux transforme le livre en objet de luxe.

De 1940 à 1960

Cette nouvelle alliance entre le monde des arts et celui des lettres se poursuit dans les années 40 et 50. Lucien Parizeau, qui fonda en 1944 parallèlement à sa maison d'édition, une galerie d'art, est probablement l'éditeur le plus représentatif de ce mouvement. Il incarne bien le phénomène de 'double vocation'[14] et occupe une position idéale pour mettre de l'avant le livre illustré. Dès

12 Claudette Hould, *Répertoire des livres d'artistes au Québec, 1900-1980*, Montréal, Bibliothèque nationale du Québec, 1982, 239 p.
13 *Ibidem.*
14 Dario Gamboni, 'À travers champ. Pour une économie des rapports entre champ littéraire et champ artistique,' *Lendemains*, no 36, 1984, 21-32.

sa première publication, *les Îles de la nuit* d'Alain Grandbois, Parizeau affiche son souci d'une présentation visuelle de qualité en confiant cette tâche à Alfred Pellan. Rappelons au passage que les années quarante voient naître, dans le domaine artistique, le mouvement de 'l'art vivant,' animé par deux des plus importants artistes de cette génération: Alfred Pellan et Paul-Émile Borduas. C'est, si l'on veut, la naissance de l'avant-garde en peinture, dont les objectifs sont de contester toute forme d'académisme ou de soumission au discours nationaliste. La liberté des sujets est revendiquée, de même qu'une facture non explicitement réaliste. Ce mouvement, issu du milieu des arts visuels, reçoit l'appui de nombreux écrivains, parmi lesquels on peut citer Robert Elie, Jacques de Tonnancour, Gilles Hénault et Claude Gauvreau. La production d'un ouvrage tel que les *Îles de la nuit* pariticipe de ce mouvement de solidarité entre les avant-gardes artistique et littéraire. Le style de l'écrivain et de l'artiste, Grandbois et Pellan, témoigne non seulement d'affinités esthétiques et d'une ouverture déclarée au surréalisme européen, mais surtout d'une identité de position dans la hiérarchie institutionnelle, celle d'une avant-garde en voie de légitimation. L'éditeur Parizeau, inscrit dans une logique de la distinction propre au réseau cultivé, privilégiait les productions marginales ou qui présentaient une quelconque originalité. Très vite, il aura recours à Robert Lapalme, l'un des caricaturistes les plus personnels de l'époque, pour créer des couvertures de livres vivantes et inusitées. Le style de Lapalme, inspiré à la fois du cubisme et de l'art déco, instaure la marque de commerce de la maison et lui sert de signe distinctif. Lapalme illustre également le texte de certains livres, dont *Ristontac* d'Andrée Maillet.

Mais Parizeau ne s'est pas limité à la publication d'auteurs québécois. Son catalogue compte bon nombre d'inédits français, dont plusieurs sont illustrés. Mentionnons *Dames étranges* de Michel Georges-Michel, lui-même illustrateur de son ouvrage, *les Années noires* de Paul Phelps-Morand, accompagné d'un bois gravé de Charles McDonald et *Cri d'alarme* d'Halina Izdebska, réalisé en collaboration avec le graveur Jean Lébédeff. *Le roman de Tristan et Iseult* n'est pas signé du nom d'un artiste, mais se présente accompagné de lettrines, culs-de-lampes et motifs décoratifs.

En dehors des romans et des recueils de poésie, les autres titres misent plutôt sur la photographie: photographies de l'écrivain et de son milieu pour la biographie de Pierre Loti, scènes de films, gros plans d'acteurs pour *la Grande mission du cinéma*, reproduction d'un portrait de William Shakespeare pour l'ouvrage critique de son oeuvre, deux planches en couleurs représentant les palettes du peintre et servant à appuyer le propos didactique de *l'Art de peindre*, ainsi qu'une trentaine de reproductions de peintures en guise de symbole de la civilisation française, dans *Esquisse de la France*.

Toujours dans les années quarante, les Cahiers de la File indienne font paraître 6 recueils de poésie, dont 4 illustrés. La maison, fondée par Eloi de

Grandmont et Gilles Hénault, était liée de près au milieu des arts visuels et à l'avant-garde picturale. Pellan illustre *le Voyage d'Arlequin* d'Eloi de Grandmont, tandis que Charles Daudelin, Jean-Paul Mousseau et Tomi Simard illustreront respectivement les recueils de Gilles Hénault, *Théâtre en plein air* (1946), de Thérèse Renaud, *les Sables du rêve* (1946) et de Pierre-Yves Le Baron, *les Équilibres illusoires* (1948) (soulignons que Tomi Simard n'est nul autre que Le Baron lui-même). Ces ouvrages (tirés à 250 exemplaires) sont tous remarquables par leur présentation et se rapprochent du livre d'artiste. Imprimés sur papier de luxe, ils offrent des images hors-texte d'une très grande netteté de reproduction.

De fait, l'évolution du livre illustré, et particulièrement du livre d'artiste, va de pair avec le développement et la diffusion des techniques de la gravure. L'enseignement des arts graphiques au Québec ne date pas de la fondation de l'École des Arts graphiques en 1942. Déjà dans les années vingt et trente, le Musée des Beaux-Arts de Montréal offrait des cours de gravure dispensés entre autres par Edwin Holgate et Simone Hudon.[15] Par contre, le développement véritable des techniques de la gravure et leur diffusion à grande échelle originent de l'École des Arts graphiques et du dynamisme de ses professeurs, Albert Dumouchel et Arthur Gladu. Cette école, qui visait à former des professionnels dans les arts d'impression, offrait des cours en gravure, en typographie, et en reliure. Elle fit paraître deux revues de luxe, *Impressions* et *Les Ateliers d'Arts graphiques* dans lesquelles les étudiants de l'école mettaient en pratique ce qu'ils avaient appris en classe et expérimentaient de nouvelles formules. La première était publiée annuellement et limitait la collaboration aux seuls étudiants de l'école. La revue *Les Ateliers d'arts graphiques* qui ne publie que deux numéros, en 1947 et 1949, reprend le même concept mais cette fois avec plus d'envergure. Le format est plus grand (32cm x 25 cm), le numéro plus volumineux et les collaborateurs regroupent des peintres et des écrivains importants de l'avant-garde culturelle: Pellan, Borduas, Jean-Paul Mousseau, Mimi Parent, Pierre Gauvreau, Jacques de Tonnancourt, Robert Lapalme, Gille Hénault, Eloi de Grandmont, Robert Elie, Roger Duhamel, etc. Tirée à 1,500 exemplaires, *Les Ateliers d'arts graphiques* participe elle aussi à la naissance de l'édition de luxe au Québec.

Si *Les Ateliers d'arts graphiques* n'a connu qu'une brève existence (deux numéros), elle a par contre suscité la création d'entreprises parallèles, dont les Éditions Erta. Roland Giguère, le fondateur de la maison, fait partie de cette nouvelle génération d'artistes et d'artisans, formés par l'École des Arts graphiques, qui vont transformer de façon majeure la scène éditoriale et artistique des années cinquante et soixante. Sa maison d'édition se distingue par un souci de

15 Jean-René Ostiguy, 'Un choix de livres illustrés par des artistes québécois entre 1916 et 1946,' Ottawa, Bulletin annuel de la Galerie nationale du Canada, 1982, 15-36.

la matérialité: typographie très variée, mise en page peu orthodoxe, illustrations originales. Giguère, partagé entre les métiers de poète, de typographe et de graveur, occupe une position idéale pour développer un modèle original de livre illustré où l'image s'affranchit du texte et propose un discours autonome. Sa première publication, *Faire naître* en 1949, réunit ses propres poèmes avec des sérigraphies d'Albert Dumouchel, son ancien professeur. Les premiers livres des Éditions Erta doivent beaucoup à l'École des Arts graphiques. Outre la collaboration d'un des professeurs, Guy Beauchamp, pour la composition, Giguère utilisa clandestinement les caractères et les presses de l'école pour imprimer ses textes.

L'originalité des Éditions Erta réside dans la conception artisanale du livre. Tout comme le livre bibliophilique en France à la fin du XIXe siècle, les livres illustrés de Giguère contestent la production industrielle et proposent un retour au livre fait main.[16] Sans qu'il s'agisse dès le départ de livres d'artiste au sens strict, les publications de la maison s'approchent du livre unique dont chaque partie résulte du travail d'un artisan. La collection de 'La Tête armée' dirigée par Claude Haeffely fait paraître 6 numéros dus au travail conjoint d'artistes et d'écrivains. *Totems* de Gilles Hénault, illustré par Albert Dumouchel, inaugura cette collection avec un tirage de 335 exemplaires. Durant les années cinquante, les livres gardent une présentation modeste. Ils sont de petit format, imprimés sur un papier de qualité moyenne et les illustrations résultent de procédés de reproduction mécanique. À partir de la fin des années soixante, Roland Giguère, revenu d'un séjour en Europe, réoriente sa maison vers une production plus luxueuse respectant tous les critères du véritable livre d'artiste.

Dans une perspective similaire, de petites maisons publient des textes poétiques accompagnés de dessins de jeunes artistes. Mentionnons *la Duègne accroupie* (1959) de Michèle Drouin, avec un frontispice de l'auteure (Quartz), *l'Ange du matin* (1952) de Fernand Dumont, accompagné d'un hors-texte de Louise Carrier (Malte), *Terres prochaines* (1958) de Guy Fournier, avec des dessins de Charles Daudelin (Orphée), *les Trouble-fête* (1952) de Sylvain et Pierre Gauvreau (Malte), *les Affres du zeste* (1958) de Diane Pelletier-Spiecker et Klaus Spiecker (Quartz) et *Poèmes de la sommeillante* (1958) de Kline Ste-Marie et Klaus Spiecker (Quartz).

L'École des Arts graphiques n'a pas contribué uniquement à la création des Éditions Erta, elle a également permis à une seconde génération de graveurs de se réunir autour d'une nouvelle maison: les Éditions Goglin. Marie-Anastasie, Richard Lacroix, Janine Leroux, Françoise Bujold et Guy Robert font paraître en 1957 *Sept eaux-fortes*, un volumineux livre d'artiste qui renouvelle la

---

16 Jean-Marcel Duciaume, 'Le livre d'artiste au Québec: contribution à une histoire,' *Études françaises*, vol. 18, no 2, automne 1982, 89-98.

conception habituelle du livre illustré. Contrairement aux ouvrages de Erta qui maintenaient un équilibre entre le texte et l'image, *Sept eaux-fortes* s'affiche avant tout comme un recueil de gravures. Il apparaît clairement que la motivation de l'ouvrage consiste bien plus à diffuser la production gravée des quatre artistes que la brève introduction de Guy Robert. Les autres publications de la maison, cinq en tout, n'auront pas toutes une orientation aussi marquée vers la dimension plastique. *L'eau, la montagne et le loup* de Guy Arsenault, accompagné de quatre bois gravés de Janine Leroux, maintient une large place à l'écrit. Françoise Bujold, qui occupe une position similaire à celle de Roland Giguère, à cheval entre les arts et la littérature, cherchera à garder constante la rencontre entre poésie et graphisme.

Mais pendant les années 40 et 50, le roman illustré se développe surtout dans le secteur de la littérature de jeunesse. Granger, Fides, Beauchemin et la Librairie générale canadienne fournissent à elles seules la majorité des titres. Pendant ces deux décennies, Granger, Fides et la LGC mettent sur le marché une cinquantaine de livres chacun, tandis que Beauchemin en publie 16. Chez Granger, le principal illustrateur demeure James McIsaac. Pour sa part, Fides fait appel à Maurice Petitdidier, Henri Beaulac, Gabriel de Beney, Cécile Chabot, Léonie Gervais et plusieurs autres. Chez Beauchemin et à la Librairie générale canadienne, les illustrateurs demeurent le plus souvent anonymes. Cette dernière maison, fondée dans les années 20 mais qui prend sa véritable expansion au début des années 40, offre un bon exemple d'une production de livres illustrés pour la jeunesse.

Il peut paraître inopportun de ranger la littérature de jeunesse dans la catégorie des productions pour grand public, puisqu'en fait, elle s'adresse à un public spécifique, celui des enfants et des adolescents. Pourtant, les tirages élevés, la modestie des matériaux utilisés et les prix plutôt bas les rapprochent souvent des ouvrages populaires. De plus, comme dans les livres adaptés à un public qui lit peu, l'image, dans les ouvrages pour la jeunesse, facilite la compréhension du texte. À la Librairie générale canadienne, la production est divisée en nombreuses collections qui visent chacune un groupe d'âge spécifique. Généralement, plus le lecteur est jeune et peu initié à la lecture, plus les illustrations sont abondantes et conçues pour redoubler le sens du texte. L'image est utilisée pour sa fonction didactique et, bien sur, comme moyen de séduire le jeune lecteur. Ainsi, elle sert non seulement à favoriser l'acquisition du langage écrit, mais elle contribue également à propager dès le plus jeune âge, les valeurs morales dominantes. *Anéatah et Deranah, les jumelles d'Hochelaga,* l'un des bons succès de la Librairie générale canadienne (le tirage indique 25,000 ex.), répond bien à la fois aux attentes du jeune public lecteur et à celles des éducateurs. Les dessins, en plusieurs couleurs, ont tout pour attirer le regard du jeune adolescent. L'iconographie, quant à elle, reproduit la vision et les codes d'un discours conservateur et souvent stéréotypé à l'égard de l'Indien. L'identité raciale ou nationale s'exprime aussi bien dans les vêtements exagérément élaborés des jeunes Indiennes que dans la représentation de la nature, où apparaissent les principaux symboles du pays: que ce soit les bouleaux, les feuilles d'érable ou les castors. Ici aussi, la fonction de l'illustration s'explique par le marché dans lequel elle s'inscrit. La littérature de jeunesse étant encore dans les années 40 et 50 largement soumise au marché scolaire, sa portée morale et didactique devient sa qualité dominante.

En conclusion, nous tenons à rappeler l'importance des composantes matérielles du livre et à insister sur leur caractère non-arbitraire. L'illustration, en tant que constituant de l'objet-livre, répond elle aussi à des impératifs dictés par le marché. Mais les différences de marchés amènent les éditeurs à produire des livres illustrés adaptés à leurs publics-cibles. Dans ces ouvrages, l'illustration est non seulement différente dans sa composition mais joue également une fonction spécifique liée à la logique du réseau dans lequel elle s'inscrit. Dans le circuit cultivé, l'illustrateur sert avant tout à légitimer le livre, à lui conférer un surcroît de capital symbolique, qui par la suite sera reconverti en valeur marchande. Dans le livre illustré de luxe, l'image séduit le lecteur grâce à ses qualités esthétiques. Elle contribue à fétichiser le livre, à le consacrer objet de culte.

Par ailleurs, le livre illustré populaire utilise lui aussi la séduction mais celle-ci joue plutôt sur l'émotivité du lecteur. L'efficacité de l'illustration réside dans son expressivité. C'est la raison pour laquelle elle utilise fréquemment la représentation de personnages en action, ce qui favorise l'identification et permet au lecteur de 'vivre' l'histoire plutôt que de la contempler de l'extérieur. La littérature de jeunesse se rapproche de cette conception mais renforce l'aspect didactique. Sa fonction première consiste à favoriser l'acquisition des grands codes sociaux: ceux de la langue et ceux de la morale dominante.

Il faudrait revenir également sur le rôle du livre illustré dans les stratégies institutionnelles du champ culturel. Dans le Québec de la première moitié du XXe siècle, le livre illustré a permis à de jeunes artistes et écrivains de se solidariser dans la lutte contre les pratiques légitimes. Pour un écrivain peu connu, la collaboration d'un artiste qui jouit d'une certaine réputation facilite la reconnaissance du milieu littéraire. L'inverse est également vrai et se vérifie durant les années 50 et 60, dans la production de nombreux livres de graveurs. La gravure étant jusqu'à tout récemment rangée parmi les arts mineurs, son union avec la littérature et plus particulièrement avec la poésie, lui permet d'accéder à un statut supérieur et d'accroître sa légitimité. C'est le mérite d'un artiste tel que Roland Giguère d'avoir initié le milieu littéraire à l'art de la gravure.

Il aurait été sans aucun doute intéressant de s'attarder aux genres littéraires privilégiés par la formule du livre illustré. La littérature de jeunesse par exemple, se conçoit difficilement sans illustrations. Le conte également, apparaît particulièrement bien adapté à l'image, qui se développe elle aussi de façon synthétique. Quant à la poésie, si on peut faire un lien entre métaphore et image visuelle, il semble que ce soit surtout pour leurs mêmes prétentions artistiques que poème et dessin se rejoignent.

Par contre, il faut bien admettre que le roman pour adultes délaisse de plus en plus la forme du livre illustré. Sans pousser plus loin l'analyse, il semble que l'avènement de l'écriture psychologique, qui mise avant tout sur la description de sentiments intérieurs et non pas sur des références visuelles, fréquentes dans le roman réaliste, se prête difficilement à la représentation graphique. Enfin, il apparaît que les versions illustrées des romans à succès adopte dorénavant une autre voie, celle du cinéma. Mais, nous entrons là dans un tout autre sujet.

Université de Sherbrooke

GEORGE L. PARKER

Publishing in Nineteenth–Century Canada: copyright and the market for books

My task in the next half hour is to tell you about a very complex subject, the publishing and copyright context for authorship in nineteenth-century Canada. As a unique form of government intervention in the literary marketplace, copyright legislation encourages authorship and stabilizes publishing: it is a way of protecting authors from unauthorized reproduction of their works, and it clarifies the legal territory for the reproducers and disseminators of those works. In the western world copyright has been the means of providing fair profits to both creator and disseminator. But copyright, like so many other cultural and industrial activities where tastes, advertising, and sales overlap from market to market, also has international ramifications. Although even a superficial knowledge of the copyright and publishing conflicts of nineteenth-century Canada is lacking these days, those situations directly bear on the infrastructure of our book market today.

Take, for example, our concern with cultural sovereignty and our cultural industries, which were topics of fear and speculation during the 1986-88 free-trade talks between Canada and the United States.[1] Without a clear understanding of the historical development of authorship, the publishing industry, the copyright tangles, and the colonial status of this small nation, many of our politicians and businessmen and possibly most of the American and Canadian public — for whom the only measuring rod is the bottom line — simply write off 'cultural nationalists' as doomsters and nervous nellies. At least the ownership

1 Charlotte Montgomery, 'Government Indicates Film, Books to Be Part of Trade Talks with U.S.,' *The Globe and Mail* (National ed.), 6 November 1985, Al, A2. See also Flora MacDonald's speech in Parliament on 16 March 1987, ['Canada's culture and culture instruments are sacrosanct and are not in negotiation'], Canada, House of Commons, *Debates*, 1987, 4221-4224.

of firms and of technology was not the issue in the nineteenth-century Canadian book trade, as were the other commercial negotiations — such as contracts between authors and publishers, as well as the network for producing and distributing books which evolved at a time when this country was a colony, in the legal, economic, and cultural senses of that word. Not only has that colonial status shaped our perspectives and those of our Anglo-American neighbours about ourselves, but it also directly shaped our publishing industry and our copyright legislation. That, in other words, is the economic institution that we are examining at this symposium. Hence the reason why some Canadians today are so sensitive about ownership and control of our cultural industries is not due to sentimental patriotism only, but to an understanding of the hard facts of history.

One of those hard facts is the story of how a 1900 amendment to the Canadian Copyright Act of 1875 gave economic and legal advantages to foreign publishers in order that local publishers could have practical control of their own market.[2] This copyright law itself was the long-awaited consequence of several alternatives open to our book trade between 1840 and 1900.

One route would have been to maintain the status quo, that is, the earlier colonial organization. For the most part, such a colonial industry would let foreigners supply their literature and their books to our readers. The publishing trade, then, would have been a marginal and regional industry whose newspaper offices would occasionally issue books by Canadian authors.

The second route could have been the one pursued by the Americans with so much success — a protectionist and unilateral one. That is, you set up barriers in the form of protectionist copyright laws and tariffs to discourage foreigners from exporting their books into your market. This is also, of course, an inexpensive way for a government to support the manufacturing sector of the book trade. It works well when there is a large population base to support that industry.

The third route, the one that did materialize, involved compromises, not simply because God made Canadians compromisers by nature, but because the set of factors to be addressed were not under exclusive Canadian control or exclusive American control or exclusive British control. I mean, we are not talking merely about the desires of publishers themselves, but about the rights of authors and the needs of readers in different nations.

What I am suggesting here is that what happens in Canada is often closely connected to events elsewhere. Some of them directly transform Canadian experiences, such as the American Revolution and the 1914 assassination at Sarajevo, but other events may only realign an existing Canadian situation. In the book trade, for example, copyright was one of several international situations

2 Portions of my book *The Beginnings of the Book Trade in Canada* (Toronto: University of Toronto Press, 1985) deal with this topic in greater detail.

that changed significantly as professional authorship became economically viable. In technology alone, everything from steamships and railways to power presses and paper manufactured from wood lowered book prices and improved distribution. At the same time the spread of literacy throughout the middle and working classes was effected by literary societies, mechanics' institutes, and provincial common schools with their uniform texts. The growing specialization of the book trade in Europe and the United States was accompanied by closer contacts between British and American houses after the Civil War, the presence of creative editors in large houses, the appearance of literary agents, and the commercialization of literature with seasonal, disposable best sellers.[3]

While all these things bear close examination in terms of the relation between our developing industrial state and cultural literacy, they are part of the reason why copyright itself became crucial and why four dates concerned with copyright legislation *outside* this country had so much to do with the structure of Canadian publishing and bookselling: namely, 1842, 1847, 1885, and 1891. In 1842 a new consolidated British Literary Copyright Act was passed — we refer to it as the Imperial Copyright Act of 1842 — and it was the basic law of copyright in Canada until the present law came into force in 1924 (this is the law that the 1988 copyright act will replace). In 1847 an amendment to that 1842 act permitted the legal entry of pirated American reprints into British North America. In 1885 the Berne Copyright Convention gave international protection to a book without regard to its place of manufacture, and the Imperial Act of 1886 implementing this Convention automatically included Canada as one of the adherents. Then in 1891 a new American copyright law was followed by a Reciprocal Copyright Agreement between Britain and the United States, and this Agreement ended piracy between the two countries. The British also included Canada in the Agreement, at the insistence of the United States.

So, keep in mind those foreign events while we look more closely at publishing and copyright in nineteenth-century Canada. You will remember that a few minutes ago I said that the publishing industry had three choices of direction — to remain colonial, to become independent, or to adopt some compromise route between the others.

II

Compared with the vitality and the large volume of bookselling in Britain, the United States, and France, Canada's looked very insignificant. Thousands of books were issued, but most of the literary titles consisted of religious works,

---

3   This topic is examined in Richard Altick, *The English Common Reader* (Chicago: The University of Chicago Press, 1957), and in Q.D. Leavis, *Fiction and the Reading Public* (London: Chatto and Windus, 1932). See also [W.W. Campbell], 'At the Mermaid Inn,' *The Globe*, 4 February 1893.

local histories, poetry, and a small amount of fiction. Local publishing emerged from the newspaper offices in eastern Canada and from a handful of book-sellers, for entrepreneurial publishing was almost non-existent before the 1880s. Retail bookselling was more visible, and certainly more viable, than book publishing because the book trade was chiefly devoted to selling imported books and periodicals. Attempts to offset the import business by the publication of local authors or local editions of foreign authors — which you would assume to be the goal of an autonomous book trade — simply created more problems in the form of lost profits and international quarrels.

Let's look at Joseph Howe's problems as a publisher. He could see the intri-cate connection between an educated electorate and its political sophistication. If there was to be a provincial literature that reflected the life and aspirations of society, then he would have to 'create' its writers and its audience. And what happened when he found a talented humorist in Thomas Chandler Haliburton? Well, the popular Halifax edition of *The Clockmaker* (1836) was pirated in Lon-don by Richard Bentley, whose edition became an international best seller. Bentley and the British publishers argued that first publication in a colony did not really count outside that colony. Soon Haliburton's annoyance melted into delight at finding a large audience and big royalties, and he and Bentley then did their best to ignore Howe.[4] The moral of this story? British and American publishers did not want to negotiate with colonial publishers on joint ventures. The colonial publisher on his own was not likely to risk his own capital (if he had any) in a small, precarious market. Often the author was asked to pay the production expenses. Professional authors such as Haliburton, Richardson, Moodie, Traill, De Mille, and Fleming sought out publishers in London and New York, and their books circulated in Canada as foreign editions. Thus, this phase of colonial publishing, roughly up to 1870, was characterized by extreme caution.

The next phase of publishing, between the late 1860s and 1890, was domi-nated by publishers who were essentially printers with large plants that had to be kept busy all day in order to make a profit. John Lovell of Montreal was one of that generation of printers and manufacturers who persuaded the Province of Canada in 1858 to establish protective tariffs in order to nurture the infant industries. These tariffs (which included books) had the same intention as the better known 1878 tariffs — part of that package known as the National Policy —

---

4   I have written on the Haliburton-Howe relation in 'Another Look at Haliburton and His Publishers Joseph Howe and Richard Bentley: The Colonial Author and his Milieu,' in *The Thomas Chandler Haliburton Symposium*, ed. Frank M. Tierney (Ottawa: University of Ottawa Press, 1985), 83-92; and ' "To Foster and Extend Our Provincial Literature": Joseph Howe and the Market for Books in Nova Scotia, 1828-1841,' *The Proceedings of the Joseph Howe Symposium*, ed. Wayne Hunt (Sackville, Centre for Canadian Studies, Mount Allison University; Nimbus Publishing, 1984), 103-115.

whose principle was that what was good for Quebec and Ontario was good for the whole Dominion. Like Howe, Lovell had his vision for the literature of this country, but he always seems to have spoken of this in terms of economics and industry, as if literary culture would naturally flower if there were a strong book manufacturing base.

In 1858 Lovell, wanting to print more than city directories and government documents, tried three new kinds of publishing. First of all, he launched into original textbook publishing with some success. Second, he had little luck encouraging local fiction writing, and even less trying to market it. Third, he was threatened with court proceedings when he tried to reprint a Canadian edition of a successful British textbook. After Confederation, Lovell decided it was time to do things the way American publishers did them—by reprinting popular British fiction. He could do this either by getting permission for a local edition or by simply pirating the book (which was the American way). But because it was illegal to pirate a British copyright work within the British Empire, Lovell ran the risk of expensive court trials. The first book Lovell chose was appropriately entitled *Foul Play* (1869), by Dion Bouciault and Charles Reade; he was duly threatened with a court case and got the reputation as a Canadian pirate.

Resigned to the fact that the Foreign Reprints Act would not be repealed, in 1871 Lovell built a huge modern printing plant at Rouse's Point, New York, about 50 miles south of Montreal. He intended to pirate British works on the American side and then ship them into Canada, for this was permitted if he paid the British copyright holder a small duty. Actually, he got so many orders from American publishers that the piracy operation was soon superceded by legimitate printing.

Yet he was convinced that there also would be in time a profitable market in Canada for reprints of popular books.[5] So he and other reprinters persuaded the Canadian government to pass protectionist copyright acts that required Canadian manufacture as a condition of copyright; among these were two abortive acts (one in 1872 and another in 1889) that proposed a licensing system whereby the reprint could be made if necessary without the consent of the original copyright owner. The Canadians argued that this was the way to strengthen printing and publishing, and that in time they could export these same reprints to the United States at a competitive price.

A whole generation of Montreal and Toronto reprinters from the 1870s until the early 1890s issued cheap series of books that were either pirated or whose copyright was in some doubt, along with a leavening of legitimate titles and even some Canadian ones. These gentlemen included the Belford Brothers; John

---

5 [John Lovell and Graeme Mercer Adam], *A Letter to Sir John Rose. . .on the Canadian Copyright Question*, by Two Members of the Native Book Trade [pseud.] (London, 1872), 8.

Ross Robertson, the founder of the *Toronto Telegram*; and Hunter, Rose, the printing and binding firm that went out of business in 1985. It would be inaccurate to say they served a 'mass market' but this was the Canadian equivalent of one, and they certainly printed millions of copies. In their efforts they had the support of the Toronto Board of Trade, the Canadian Manufacturers' Association, and even Prime Minister John Thompson; and they certainly had the support of booksellers and the public at large. This was, after all, the era in which the cry of cheap reading for the masses was an important plank in the liberal program for the spread of literacy.

III

But at the heart of the problem with Canadian publishing in the last quarter of the century was the anomaly that permitted pirated reprints to be sold legally in this country. This situation existed because booksellers had always imported books from Britain and the United States. But by 1840 a great many of the American imports were not works of American origin but cheap pirated reprints of British copyrights. British publishers had inadvertently handed over the British North American market to the Americans, for costly British books were very slow in getting to Canada and then were prohibitively expensive when they got here. The Americans, with the largest market in the English-speaking world, exploited their situation by printing large editions that were sold at low prices. Naturally, Canadians bought these cheap books. Why pay 30 shillings if you can get the book for 5 or 6 shillings? These reprints ranged from textbooks, scientific treatises, and histories, to the novels of Scott and Dickens. While American printers and publishers grew rich on authors to whom they paid no royalties, other Americans, unhappy with the ethics of this practice, spent fifty years negotiating with the British for fair treatment for authors.[6]

In 1842 the new Imperial Copyright Act excluded the pirated reprints from all British territories, which included British North America. The outcry[7] from the colonies soon reached Whitehall, but five years passed before the new Whig Government accommodated the British North American need for cheap educational reprints from the United States by passing the Foreign Reprints Act of 1847. This Act permitted the pirated reprint into each province when a 12½% duty was collected at the border for the British copyright holder.

6   This subject is treated at length in James J. Barnes, *Authors, Publishers, and Politicians: The Quest for an Anglo-American Copyright Agreement 1815-1854* (London: Routledge & Kegan Paul, 1974).
7   The outcry led to the first government enquiry into the book trade, and its findings are reported in 'English Copyrights Act: Report of the Select Committee...,' Canada (Province), Legislative Assembly, *Sessional Papers, No 2...of the Journals, 1843*. Appendix PP (Kingston: Barker 1844).

There were all kinds of unforeseen consequences from this philanthropic desire to help the poor Canadian population. In 1857 British publishers claimed angrily they had never heard of it, and they never did get very much from those duties. In fact, had the duties been collected scrupulously, British publishers might have been more sympathetic to the plight of the Canadian reprint publishers later in the century — but this is purely hypothetical. Meanwhile, Canadian booksellers imported thousands of these reprint editions (and not all of them were pirated works).[8] For their part, the Americans became accustomed to supplying the Canadian market with roughly ten per cent of their runs. By the 1870s American publishers frequently persuaded British authors to include Canada with the American market rights. In this way the Americans protected themselves from Canadian reprints because then the British author would not be able to sell Canadian rights to a Canadian publisher.[9] But by the 1880s, when transport across the Atlantic was faster and cheaper, the British imitated the Americans by issuing cheap series for their colonial markets, for British publishers assumed that the Canadian market was *theirs* — to be supplied with books from the Mother Country. That is what colonies are for.

In the light of these circumstances, the frustration and anger of Lovell, the Belfords, George MacLean Rose, and John Ross Robertson becomes understandable. We may almost forgive them for their piracies. If Canada were to be an autonomous nation after 1867, which could and did make its own copyright laws, why, then, could not the Canadian printer and publisher control and supply his own market? Why should American publishers have an extraordinary privilege that was denied to Canadians? Well, Canadian copyright law in 1868 and 1875 stipulated that you must print and publish in Canada to get *Canadian* copyright, but in fact this law tended to apply only to residents of Canada. A British copyright book, and even an American copyright that was offered for sale in London, could be protected in Canada under the 1842 Imperial Act because we were part of the Empire; and the Colonial Laws Validity Act of 1865 ensured that future colonial legislation would not remove or restrict rights that existed under prior British legislation. The Canadian courts always maintained this principle of imperial protection in Canada.

---

8   In 1865 William Chewett of Toronto imported about 10,000 copies of British magazines; as noted in J.M. Trout, *Annual Statement of the Trade of Toronto. . .1865* (Toronto: The Leader, 1865), 50.

9   This was the point of James Anthony Froude's comments before the Imperial Royal Commission on Copyright. See Great Britain, Parliament, Copyright Commission, *Minutes of the Evidence taken before the Royal Commission on Copyright Together with an Appendix. Preceded by Tables of the Witnesses and of the Contents of the Appendix* (London: Eyre and Spottiswoode, 1878), 273-274.

IV

Two events helped resolve the situation to the satisfaction of the British author and the Canadian publisher: the Berne Convention of 1885 and the Anglo-American Reciprocal Copyright Agreement of 1891. We ended up with the agency system, which meant the presence of branch-plant and subsidiary publishing. Colonialism has many guises.

Although the Berne Convention was an important step forward in protecting authors' rights internationally, it was not welcomed by the Canadian publishers, who could only see their market carved up even more. There had been a decade-long depression and there were dozens of bankruptcies among book firms each year. In fact, some Canadian publishers only survived because they had textbooks and subscription books to fall back on.[10] The American Copyright law of 1891 and the subsequent Anglo-American Reciprocal Copyright Agreement also put authorship on firmer grounds, and even Canadian authors benefitted from this act. It immediately ended the American piracy of British books, and thus turned the 1847 Foreign Reprints Act into a dead letter. In time the new American law was probably the salvation of Canadian publishing,[11] but nevertheless it was a protectionist Act and Canadian publishers wanted the same kind of protection in the Canadian Act. For five years the Canadian trade was in a state of crisis because now that there were no more pirated editions to worry about, all the foreign editions in our market were legal! It was possible to buy a best seller such as *Trilby* (1895) in three different national, legal, editions—British, American, and Canadian.[12] When this situation was shown to them, even the British publishers conceded that changes must be made and some conciliations were agreed to at a Copyright Conference in Ottawa in November 1895. Although these arrangements took five years to be legislated, other fortunate changes came about in the marketplace.

With piracy removed by the 1891 American law, both British and American firms were inclined to make legal arrangements and joint ventures with Canadian publishers, for issuing books by Canadian and non-Canadian writers—a far cry from the days of Howe and Lovell. These changes were put into

10 Sir George Foster commented on hard times in the 1890s in a speech in Parliament: Canada, House of Commons, *Debates*, 1894, 221-222. See also George Doram, *Chronicles of Barabbas* (New York: Harcourt, Brace, 1935), 13.
11 William Gage's annual report for 1900 of the Booksellers' and Stationers' Section of the Toronto Board of Trade, in 'Canada May Supply Britain with Paper,' *Bookseller and Stationer*, XVII (February 1901), 22-24.
12 Canada, Sessional Papers (No. 8B), Appendix to the Report of the Minister of Agriculture, 1895, *Conference on the Copyright Question* (Ottawa: Queen's Printer, 1896), 6.

practice by a new generation of young Canadian publishers and young French- and English-speaking authors. Both groups persuaded Laurier's cabinet to listen to the message of British and French publishers, which was this: that the Canadian reprinters—who represented the manufacturing sector—should no longer call the tune as far as authors' rights were concerned; that Canada must not be allowed to withdraw from the Berne Convention; and that flexible arrangements be made for issuing books in Canada, either by importing plates, sheets, or books—depending on their sales prospects—rather than rigidly insisting on all stages of manufacture in Canada.[13]

The authors, for their part, supported the entrepreneurial publishers such as William Copp, William Briggs of the Methodist Book and Publishing House, and George Morang, a young American who threw his lot in with twentieth-century Canada.[14] I think that when it came to the economics of publishing, Copp, Briggs, and Morang were as hard-nosed as John Lovell, but they also had something of Howe's vision. These turn-of-the-century publishers understood that literature reflected the aspirations and the identity of the community. They were fortunate in having the trust and friendship of Canadian authors who had international reputations, and fortunate in the contacts they made with London and New York houses.

At the Third International Congress of Publishers, held in London in 1899, Morang in effect told the British and Americans, this is our market, our territory. We know it best because we are on the spot all the time. Now, in return for protecting your book in Canada, we will hold the Canadian copyright. We will either publish the work here by renting your plates or we will import the sheets or the bound book. If you will not let us publish your book, then we will act as the legal agent for one book or preferably for all your lines.[15] This is the way the Canadian-owned firms began to operate, and this is the way the branch-plant publishers operated; firms such as Oxford (1905) and Macmillan (1905) came to distribute the books of their parent firms, but they too undertook Canadian publishing programs. Oxford was managed by a former employee of Briggs, S.B. Gundy. Macmillan of Canada was managed by an Englishman, Frank Wise, who was sent to Toronto from the New York firm of Macmillan.

13 The founding meeting of the Canadian Society of Authors discussed all these points, which were the work of the Society's founders, James Mavor, Bernard McEvoy, George W. Ross, and Goldwin Smith. See 'For Copyright,' *The Globe*, 7 February 1899.
14 Copp negotiated for a separate Canadian Copyright edition of Gilbert Parker's *The Seats of the Mighty* (1896), which was issued simultaneously with the London and New York editions. Morang negotiated with Hall Caine, Arthur Conan Doyle, and Rudyard Kipling for Canadian editions of their novels. See George N. Morang, *The Copyright Question: A Letter to the Toronto Board of Trade* (Toronto: Morang, 1902), 20.
15 George N. Morang, 'The Development of Publishing in Canada and the Canadian Copyright Question,' *Publishers' Circular*, LXX (10 June 1899), 654.

Thus in 1900 Canada amended the 1875 Copyright Act so that local manufacturing and local publishing were no longer the only conditions for protection
in Canada. Now the publisher (who was sometimes only a glorified wholesaler)
had some flexibility in handling foreign titles, and the foreign publisher still ex-
ercised some control over the Canadian market.

V

As Canada changed from a mainly rural and resource economy into a more
urbanized, industrialized society, its book trade became more specialized.
Meanwhile, Anglo-American copyright laws underwent revamping and reinter-
pretation, and in Canada likewise there was a shift away from the assumption
that copyright was a monopoly for the reproducer of a work to an acceptance
of the principle that copyright protects the author first of all. But the evolution
from the status of a series of loosely linked colonial trades to a national one by
means of copyright legislation was slow, and indeed our book trade is not autonomous even today. Whereas the value of the domestic book market in 1984
was $1.3 billion, the value of books published in Canada accounted for 24% of
this, or $323.7 million. Hence the compromise of 1900, while it had positive re-
sults for publishers and writers in this country, also perpetuated a situation
whereby foreign firms controlled their copyrights in the Canadian market, and
eventually established their branches here to distribute their books.

Royal Military College of Canada

NAÏM KATTAN

Le rôle des gouvernements dans le financement des arts

Dans la société féodale les arts de la cour étaient financés par les princes. Il y avait cependant tout un domaine de l'art qui ne demandait au prince ni son avis, ni son argent. Fêtes populaires, carnavals, artisanat, ou du moins ce que l'on qualifierait aujourd'hui comme tel. Ils constituaient une dimension de la vie quotidienne et des sources d'où les artistes de la cour puisaient des éléments de leurs produits. La société bourgeoise, notamment celle de l'Europe du dix-neuvième siècle, modifia les rapports de l'art et de la société. Le produit artistique est devenu commercial. La société assigna un autre rôle à l'artiste. Héros, victime, porte-parole et serviteur, il était, tour à tour, honoré et honni, menant une existence somptueuse ou misérable. Les arts populaires étaient toujours là. Il y avait désormais des produits que seule une élite instruite, au goût cultivé, pouvait apprécier ou comprendre.

La société industrielle et surtout la société post-industrielle bouleversèrent à nouveau les rapports entre l'artiste et la société. Les progrès de l'enseignement, ainsi que le développement de nouvelles technologies ont donné naissance à une culture de masse. Ai-je besoin d'en mentionner les produits? Livres de poche, disques, cassettes, télévision, chansons populaires. Par ailleurs, l'élite instruite et cultivée s'est élargie. Elle n'appartient plus à une place en particulier, ses membres se recrutent dans toutes les classes de la société. Ainsi, d'un côté, une culture de masse qui cherche à atteindre le plus grand nombre, sans tenir compte des frontières géographiques ni même linguistiques et d'autre part, une expression vitale d'une société qui cherche à se donner une cohérence culturelle pour se comprendre et pour survivre. Car la culture de masse multi-nationale et industrielle réduit société et individu à l'anonymat. Il ne s'agit pas là d'un complot pour tuer les diversités et les dissidences mais d'un besoin naturel à l'industrie qui ne peut survivre sans expansion, sans continuelle conquête de nouveaux marchés.

Dans cette société, le rôle de l'État a changé. Il n'est plus simplement arbitre, régulateur. Il est acteur. Il s'occupe des routes et des parcs, de la sécurité et de l'enseignement. Il est dispensateur de services publics et l'un de ces services est la culture. À côté, au même titre que la santé, l'éducation, la sécurité et le transport, la culture est un besoin social. Elle n'est pas marginale à la vie et elle n'est pas là pour embellir l'existence, elle est une dimension de la vie sociale et individuelle. Aussi, l'État n'est pas appelé à aider la culture, c'est un service social qu'il doit dispenser à la population. De quelle manière? C'est là où les complications commencent. Une manifestation artistique peut être un produit commercial, une marchandise. Une personne la fabrique, la propose à la vente et une personne l'achète. L'État n'a pas de rôle à jouer à ce niveau. Mais la manifestation artistique peut être autre chose: une expression culturelle, une dimension de la vie, un produit peut-être, mais qui n'est pas simplement à vendre et à acheter. La société suscite les artistes, leur donne naissance et ceux-ci, par leur activité, participent à sa vie. Il y a là un circuit d'échanges, un dialogue perpétuel et l'État n'a d'autre rôle à jouer que d'en favoriser le déroulement. Il est la courroie de transmission. Il doit rendre la vie de l'artiste possible pour qu'il puisse avoir accès à la société et en même temps il doit permettre au public d'avoir accès au propos de l'artiste. Concrètement, c'est la société qui choisit ses artistes et c'est l'artiste qui, librement, propose à la société les résultats, toujours partiels, de sa quête et de sa démarche. Le circuit peut opérer commercialement. Le danger est d'imposer à ce circuit le critère d'une rentabilité marchande qui le pertube et en dévie le déroulement, d'où le besoin de la présence de l'État. Mais là, on fait face à un autre problème. Comme je viens de le dire, l'État n'a de rôle que celui d'une courroie de transmission. Or, pour s'imposer et se perpétuer, les responsables politiques, les gouvernants en place peuvent prétendre à jouer un rôle visible, un rôle de direction. Ils imposent alors une idéologie qui perturbe le circuit et réduit la liberté d'échange entre l'artiste et la société. Entre les directives marchandes et les directives politiques, le champ de la liberté se trouve restreint, limité. Je ne prétends point que la production culturelle s'effectue dans une pureté virginale où ni commerce, ni politique n'interviennent. J'irais même jusqu'à dire que la liberté de l'échange entre public et artiste nécessite la présence et du commerce et de la politique, à condition que ni l'un ni l'autre n'en modifient le processus et n'en changent la nature.

Le Canada a l'avantage d'avoir deux cultures, c'est-à-dire, deux richesses et de disposer de plusieurs marchés régionaux. Or, divisée en cultures et en régions, notre population ne peut pas faire vivre commercialement sa culture, d'où le danger de la marginalisation de celle-ci, de sa provincialisation et surtout la menace non pas de la présence d'autres cultures qui est toujours souhaitable mais de leur envahissement. Et quand je parle d'autres cultures, je songe surtout à une culture de masse, anonyme et multi-nationale, qu'on dit américaine parce que c'est là d'abord qu'elle se trouve, se fabrique et se manufacture. Mais il y a une culture américaine avec laquelle on peut et on doit établir des échanges comme on doit le faire avec toutes les grandes cultures mondiales.

Donc, le rôle de l'État dans le financement des arts au Canada est d'abord celui de dispenser le service public qui est la culture. Et chez nous, l'État doit jouer aussi deux autres rôles. D'abord celui de permettre la vie et l'épanouissement des deux langues et de toutes les cultures de toutes les régions du Canada. Là encore, l'État doit être la courroie de transmission pour permettre l'échange dans la liberté mais il y aussi un autre rôle, c'est celui de protecteur. Nos cultures sont fragiles et vulnérables. Parce que nous vivons dans une société développée et parce que notre population n'est pas très grande. De plus, sur le plan de la langue, nous appartenons aux trois plus grands producteurs culturels du monde occidental, à savoir la France, la Grande-Bretagne et les États-Unis. Cela ouvre certes les marchés de ces pays à nos artistes mais cela ouvre encore plus nos marchés aux artistes de tous ces pays. Plus un pays est développé, moins sa culture est archaïque et plus les artistes éprouvent de la difficulté à se distinguer, à se faire reconnaître comme appartenant à leur pays. Il est merveilleux d'être un artiste international mais on ne peut pas l'être dans l'anonymat. Le rôle le plus important, à mon avis, et le plus délicat de l'État est donc celui-là même de financer les arts dans la liberté pour qu'ils puissent par leur dynamisme propre se projeter dans le monde et proposer à leur société et à toutes les sociétés une quête et une démarche particulière.

On a beaucoup parlé de la distance qui doit prévaloir entre l'État et la communauté artistique. Cette distance ne doit pas être trop grande car les gouvernants doivent comprendre les artistes, les sociétés qui les élisent et les choisissent pour tenir compte de leur rôle et de leur importance. Et c'est l'État qui doit susciter les organismes qui établissent cette distance. Il est essentiel que l'artiste soit accepté et reconnu, qu'il y ait intimité entre le pouvoir et l'expression artistique mais que ce ne soit pas aux dépens de la liberté. Il faut que ces organismes acceptent, et ce n'est pas toujours facile, que dans cette expression libre, l'artiste puisse aller jusqu'à mordre la main qui le nourrit.

Ottawa

BYRNA BARCLAY

Breaking Trail In Saskatchewan: funding the literary arts

The legend

Not so long ago, in a place where it rained gophers, the umbrella was invented by three people. The first was a visual artist who lived on an island in the middle of a fast-flowing river. He hated ploughing and seeding and threshing. When he left his island he was too shy to ask anyone to look at his work. The second person didn't want to spend all her time rocking the cradle. She played many instruments. She acted out stories, but no one would pay to see her perform. The third individual had bits of paper stuck in his hatband, papers falling out of his coat sleeves, sheaves of papers spilling out of his pockets. He never came out during the day. He was always scribbling and muttering to himself.

The three artists were lonely, isolated from other people and from each other. Although they had to be alone to create, they needed other people to see and hear and read their work. They were cold and bruised because they had nothing to cover them when it rained bears and beaver.

The visual artist discovered others living on islands. He called out to them: 'Come see my work. Let me see yours.' He gathered them together, then searched out the performing artists who were easy to find because they were always jumping out from wheat fields, from behind trees, from under rocks. 'Look at me!' they said. 'Listen to us!' It took a long time to find the scribblers because they hid in closets and attics and haylofts.

One night, the visual artist, the performer, and the writer huddled in the middle of the island, cold and hungry and tired of showing their work to each other. It was raining squirrels. 'This is crazy,' the artist said. 'We need something to shelter our work.'

The performing artist stopped dancing and held her feet in first position. 'We need a covering with spokes, one that will open and spread.'

The writer said, 'We need to get a handle on this problem. We need money to design, build, and maintain our umbrella.'

'Let's ask the Boys under the Dome to help,' the visual artist said.

So they went to the Dome and wrangled and bangled with the Boys who finally declared to all and sundry that the new structure would be called The Saskatchewan Arts Board. It would shelter the arts, promote its excellence. They gave the Board some money, not *too much* of course, but enough to build the base. That first year, the best art was collected; it toured throughout the land. Art camps were set up in the parklands. They did so well, the Boys under the Dome cut their funding in half.

Undaunted, they built another umbrella, then another, and still another, until there was a symphony in both cities, galleries, theatres, and museums.

One summer, the Big Boy from under the Dome, the Leader himself, visited the music camp. The children sang and danced and played their instruments for him. He shared their beans. 'This isn't good enough for tomorrow's artists,' he said. 'We're closing the institutions for the consumptive and mentally ill. You can have the one in the magic valley forever. It will be a year-round School of the Arts.'

'We better start small,' the Board said. 'We'll teach the arts only in the summer.'

'You need a performing arts theatre,' the Leader said, 'so people can come and see and hear you.'

'Later,' they said.

So the Leader started building bigger and better roads. That stirred the dust. 'You're neglecting the arts!' they cried. 'Give us a mile of highway!' the artists yelled. After all, they were the trailbreakers.

By now, the story-tellers had gathered in that magic valley, at the School of the Arts. They created the Saskatchewan Writers' Guild, started a readings and workshop programme, set up a writers' retreat. Some bound pages together so all could read the stories and poems. They called themselves Thistledown and Thunder Creek and Fifth House.

'It's all wonderful,' the writers said, 'but our children learn about kings and their battles that took place in other lands. They don't know anything about their own history or culture.' So they started visiting schools, singing their songs.

Some say it all happened because of the Mother Poet, that larger-than-life lady who can see further into tomorrow than most people. Others say it was the man with pens growing out of his head. Still others say it was the first person who got paid for putting words on paper. But everyone agrees: it all happened because those original artists knew the difference between bones and feathers when it rained crows.

Of course that isn't the end of the story. The trouble with an umbrella is you've got to build a new one every year, especially when you never can tell whether it's going to rain mice or horses or buffalo. Sometimes the spokes are uneven, they rust, bend, even break during times of drought. The cloth wears and tears. It can flip inside out if you don't watch out for high winds over the Dome. Never let it carry you away.

The trick is to carve a solid base and maintain it. The trick is to design a bigger and better covering every year.

Interpretation

I'm a writer. I don't know what a polysystem is, and I'm afraid Deconstruction is what's going to happen to the School of the Arts if we receive a major cutback in 1987. But I do know what an umbrella is, what a network of support means, what constitutes a literary institution.

I'm one of the many writers who was nurtured and inspired at the Saskatchewan School of the Arts by literary artists like Rudy Wiebe, Robert Kroetsch, Eli Mandel, Anne Szumigalski, Jack Hodgins and Leon Rooke, to name a *few* who are devoted to the development of literature in Canada. I'm one of many who has worked for the arts through the creation and expansion of literary programmes offered by the Guild and who has benefited from them. I often wonder: without the network of the School, the Guild, and the Individual Assistance Grants offered by the Arts Board would I have become a writer? I doubt it. Few authors have emerged in my province who have not received that kind of support.

Since its creation in 1948, the Saskatchewan Arts Board, first of its kind in North America and second in the world after the British Arts Council, has formed the umbrella for the professional arts community, including the literary. Its mandate under the Act is to promote excellence in the arts. An arm's-length agency, it has the responsibility and role to act as an advocate for the arts by maintaining constant awareness of the growing needs of the arts organizations and individuals, and by securing funding for operational, project, and individual assistance for them. In the literary area, this means providing operational grants to the Writers' Guild, to three publishing houses, and to one literary magazine. It means providing Individual Title Assistance to any house in Canada that publishes a literary book by a Saskatchewan author. It means offering three kinds of individual assistance grants to buy time for creation, research, study, travel. It means overcoming the current problems in funding.

The legacy: funding problems

The literary institution in Saskatchewan is made up of individual writers, the Guild, publishing houses and literary magazines. It is unique insofar as it emerged from the grass roots and remains separate from the universities which only now offer classes in Canadian literature, host the odd reading (unattended by English professors), and leave the writer-in residence programmes to libraries, the Canada Council, and the Writers' Guild.

Historically, the literary arts, as a formal, funded institution, were the last to receive recognition and funding from national, provincial, and civic governments. Although Saskatchewan has provided a leadership role in funding literary organizations such as the Writers' Guild and literary publishers, we experience the same problems as other provinces in attempting to correct historical inequities. Without an infusion of new funds earmarked for the literary discipline it is difficult to raise operational levels to match performing and visual funding. In May 1984, the Saskatchewan Arts Board committed itself to solve this problem. It started by raising a new publishing house from project status to operational, with a grant increase·that has begun to lift that House to the level of the others. While the performing arts necessarily cost more to produce and therefore will always require more funds, the Board has corrected the division of funds available to individual literary and visual artists: now, monies are allocated according to the number of applications in each division; no discipline shall ever receive less than 25% of the Individual Assistance Fund.

Funding problems arise out of the necessity to meet the needs of individuals and groups within the literary institution, and they are not separate from the problems facing other disciplines funded by other agencies and councils in Canada. Some of the major problems are listed below:

1. The arm's-length principle must be upheld and preserved.

2. The problem of too many agencies and councils on too many levels creating a diffusion, over-lap, and an insecure economic basis for the arts must be addressed.

3. Inequities between professional and non-professional groups and individuals have never been examined, nor has the problem of unfair competition for funds between them.

4. Provision for the emerging professional artists must be ensured.

5. The controversy of tax-based dollars vs. lottery funds, government allocations vs. private sector patronage makes no sense in provinces whose economy is based upon agriculture or the fishing industry.

6. Deficit reduction and prevention — a severe problem for the performing arts which has recently been addressed in Saskatchewan through a financial aid programme set up by the Department of Culture and Recreation and administered

by the Arts Board—will creep into the literary institution if a long term solution to the funding crisis is not met.

7. Cultural agencies and the clients they serve are unable to create new programmes or expand existing ones under a system based on year-to-year survival depending on government allocations. The need for a long-term plan with a sound economic base and graduated annual increments is the only way to prevent the arts from becoming a static entity.

The lighthouse

Every performer needs an audience. Every visual artist needs someone to exhibit the art, people to purchase it; every writer needs a publisher and *readers*. These truisms still yield some questions, the first of which is: Whom are we writing for? Other writers? Academics? Certainly not critical reviewers!

A true literary artist writes for the populace. A lawyer said to me recently, 'I read a novel once.' I know professional people who — if they read literature at all — stock their libraries with British and American books. These are people who were denied their own literature during their formative years, who have not been properly exposed to their own literature; consequently, I applaud the universities, colleges, and schools which have begun in the last decade to offer classes in Canadian literature.

However, I have to special order new literary books because they are not available in local bookstores. When I give readings in rural areas people line up to buy signed copies of my novels.

Should we provide incentives for people to buy books? Tax deductions?

Who is responsible for the preservation and growth of our literature?

In May 1984, a gentleman from Holland toured Canada. He told me this story: In celebration of the anniversary of the Canadian liberation of Holland the Holland Festival ordered 12,000 books, representing fourteen Canadian authors, from two mainstream publishing houses. Neither house bothered to fill the order or even reply to the letters. 'It seems that Canadian publishers are so heavily subsidized by government grants,' he said, 'they don't need to sell books.'

Publishing is an industry, but it is also the lighthouse of our literature, and the responsibility of preserving that literature is falling more and more on the shoulders of the alternate, literary presses. In Saskatchewan our mandate is to promote excellence in the arts, and The Arts Board therefore only provides funding for literary work. Although operational grants ideally cover promotion and distribution, in 1985 the Board provided special Promotion and Distribution Grants to three Saskatchewan-based publishing houses. This grant was only a short-term solution to the problem of readership, and it did not address the larger audience issue, the need for a perpetual motion mechanism that not only would stabilize the arts but would ensure its growth.

The funding crisis: Maxwell's million

In 1987 we are faced with deficits at national and provincial levels due to loss in revenues, inflation, and low interest rates. At the same time, we have received reports from commissions: we know the economic impact of the arts, recognize it as a viable industry with the potential for even greater job creation. The political will seems to be there, but here in Saskatchewan we are faced with a predicted percentage cutback across the board.

As a taxpayer I want my money to go to Health, Education, and the Arts. As an individual I am committed to preserving the operational, project, and individual assistance which have become the foundations of the preservation and growth of our culture.

If rural hospitals are closed, urban hospitals and university budgets are frozen, who will be concerned if theatres and symphonies shut down, and if the Saskatchewan School of the Arts closes on its twentieth anniversary?

On March 7 1987, the Premier of Saskatchewan said, 'Art is the soul of our society. We must preserve it.' Through the Department of Culture and Recreation, the portfolio responsible for the dispersement of lottery dollars, Hon. Colin Maxwell allocated one million dollars to the Saskatchewan Arts Board for individual assistance, operational and project grants, as well as $500,000 towards deficit reduction and prevention in the performing arts. This short-term infusion of new money has stabilized the arts.

Now, let's talk long-term planning at the national and provincial levels.

Let's not only examine what has become a literary institution, and correct historical inequities, but also lay down concrete mid-term and long-term plans based on a viable vision for the arts that is shared by writers, publishers, literary organizations, universities, and schools.

Without stabilization strategies shared by government and the people it serves, funding crises will continue.

Note: The views expressed in this paper are the author's and are not representative of any one agency or organization.

Regina

RAY ELLENWOOD

Government Funding: the effect on writers, translators and their associations

The entire literary industry in Canada, including writing, translation and publication, is highly subsidized in various ways by different levels of government. The reasons for this have to do with the economics of the book industry in this country, as other commentators have already explained. Thus, the writers, manufacturers-distributors, sellers and readers make up one basic and complex polysystem, but we also have a sub-system of government agencies whose interventions affect the whole polysystem, no matter where they are applied. If government funding to publishers affects the number and even the nature of books printed, this obviously has repercussions on the sub-system of writers, and if government funding makes it possible for writers to communicate and organize, this can have an impact on relationships between writers and publishers. Finally, the changes in sub-systems and dynamics which result from government funding can, in turn, rebound to affect the government agencies themselves. To give some idea of how this works, I offer a very general overview of government funding of literature, then look more specifically at writers' groups, and finally examine the impact of government funding on literary translation as a recent and obvious case in point.

Government funding to Canadian literature has come primarily from federal agencies: the writing and publications section of the Canada Council, the Multiculturalism Directorate of the Secretary of State, the Department of Communications and the Department of External Affairs. There are also provincial agencies, such as the Ontario Ministry of Citizenship and Culture, the Ontario Arts Council, the Saskatchewan Arts Board, Alberta Culture and others. Finally, there are civic institutions, from local governments to schools and libraries, which contribute a small share. The methods and targets of subsidization are so many and so varied that they would be material for a study in themselves.

Various levels of government give financial assistance to publishers of books and periodicals. Once a publishing house or periodical has established itself by printing a given number of titles or issues, it can apply for assistance, first in the form of title-by-title project grants and then in the form of larger block grants. Applications on both the federal and provincial levels are submitted to juries which decide once a year on the distribution of available funds. Not all books or periodicals supported by one level or branch of government are eligible for assistance from another. Procedures and rules can be very complicated, varying markedly between federal and provincial agencies. The federal government also assists publishers of Canadian literature with promotion costs and has even instituted occasional buy-back schemes whereby a number of recommended titles are purchased for distribution in embassies abroad.

The Multiculturalism Directorate of the Secretary of State distributes some funds to publishers of ethnic literature in much the same way as the Canada Council. At times, the distinctions between Jurisdictions of the Canada Council and Multiculturalism Directorate are not very clear. Generally, Multiculturalism concerns itself with literatures and cultural events in the non-official languages, but there are authors such as Joseph Skvorecky whose work (in the original and in translation) was first published with grants from Multiculturalism but who now is assisted by the Canada Council.

One Ontario publishing enterprize with which I am associated comprises a literary magazine and a small publishing house. The periodical receives almost an equal share of assistance from the Canada Council and the Ontario Arts Council (approximately $14,000 from each in 1986), the amount being subject to jury decision and to available funds. Last year, the house received, in approximate figures, $34,000 in Canada Council grants and $6,000 from the Ontario Arts Council. It also recommended the names of authors to whom almost $25,000 of Ontario Arts Council money was distributed. Note that this is a small operation, publishing ten to fifteen titles per year, which could probably not survive without government assistance, yet one that has had an acknowledged impact on Canadian writers and Canadian literature not only by getting words printed but also by funneling money to writers.

Of course, Canadian governments also make grants directly to authors. Most of these come from the Canada Council, with its Explorations Grants for beginning writers and its 'A' and 'B' grants for more established authors.[1] These provide subsistence, research and travel funds for a given project or over a given period of time. The Canada Council also supports an extensive cross-Canada programme which pays honoraria and travel expenses to authors reading their works in public. Application is made to the Council by the host organization.

1   See, for example, the brochure entitled *Aid to Artists* published annually by the Arts Awards Service of the Canada Council.

Some writers' groups also operate a portion of this programme for their members, acting as mediators between the host organization and the government. Canadian authors on reading tours abroad sometimes receive travel assistance from External Affairs. There are also Writer-in-Residence programmes, assisted by the federal government, which pay writers a salary to be available for consultation, usually over the period of a year. At first, these were restricted to universities, but now some public libraries have instituted them. The Ontario Arts Council, as has already been mentioned, also gives grants to writers on the recommendation of publishers or editors of established literary magazines.

Finally, we should not forget the recently instituted reprography collective in Quebec and the Public Lending Right Commission. The former distributes $1,000,000 of provincial money to Quebec authors for the photocopying of their books in schools and universities; the latter compensates authors with $3,000,000 of federal money for the use of their books in libraries across Canada. Although these must be clearly distinguished from the grants and bursaries mentioned earlier, they are nonetheless sources of government money for Canadian authors and, from the point of view of a theory of literary polysystem, they are particularly interesting because they result from writers' groups lobbying governments, affecting policy and thereby giving a new dynamic to the network of systems.

Government funding of writers' groups usually takes the form of assistance with operating costs, as well as with special projects, including travel costs for annual general meetings. Canada Council grants to writers' organizations, French and English, for the fiscal year 1986-87 totaled $186,887 in operating grants, $158,120 for readings ond $19,400 for conferences and special events.[2] The original purpose of this assistance was to make it possible for writers to meet, communicate and deal collectively with the problems facing members of a solitary profession in a large country of small population. It has obviously succeeded. There are more than a dozen writers' groups across Canada, including large associations such as The Canadian Authors' Association, The Writers' Union of Canada, The Periodical Writers' Association and the Union des écrivains québécois, as well as a number of smaller groups, including (and this is no doubt an incomplete list) The League of Canadian Poets, Playwrights' Union, The Nova Scotia Writers' Federation, the Association des écrivains acadiens, The Newfoundland Writers' Guild, the Writers' Federation of New Brunswick, The Prince Edward Island Writers' Association, The Manitoba Writers' Guild, the Saskatchewan Writers' Guild, The Writers' Guild of Alberta and The Federation of British Columbia Writers. Some of these groups

2   This information derives from the Canada Council's *Annual Report*, courtesy of Katherine Benzekri of the Writing and Publications Section.

obviously represent regional constituencies or writers of specific genres, others are cross-disciplinary and national.

To gain some idea of government funding, consider that The Writers' Union of Canada, one of the largest English-language groups with a membership of over 500, operates on a total budget of about $400,000. Approximately 42% of their operating costs, including the cost of their Annual General Meeting, comes from various governments. Of that 42%, approximately 28% comes from the Canada Council, 12% from the Ontario Ministry of Citizenship ond Culture, about 1.3% from Alberta Culture (the Alberta government has funded TWUC since its beginning) and .2% from the Saskatchewan Arts Board. The remaining expenses are met from membership fees and other sources.[3] These figures are probably quite representative of the 'national' organizations.

The Union des écrivains québécois is an umbrella organization which represents a majority of Quebec writers working in all genres, whereas writers in English tend to be represented by specific, independent organizations such as the League of Canadian Poets. These organizations cooperate, however, by sharing accommodation in some cases and by presenting a united front for publicity and lobbying. The result is a collection of associations which can provide many kinds of specific professional assistance for members (on matters ranging from contract disputes to computers), but may also exert collective pressure on the other sub-systems through special committees devoted to copyright, reprography, book distribution, tax reform and other issues of concern to writers.

Over the years, as the writers' groups have gained members and strength, these same associations have been pushing more and more for autonomy so that, while accepting assistance from the various governments, they also tend to question government agencies on their policies and methods while lobbying for the special interests of their members. It was largely through the efforts of the Union des écrivains québécois that the Quebec government was persuaded to institute compensation for reprography. The writers' groups have also managed, as was mentioned earlier, to obtain some control of the organization of reading programmes and have persuaded the Canada Council to fund readings by authors of works other than fiction or poetry. But the clearest example of complicated relations between writers' groups and government funding agencies may be seen in the ongoing dispute over who should control the recently established Public Lending Right Commission.

It was the Canadian Authors' Association which first called for public compensation of authors whose works were available through the public library system. These efforts began over forty years ago, but early reactions were discouraging. The issue was raised again in 1973 by members of The Writers'

---

3   This information comes courtesy of Penny Dickens, Executive Director, Writers' Union of Canada.

Union, who fought a long campaign against opposition from various quarters, finally arriving at a general consensus among writers' groups, publishers and librarians. At that point, the Canada Council decided to take the concept under its wing, as Andreas Schroeder explained:

> It will probably always remain a bit of a mystery why the Canada Council chose at this point to pre-empt TWUC's campaign by denying the Union's application and undertaking both a PLR study and pilot project on its own. Possibly certain Council mandarins feared that TWUC's inclination to manage and control the eventual PLR Fund might have jeopardized the political viability of the scheme in the eyes of Ottawa MP's (i.e. conflict of interest). It may have been that these same mandarins considered any administration and dispersal of public funds to the Arts – traditionally a function of the Canada Council – more appropriate to themselves than to the Writers' Union.[4]

In 1981, the Canada Council eventually did publish a *Proposal to Establish a System of Payments for Public Use* but nothing came of it. All activity was suspended by 1982 because money to pay for the scheme was not forthcoming. It was only after a vigorous public campaign by the writers' groups that the government was finally persuaded, in 1986, to make money available for PLR, and that was when rivalry between the funding agencies and the writers' groups came to a head.

The money for the scheme was to come from the office of the Secretary of State, through the Canada Council, to a commission which would distribute it to authors. The question remained: what would be the constitution of the Commission? In the first organizational meeting of 29 April 1987, it was abundantly clear that the Canada Council wanted to retain as much control as possible while the Writers' Union and the Union des écrivains québécois believed that the commission could be more efficiently and energetically run by the writers' groups themselves.[5] There was heated debate in which representatives of some writers' groups decried the paternalism of the Canada Council, but eventually a composition was arrived at which was acceptable to the Writers' Union and other groups including librarians and publishers, but not to the Union des écrivains québécois, which continued to argue that writers' groups should run the commission more independently. A communiqué by UNEQ, dated 23 Octobre 1986, read:

> Le programme de Paiment aux auteurs pour utilisation publique aurait pu aider les associations d'auteurs à se développer, leur permettant ainsi d'offrir de meilleurs services à la

---

4 'A Brief & Irreverent HISTORY OF PUBLIC LENDING RIGHT (alias 'Payment for Public Use') IN CANADA,' Writers' Union symposium on Payment for Public Use, Toronto, 14 May 1985.
5 For a thoroughly biased view of the proceedings, see Ray Ellenwood, 'Paying the Piper,' *Books in Canada*, 15:6 (Aug.- Sept. 1986):3-4.

communauté littéraire, tout en générant de l'activité économique dans le milieu même des auteurs. Le ministère fédéral des Communications et le Conseil des Arts du Canada ont malheureusement choisi une formule qui ne fait qu'accentuer la dépendance des auteurs à l'endroit du Gouvernement, en avalisant le principe de la centralisation étatique à une époque où les pouvoirs publics sont les premiers à remettre ce 'modèle' en question.

Nonetheless, an executive was elected for the commission and, indeed, the first Public Lending Right cheques were sent out to writers in mid-March 1987.

At a meeting of the full public Lending Right Commission which took place in June 1987, the issue of UNEQ's participation was raised again and a debate went on concerning the balance of power not only between writers, associations and government agencies, but also between the different writers' associations. This, then, is a good example of how difficult it can be to reconcile the perceived need of writers and writers' groups for government assistance, with their determination to be as independent as possible from government policy and indeed to influence it.

But as a specific case in point, nowhere has the impact of government funding on Canadian literature been so obvious as in the history of literary translation in this country. The Canada Council's system of grants in aid of translation, begun in the late sixties, has actually created a small industry of translation of Canadian literature because it made publication of literary translations economically viable.[6] In the publication of a literary translation, all costs are the same as for any other book, but there is an additional fee for the translator's work, which simply raises the unit cost per book, cuts down on potential profit and therefore discourages publishers from considering translations unless they are assured of a large sale. By giving a grant of a flat fee per word through the publisher to the translator, the Canada Council made it possible for some new and experimental writing, not just the usual best-sellers and 'classics,' to be published in translation. Under the present system, requests for grants come from publishers. New translators are required to submit a sample of their work to the Canada Council for approval. The translator's fee is paid according to contract, but also in instalments controlled by the Canada Council. Note that these grants are for work done, as opposed to 'A' and 'B' or exploration grants paid to authors.

Thus, the positive side of the picture is that over 600 titles of literary translation have been published since 1971, when the translation grants were introduced, whereas very little translation of literary works was done in Canada

6   This has been documented in Philip Stratford's Introduction to his *Bibliography of Canadian Books in Translation* (Ottawa: Humanities Research Council of Canada, 1977) and in my article, 'Some Actualities of Canadian Literary Translation,' *Translation in Canadian Literature*, ed. Camille R.Labossière (Ottawa: U. of Ottawa P, 1983):61-71.

before 1950. And there has been a consistent 50 to 60 titles, French and English, published every year since 1974. It is no accident that the Literary Translators Association was founded in 1975, mainly by people who had received grants in aid of translation, at a meeting assisted by a project grant from the Canada Council. Since then, the Association has received an operations grant which includes assistance with members' travel to the Annual General Meeting. A small association with about 80 members, the ATL/LTA now receives about $4,000 per year from the Canada Council, with rare grants from Multiculturalism for special projects and from External Affairs for members' travel to conferences abroad. But the group also hosted an international gathering of literary translators in Montreal in October 1986. That event was assisted by government agencies to a total of $39,000, most of which came from the Canada Council, External Affairs and the Department of Communications, with about 10% from the Secretary of State (Official Languages and Multiculturalism) and Quebec Cultural Affairs. This is roughly ten times the normal operating budget of the Association, which would obviously have great difficulty sponsoring such an event without government assistance.

The importance of government funding to literary translation and translators is therefore obvious. This does not mean, however, that government policies go unquestioned. In the first place, the system of payment through the publisher to the translator has been criticized because it does not recognize that translators usually know more about books and authors in the source language than do publishers. Also, the present method of payment affects the kind of work translated. Since it is based on word count, the current rate being 10 cents per word, it means that anyone who depends to any extent on literary translation for a living can ill afford to translate poetry. But no amount of argument or complaint has brought any change in these policies.

Over the years, it has become more and more obvious to the Literary Translators Association that Canada Council policy begins, not with the primary intention of encouraging and improving literary translation itself, but of encouraging the dissemination of Canadian authors' works through translation. The translator is seen as a medium, which is why the Canada Council maintains control in the hands of the publisher. Canadian translators are not encouraged to initiate projects or to apply for grants independently, whereas in the United States bursaries similar to Canada Council exploration grants are available to translators, allowing them to work on projects, as authors do, and to find a publisher upon completion. But the clearest evidence of an unstated policy behind Canada Council intervention is the fact the it will not give grants in aid of a Canadian translation, even of a Canadian author, if the publisher is not Canadian; nor will it consider subsidizing a translation by a Canadian, published by a Canadian publisher, if the author translated is not Canadian. Yet it gives financial assistance to foreign publishers of Canadian works translated into a selection of languages.

These are issues which the Literary Translators Association has raised many times with the Canada Council, often with the support of groups such as the Writers' Union and the Union des écrivains québécois. But, just as the process which first gave rise to Canada Council policy in such matters remains mysterious, the ways of bringing about change in policy are not at all clear. Pressure, it appears, is essential.

For the past fifteen years, literary translators have been working to convince government agencies and indeed the whole Canadian book industry that a literary translation is indeed a work of Canadian literature and that translators are part of the sub-system of writers, rather than appendages to the publishing industry. If translators should be successful in changing government policy, then publishers, writers and indeed the whole network will be affected. There may even be small repercussions for the international literary polysystem of which Canada is a part.

York University

KEN NORRIS

Little Magazines and Literary Periodicals

When *The Little Magazine in Canada 1925-80* was published in 1984, it received its fair share of favorable, unfavorable and indifferent reviews. In writing a history of little magazine activity in this country I knew I would please some critics, outrage others, and be found by still others to be documenting a marginal or peripheral activity. 'What, after all, is the *value* of a little magazine?' some asked. 'Aren't the works of individual authors more important in establishing a literary tradition than the mimeographing of limited circulation magazines by small circles of rabid young poets?' I consider these questions valid and valuable, and I will try to address them later in this paper. But first let me express my primary dismay about the only common factor in virtually all the reviews of my literary history: most of the critics reviewing the book could not make or chose not to make a distinction between a little magazine and a literary periodical. To some this may not seem like an important distinction. As far as I'm concerned, not being able to distinguish a literary periodical from a little magazine is the same as not being able to distinguish night from day. There are significant aesthetic, political, social and cultural differences between a little magazine and a literary periodical.

Much of what I'm about to say, and the distinctions that I want to make, have been said and made before; in 1967, Wynne Francis published an article, 'Literary Underground: Little Magazines in Canada,'in *Canadian Literature*[1]; in this article she gave some very precise definitions of what constitutes a commercial magazine, a literary periodical, and a little magazine. The problem with her article, however, is that she didn't call these publications 'commercial magazines,' 'literary periodicals,' and 'little magazines': she called them 'Big magazines,' 'Small magazines,' and 'Little magazines.' One can see how the

---

1   Wynne Francis,'Literary Underground: Little Magazines in Canada,' *Canadian Literature*, 34 (Autumn 1967), 63-70.

distinction between 'Small magazine' and 'Little magazine' didn't become part of every Canadian critic's operative vocabulary. Nevertheless, Francis's definitions are substantively useful. It strikes me that 'literary periodical' can serve as a much more useful term than 'small magazine' when one attempts to distinquish a publication that is very different in intention and operation from the little magazine.

Before getting to a discussion of the differences between the literary periodical and the little magazine, perhaps it would be useful to divorce them entirely from any relation to the commercial magazine, the Big magazine. As Francis tells us,

> Big Magazines are commercial enterprises thriving on advertising, public sales and wide circulation. They appeal to a large segment of the general public whose opinions they tend to reflect and perhaps to mould. Their range of material is broad, with an emphasis on current affairs. Their interest in literature is minimal or peripheral, exploiting the sensational or human interest angle of the contemporary world of letters. Occasionally they include original creative pieces but these tend to be selected as bait for public controversy or because the writer is a celebrity.[2]

Magazines such as *Saturday Night*, *Chatelaine*, and *Maclean's* can be easily identified as magazines of this stripe.

When it comes to offering a definition of what we'll call the literary periodical, Francis notes some very specific distinguishing characteristics. In comparison to the mass-oriented commercial magazine, the literary periodical 'appeals to a more select segment of readers. These are most often college-bred with a developed taste for 'the Arts' and for 'Literature' in particular.[3] She rightly then goes on to distinguish between two types of literary periodicals: 'the scholarly or critical journal which is academically oriented and the independent periodical which mingles contemporary imaginative writing of various kinds with criticism and reviews.'[4] The production values for both types of magazines are quite high and both rely upon grants and subsidies, the critical journal having its deficits underwritten by its university of affiliation and by the Social Sciences and Humanities Research Council of Canada, and the independent periodical having its deficits underwritten by its university of affiliation (if it has one) and by the Canada Council, the Ontario Arts Council, the Saskatchewan Arts Board, etc. Both types of magazines are diligent about subscriptions, which provide some degree of revenue.[5]

---

2 Francis, 63.
3 Francis, 63.
4 Francis, 64.
5 Here I've incorporated some features provided by Francis (64) with developments that have occurred in the past twenty years.

Even though it relies very heavily upon subsidies, the literary periodical of imaginative writing tends to be run in a business-like fashion; this has become especially true in the light of the various Arts councils' aid-to-periodicals programs. Professionalism is constantly emphasized by these programs, and so the literary periodical must exhibit a concern for design, circulation, and distribution, even if the periodical's potential audience is small and limited, which it usually is. The editors attempt to get the magazine out on a regular schedule and to offer at least some token payment to its contributors; payment to contributors is now, in fact, often part of the subsidy apparatus.

As far as the tenor and content of the literary periodical are concerned, Francis defines them as follows:

> The tone of such a magazine is mature, urbane, liberal; its policy is clear and consistent; its material is drawn from the best established contemporary writers. Though it occasionally publishes the work of an unknown, it displays an uncanny ability to pick up-and-coming talents on the eve of their public success. The longer it lives the more such a magazine tends to acquire an air of wisdom, dignity and stability and the less likely it is to reflect the sensibility and aspirations of the young or the avant-garde.[6]

Given these defining characteristics, it is very easy to identify examples. Publications such as *Queen's Quarterly*, *Canadian Literature* and *Essays on Canadian Writing* offer examples of the scholarly literary periodical, while *Descant*, *Malahat Review* and the now defunct *Tamarack Review* exemplify the literary periodical devoted to imaginative writing.

Francis's final comment on the literary periodical is that it 'reflects the sensibility of the intelligent liberal bourgeois and as such it constitutes The Establishment — a veritable *bête noire* of the Little Magazine world.'[7] Whereas, in 1967, Francis could see the literary periodical as a manifestation of 'The Establishment,' perhaps in 1987 we can feel more comfortable with perceiving 'an Establishment,' given that Canadian literature has grown beyond the possibility of its being the fiefdom of one small select group. Certainly the literary periodical comes to represent something that is *established*; once it gains credibility with the granting organizations its continued existence is, more or less, assured, although the magazine's financial stability will always remain precarious.

For a succinct definition of the little magazine I'd like to quote Thrall, Hibbard and Holman's *A Handbook to Literature*; they define little magazines as 'literary journals of small circulation, very limited capital, and usually quite short lives, dedicated to the fostering of avant-garde aesthetic ideas and to publishing

6 Francis, 64.
7 Francis, 64.

experimental poetry and prose."[8] Whereas the literary periodical represents an establishment or orthodoxy, the little magazine is revolutionary and experimental, devoting itself to aesthetic exploration, pathfinding, innovation, and invention. According to Wynne Francis, there is a heretical and subversive intent at work in the little magazine:

> The Little Magazine is essentially subversive — not in a narrow political sense but by its profound and radical aversion to prevailing cultural values. It is significant that its proliferation has been concurrent with the spread of modern urban culture — the type of society, that is, wherein commercialism, mass-production and middle-class conformity combine to correct and inhibit the creative imagination. Little Magazines emerge in defiant relation to such a culture wherever it is established. Their function — indeed their mission in regard to it — is at once subversive and redemptive.[9]

Looking back over recent literary history it is easy to spot the significant little magazines in Canada: *Preview, First Statement, Contact, Tish, CrOnk, blewointment*. All these magazines presented radical challenges to their society and to the accepted aesthetic norms of their day. But what about little magazines today? Well, there are a few out there, existing as part of a literary underground, with names like *Industrial Sabotage, Zymergy, The Hanged Men Dance*, and *Mondo Hunkamooga*. These magazines are published on an irregular basis, have a small coterie of readers, and, as far as I know, are totally self-financed. Needless to say, they are rather scruffy in appearance. Whether they'll have any lasting impact on Canadian literature will depend upon whether they have anything genuinely new and lasting to offer in their aesthetic programs.

Having established these definitions we can see that the literary periodical and the little magazine are, in fact, worlds apart; they actually exist in something of an antagonistic relation. The literary periodical helps to establish and buoy up prevailing aesthetic trends while the intention of the little magazine is to aesthetically advance the art form and topple the orthodoxy. Often what's heretical becomes the new orthodoxy ten or fifteen years later, and then the process begins all over again. What we seem to witness in this century and in this country are, on the one hand, a history of resentments, and on the other, a constant debate between poets of Modernist and anti-Modernist persuasions. What we have also been witnessing in the past twenty years is the rise in importance of the literary periodical and the diminishing impact of the little magazine.

Before going any further with this last point, let me cover one possibly troubling concern. Surely one reaction to what I've been saying is that these definitions are well and good, but what have they got to do with the reality of periodical

---

8 William Flint Thrall, Addison Hibbard and C. Hugh Holman, *A Handbook to Literature* (New York: Odyssey, 1960), 263.
9 Francis, 67.

publishing in Canada? Such a black and white way of looking at things doesn't necessarily reflect the eclecticism of many Canadian productions. I'm willing to concede that a great many Canadian literary magazines, especially in their early years, tend to inhabit the twilight zone between the literary periodical and the little magazine. In her article, Wynne Francis is also painfully aware of this state of literary limbo. She states:

> It is actually in this limbo, suspended between two worlds, that we find most of Canada's literary journals. By limbo I mean that state in which a literary magazine is uncertain of its direction, is unsure of the nature and potential extent of its public and therefore displays a wavering, eclectic or ambivalent policy...As financial pressures increase, however, these magazines in limbo have only this choice: to perish, or to conform more strictly to literary periodical standards – which means in effect to abandon their flirtation with the world of the Little Magazine.[10]

The point Francis is making here is essentially sound; especially in the light of their requiring subsidies, magazines that are wavering in their policies (or, quite frankly, have no coherent editorial policy) have little choice but to jump in the direction of the literary periodical or else be pushed by the arts councils into oblivion. I do not intend to depict the Canada Council or the Ontario Arts Council as the Wicked Witch of the West in this equation; it is just that they have very specific criteria that a periodical must adhere to if it expects to be eligible for funding.

When I was writing my history of the little magazine it was quite apparent how important the little magazine had been to the evolution of Modernist and early Post-Modernist aesthetics in Canadian poetry. When John Sutherland began publishing *First Statement* in 1942 there were very few outlets for the working-class social realist poetry he wanted to encourage. Similarly, in 1952, if Layton, Souster, and Dudek wanted to see their Modernist work in print, then Souster had to be cranking the handle of the mimeograph machine in his basement to produce *Contact*. Later magazines like *Tish* and *GrOnk* were faced with the same task: venues had to be created so that work of a new kind could see the light of day.

When it came to documenting little magazine activity in the late sixties to early seventies, however, I found that the situation had begun to change. Much of the energy that had gone into the founding of little magazines was not going into the creation and operation of literary presses. There was also a decrease in the number of fighting little magazines and an increase in eclectic literary periodicals.

Well, perhaps all the important aesthetic battles of this century had already been fought; therefore, there was no longer any need for the fighting little

10 Francis, 65.

magazine. This may be true, but I tend to doubt that this has been the source of the change. What I believe has happened is that, due to the availability of grants and subsidies, an extensive and substantial middle ground, the like of which has never before existed in Canada, has come into existence. I would go so far as to say that this created middle ground, contrary to the claims of certain large commercial publishing houses, essentially *is* the publishing apparatus of Canadian literature. What we are facing now is a new situation with transformed and transforming rules and requirements.

Whereas an early literary press like First Statement Press published eight titles in its six years of existence, and Contact Press some fifty titles in its amazing run of fifteen years with the assistance of the Canada Council, what were once upstart small presses like Coach House, Oberon, House of Anansi and Talonbooks are now all passing the twenty-year mark, having published hundreds of books, all with no end to their existences in sight. Similarly, when we turn to the literary periodical, we discover a number of magazines that have been in existence for over ten years: *Descant, Malahat Review, Ellipse, Event, Quarry, Matrix, Contemporary Verse 2, The Antigonish Review, Grain, Prism International, Capilano Review, Waves,* and of course the venerable *Fiddlehead.* To have so many active literary periodicals of such longstanding in operation is unprecedented in the history of Canadian letters. What's more, the four literary presses I've mentioned only begin to suggest the present activity of literary presses, and the situation is exactly the same when we consider the literary periodical.

With so much access to publication available to writers, it's easy to see how the fiery necessity for the little magazine has been eroded. If you add to that a climate of economic recession, which precipitated a new conservatism in politics and also aesthetics, you witness the virtual disappearance of any new gestures towards an avant-garde.

We've passed from a period in our literary history when the little magazine was of the utmost importance, to a period in which the literary periodical now predominates. Whereas Canadian literature was once plagued by a paucity of outlets for imaginative writing, there are some who suggest that we are now facing a locust plague of small presses and literary periodicals. Judging the situation by the values of the marketplace, one can only conclude that we are at present producing more literary works than anyone can read and more literary periodicals and books than anyone cares to buy. For all of the professionalism evident in the production of literary books and periodicals, what is also evident is the lack of an adequate audience. A number of literary periodicals have suffered a drop in their circulation, just as a number of literary presses have noticed a drop in the sales of individual titles. Canadian literature, as we have known it for the past ten or fifteen years may have, in fact, peaked, or have begun to spread itself too thin.

What we are now faced with, if we are interested in recent Canadian literary history, is assessing the impact of subsidization upon Canadian literary productions. I believe that the impact has been enormous and that evidence can be found to support many different points of view. I prefer to dwell upon the more positive aspects. There is now an active publishing community where once there was a very minimal one. There are a number of literary establishments where once there was only relative obscurity for all. There are thousands of published poets where once there were only those who had been published by Ryerson Press. I confess that I long to see nasty aesthetic debates between a *Preview* and a *First Statement*, but if one wants bitchiness one can always read *Books in Canada*. But seriously, I think there are still important aesthetic debates to be posited and contested; however, I now find it difficult to predict in what forms they will take place, or if they *will* take place. Perhaps what we are currently witnessing is the death of the little magazine in Canada; then again, perhaps some wild-eyed poet has just switched on the company xerox machine after hours and is starting up production of a new little magazine that will change Canadian literary history forever.

University of Maine

SHERRY SIMON

Alliances stratégiques: Le féminisme et les revues littéraires au Québec

À la mémoire de Suzanne Lamy

'Le féminisme, ce révélateur privilégié des enjeux de notre temps'
— Françoise Collin

Pour qui s'intéresse au rapport entre les idées et les pouvoirs, aux entrechoquements des courants littéraires et des institutions, et aux lieux de parole que sont les revues, il n'y a pas sujet plus pertinent, me semble-t-il pour le Québec de ces dernières années, que celui du féminisme. Parce que le féminisme n'existe qu'articulé à un projet: à un mouvement socio-politique, à une pratique littéraire, ou à une recherche de nouveaux savoirs. Et parce que le féminisme comme toute mise en question des schémas conceptuels, se voulant à la fois transgression et permanence, force les portes de l'institution et indique ses seuils de résistance. Je voudrais ainsi explorer dans cet exposé le champ des revues littéraires et culturelles au Québec à travers le prisme particulier qu'est le féminisme littéraire. Ce faisant j'espère montrer d'une part comment le féminisme trouve sa place dans le monde des idées et des écritures au Québec et d'autre part comment les revues sont reliées aux autres instances du monde littéraire.

Très nombreuses, ces derniers temps, ont été les publications qui ont eu comme sujet l'institution littéraire au Québec. Du féminisme, cependant, on a très peu parlé. Un seul article de fond a jusqu'ici, que je sache, traité ce sujet.

Il s'agit de la contribution de Suzanne Lamy au recueil *Trajectoires: Littérature et institutions au Québec et en Belgique francophone.*[1] Ni le numéro de *Liberté*, 1981 (134), consacré à 'L'institution littéraire québécoise,' ni *L'Avant-garde culturelle et littéraire des années 70 au Québec*, ni les 17 communications de *L'institution littéraire* qui a paru en 1986 ni l'ouvrage collectif *Le Spectacle de la littérature* (1984) ne se penche sérieusement sur le sujet.

Dans son article qui dessine le portrait du féminisme institutionnalisé, oui, mais institutionnalisé dans la marge au Québec, Suzanne Lamy constate que du côté des revues les écritures féministes se sont taillés une place à l'intérieur de revues *mixtes* au Québec (p. 97) c'est-à-dire qu'il existe peu de revues québécoises définies exclusivement à partir d'un projet féministe. Les revues qui font exception à cette règle sont les revues militantes, celles qui sont mortes: *Québécoises debouttes (1972-74) et Têtes de pioche (1976-79); Plurielles* (1977-78); *Des luttes et des rires de femmes* (1978-81); comme celles qui existent toujours: *La Gazette des femmes* (1979-), *Communiqu'elles* (1981-), *Amazones d'hier, lesbiennes d'aujourd'hui* (1982-), le *RAIF* (1973-). Trois autres revues aussi, cependant, se définissent par leur projet féministe: la revue de création *Arcades* (1982-) qui depuis 1984 se consacre à l'écriture féministe, la revue *Tessera* (1984 -), qui n'est qu'en partie une revue québécoise, et *La Vie en Rose* (1980-).[2]

Ouvrons une parenthèse pour parler de *La Vie en Rose* parce qu'il faut saluer tout spécialement cette revue née en 1980 et qui aujourd'hui a un tirage de 20,000.[3] Il s'agit d'un rejeton en quelque sorte du magazine contre-culturel *Le Temps fou* (puisque une revue socialiste, féministe et écologiste), qui avait la prétention de parler de l'actualité vraie (même la Constitution et autres événements de la politique *platte*) à partir d'une perspective féministe. La revue a réussi à créer un lieu de parole féministe mais l'identité de ce lieu a bougé beaucoup. Au début le 'nous' qui parlait était nettement celui d'une communauté (et cette communauté était en gros la même que celle du *Temps fou*). Avec le temps le 'nous' est devenu de plus en plus la voix de l'équipe éditoriale. Depuis un an la revue a pris le risque de la commercialisation à outrance: couverture

---

1   Lamy, Suzanne, 'Un goût de perversion,' *Trajectoires: Littérature et institutions au Québec et en Belgique francophone*, sous la dir. de L. Gauvin et J-M Klinkenberg, Bruxelles, PUM-Labor, 1985.

2   Une liste de périodiques féministes préparée par *Communiqu'elles* fait état de 53 publications à travers le pays, dont 11 sont du Québec.

3   Après une campagne financière en 1986 qui a récolté des sommes substantielles et un appui public très chaleureux, l'équipe de la *Vie en Rose* a été obligée en juin 1987 d'en suspendre la publication. Une dernière campagne d'abonnement au cours de l'été devait décider du sort de la revue, mais les pronostics étaient bien noirs. Si ce sont l'habilité journalistique et la débrouillardise de l'équipe éditoriale qui ont permis à la revue d'atteindre des résultats tout à fait étonnants, c'est peut-être le rêve d'avoir vu trop grand qui aurait mis fin à cette aventure.

ultra-glacée, promotion agressive (le slogan 'le magasine culotté'), articles de dimension limitée. Tout de même la revue fait un excellent effort pour couvrir l'actualité internationale et a réussi à créer et à maintenir l'idée d'une actualité 'au féminin.' Reflétant bien le contexte actuel, la revue ne représente plus ni un projet féministe bien défini ni l'image d'une culture spécifique. Elle se caractérise maintenant plutôt par un choix d'objets inédits (souvent des personnalités féminines qui ont atteint une certaine célébrité ou dans le cas de Nathalie Petrowski une certaine notoriété) et par un ton personnalisé qui véhicule une charge affective intense. Malgré son tirage impressionant, donc, *La Vie en rose* est loin d'être la représentation exclusive du féminisme actuel au Québec.

À l'exception donc des quelques revues qui s'identifient comme féministes, la présence du féminisme dans les revues littéraires et culturelles au Québec est beaucoup plus diffuse. J'essaierai de repérer les formes qu'il assume en la regardant dans la configuration générale des revues actuelles au Québec — que je présenterai sous forme de quatre séries: 1) les revues universitaires, 2) les revues politico-littéraires, 3) les revues de création et 4) les revues de critique.

1)Dans la série des revues universitaires établies on retrouve *Études françaises*; *Études littéraires*; *Voix et images*; et *Protée* (une revue de sémiotique). Il y a une absence étonnante d'études ou d'objets féministes dans les deux premières. À l'exception d'un numéro spécial 'Féminaires' de la revue *Études littéraires* on pourrait penser que pour ces deux revues l'écriture et la lecture féministes n'existent pas. Pour *Protée* le féminisme ne semble pas avoir été une perspective privilégiée non plus. Seulement *Voix et images* a été ouverte aux sujets et aux lectures féministes, avec des dossiers sur Madeleine Gagnon et Yolande Villemaire, des articles occasionnels et les comptes-rendus de livres d'écrivaines. Le fait que *Voix et images* soit la revue universitaire la plus identifiée aux études féministes résulte directement de l'importance des écritures féministes dans la production québécoise au cours des dix dernières années. Il consacre aussi le trait marquant de la critique féministe au Québec et c'est d'avoir choisi de se consacrer presque exclusivement aux écritures féminines de la modernité. Cette congruence entre le féminisme comme mode d'analyse critique et le corpus d'écritures des femmes modernes caractérise la manière dont la critique féministe a pris forme au Québec (et beaucoup moins dans le monde anglophone, par exemple).

2) La relève des revues politico-littéraires maintenant défuntes: *Cité libre* (1950-66); *Parti pris* (1963-8), *Chroniques* (1975-78) et *Stratégie* (1972-77); *Mainmise* (1970-78), *Le Temps fou* (1974-83), a été assumée par trois revues:

Possibles[4] (1976-), *Dérives* (1975-) et *Vice-Versa* (1984-). Il ne s'agit pas à proprement parler de revues politiques: politique ici prend un sens très large, évidemment, parce qu'il y a un vide actuellement au Québec là où se trouvait autrefois le discours d'inspiration marxiste. Il n'y a pas au Québec de revue culturelle qui ait un contenu politique comparable à celui de *This Magazine*, ou même à celui de la revue *Fuse*. Par contre, un des phénomènes les plus intéressants au Québec ces dernières années a été l'émergence de lieux de réflexion sur l'interculturel ou le transculturel.

Dérives existe depuis 1975 et a pu à partir d'un groupe de collaborateurs réguliers autour de Jean Jonassain servir de point de ralliement 'anti-nationaliste' dans un climat québécois qui ne s'y prêtait guère. La réflexion féministe était assez étroitement liée à *Dérives* au moins durant les premières années et Madeleine Gagnon, par exemple, a contribué assez régulièrement à la revue. Depuis quelques années cependant le projet de *Dérives* s'est quelque peu dilué; la revue, qui conserve une haute qualité de réflexion, consacre des numéros spéciaux aux sujets les plus divers. La problématique transculturelle a été en très grande partie appropriée par *Vice-versa*.

Vice-Versa, née d'une revue culturelle italienne, existe dans sa forme actuelle depuis 1984 et est certainement la revue la plus dynamique au Québec actuellement: elle représente un projet et une philosophie bien articulée (le Québec transculturel fondé sur une conception postmoderne de l'ethnicité, c'est-à-dire une mise en question des origines à l'intérieur d'un Québec francophone) et est très présente sur la scène publique à travers un graphisme et une publicité agressives et accrocheuses. C'est une revue qui comme *La Vie en rose* a assumé le parti-pris de la *vente*, mais contrairement à *La Vie en rose* qui a sévèrement compromis la qualité de ses articles, *Vice-versa* présente un contenu qui est parfois recherché et difficile d'accès. Contrairement à *Dérives*, *Vice-versa* n'a aucun lien continu avec le féminisme et a publié très peu d'articles d'inspiration féministe.[5]

4 *Possibles* a publié deux numéros spéciaux consacrés aux femmes dans une perspective socio-politique et publie régulièrement des articles dans une perspective féministe. Mentionnons aussi l'excellent numéro de *Sociologie et sociétés* consacré aux femmes: *Les femmes dans la sociologie*, sous la direction de Nicole Laurin-Frenette, Montréal, PUM, 1981.

5 L'affiliation entre ethnicité, marginalité et féminisme semblerait pourtant devoir s'imposer, surtout dans le contexte québécois où les questions de langue sont privilégiées. Plusieurs écrivaines au Québec et au Canada, comme Daphne Marlatt, Smaro Kamboureli et Régine Robin ont comme Françoise Collin articulé ce lien: 'Même si la situation culturelle des femmes ne peut être identifiée à celle des immigrés, ou d'une manière générale à celle des minorités, elle comporte cependant le même caractère d'irréductible étrangeté – pour ne pas dire d'exclusion – dans la familiarité' (*Lettre internationale*, no. 11, hiver 86/87, 63). Et Marco Micone a donné une large place dans ses pièces aux questions spécifiques à l'immigrante.

Il est intéressant de contraster sur ce point les revues *Border/lines* et *Vice-versa*. Toutes deux ont opté pour un format semblable, un graphisme agressif et un contenu culturel théorique exigeant et interrogateur. *Border/lines* intègre de façon importante des articles féministes au point où on peut dire que la critique culturelle sur laquelle la revue s'appuie s'inspire *également* du féminisme et des théories critiques britanniques et américaines.

Comme si le rapport entre féminisme et ethnicité s'imposait quand même au Québec, une nouvelle revue portant le titre *La parole métèque, pour un renouveau féministe* vient de voir la lumière au Québec. Il s'agit d'une revue littéraire et culturelle qui propose de donner la parole à la femme immigrante. Quel avenir peut-on lui prévoir? Du fait qu'elle entre en compétition directe avec *La Vie en rose*, d'une part, et *Vice-versa* de l'autre, son projet risque d'être sévèrement compromis.[6]

3) C'est avec les revues de création (qui sont parfois en partie des revues de critique) que l'on retrouve l'expression fondamentale du féminisme. Il s'agit des *Herbes rouges* (1968-); *Estuaire* (1976-); *nbj* (1977-); *Moebius* (1977-); *XYZ* (1985-); *Arcade* (1982-); *Solaris* (1979-); *Imagine* (1979-). Ce sont surtout les *Herbes rouges* et la *nbj* qui ont accueilli le féminisme, comme écriture et comme lieu de réflexion dans le sens où fiction et théorie se sont annulées l'une dans l'autre. (La *nbj* publie depuis 1975 un numéro par année consacré à l'écriture des femmes.) Mais il faut aussi souligner l'essor du fantastique et de la science-fiction au Québec. Sans que cette écriture soit située dans une théorie explicitement féministe, l'écriture d'Esther Rochon par exemple a de profondes résonances féministes.

4)Les revues critiques: *Liberté* (1959-); *Spirale* (1979-); *Lettres québécoises* (1979-); *Nuit blanche* (1982-); *Jeu* (1976-); *Trois* (1985-). Le rapport difficile de *Liberté* au féminisme est notoire. À part un numéro spécial sur le féminisme, la revue est peu ouverte à la réflexion féministe. De la liste de revues critiques il n'y a que *Spirale* à avoir intégré le questionnement féministe de façon continue et explicite à ses pages et cela depuis 1979.

---

6 Évidemment la disparition éventuelle de *La Vie en rose* donnerait toute une nouvelle place à cette revue. Du fait qu'elle relève d'un projet individuel plutôt que d'un mouvement, elle n'aurait certainement pas le même poids social que *La Vie en rose*. Elle semble tout de même avoir touché des femmes vivant au Québec depuis de nombreuses années qui cherchait 'une tribune où les femmes de différentes origines puissent partager leurs expériences et actualiser le dynamisme qu'elles représentent pour la société québécoise.' (Éditorial, no. 2) Il est cependant trop tôt pour savoir si ce lieu de parole va s'établir et durer.

L'instance de la revue

Pour *Spirale* le féminisme — et sa conjonction avec la modernité — ont long-temps identifié en grande partie le projet et le *lieu* de la revue[7]. Avant d'entre-prendre l'analyse du féminisme tel que traité dans *Spirale*, je voudrais essayer de définir plus spécifiquement cette idée de la revue comme un *lieu* de parole.

Le monde des revues littéraires en est un de mouvance continuelle. Près de 140 périodiques littéraires et culturels sont nés entre 1945 et 1984 au Québec, dont 60 environ sont aujourd'hui disparus (*nbj*, (hiver 1985):11). Pour durer une revue doit réussir à créer, autant qu'un style, un *lieu* identifiable de parole, dans le sens où Suzanne Lamy a écrit: 'Le lieu dont on parle est parfois aussi impor-tant que ce qu'on y dit.' (Lamy, 101)

Une revue qui dure devient en quelque sorte un *auteur*, une signature col-lective qui englobe la totalité des signatures individuelles qui se manifestent dans ses pages. Cet auteur se définit bien sûr par son projet culturel et intellec-tuel, mais aussi par sa position sociale. L'analyse qu'a faite Anna Boschetti des *Temps modernes* montre assez paradoxalement qu'il est difficile de compren-dre la spécificité doctrinale de la revue si on regarde seulement son contenu. 'Les différences doctrinales par lesquelles les individus et les groupes se sont démarqués et ont justifié exclusions ou alliances ne suffisent pas en réalité à les distinguer si elles ne sont pas mises en relation avec les propriétés qui opposent les differents groupes et leur fonctionnement.' (Boschetti, 180; et par cela elle fait référence aux origines, aux éducations, aux projets spécifiques et aux insti-tutions auxquels sont reliés les différents membres de la rédaction des revues.)

Bernard Andrès a confirmé cette thèse en examinant ce qu'il a appelé la 'fausse polémique' entre les *herbes rouges* et la *nbj* en 1983-4. (Andrès, 1985) Andrès montre que mise à part la question du retour de la religion (qui n'est quand même pas rien), le différend entre ces deux groupes du même âge, du même statut social marginal à l'université, bien installé dans les cégeps, se ré-duisait à rien. En montrant que le débat était plutôt une opération de relations publiques, dans un sens très positif, Andrès conclut que les deux revues définis-sent un *même* lieu mais que ce lieu s'oppose à celui de l'université, maintenant une pluralité réelle à l'intérieur de l'insitution littéraire.

Dans un petit milieu comme le monde littéraire québécois, cette pluralité est des plus salutaires. Si Jacques Dubois peut identifier la revue comme un lieu et une étape distincte parmi quatre instances de légitimation littéraire (la criti-que, l'académie, l'école) (Dubois, 89-91) il serait illusoire de croire que dans le contexte québécois chaque instance aurait son autonomie propre. Dans le

---

7   Mon analyse de *Spirale* couvre la période 1979 à 1985 et exclut de ce fait ma participation
    à la direction de la revue.

milieu québécois, où le nombre de figurants n'est pas énorme, la présence des mêmes individus dans les diverses instances (revues, université, édition) est fréquente et inévitable. Il reste vrai qu'au moins à l'origine, les artisans de *Spirale* (et certainement des *herbes rouges* et de la *nbj*) écrivaient consciemment à partir d'un lieu qu'ils considéraient non-universitaire.

Le lieu de la revue est aussi une position relative à d'autres revues. Le meilleur indicateur des complicités entre revues c'est la polémique. Au cours des dernières années, à part la polémique analysée par Bernard Andrès (et qui a eu des échos dans *Spirale* avec la démission de deux membres de la rédaction), il faut souligner la critique très importante du numéro de *Voix et images* sur la *nbj* lancée dans *Liberté* (no 159, Vol. 27, no. 3, juin 1985, 19-47) par Jean Larose; la critique de la rubrique 'légitimes offenses' de *Liberté* lancée dans *Spirale* par Benoit Melançon (no. 56, déc 85) et la critique de la *nbj* faite par Pierre Nepveu également dans *Spirale* (no 59, avril 1986).

Cette configuration définit la *nbj*, *Liberté*, *Spirale*, *herbes rouges* et jusqu'à un certain point *Voix et images* comme faisant partie d'un même sous-réseau identifiable parmi les revues. À l'exception de *Liberté*, ces revues sont celles où s'exprime en priorité l'intérêt pour le féminisme et l'écriture moderne.

D'autres commentateurs ont déjà fait l'analyse de la configuration féminisme-modernité telle qu'elle s'exprime dans la *nbj* et les *herbes rouges*. (Sabourin, 1985; Frémont, 1985 et surtout Nepveu, 1985). Je voudrais dire quelques mots sur l'approche spécifique de la revue *Spirale* entre 1979 et 1985.

Le féminisme dans Spirale

La naissance de *Spirale* (sept. 1979) correspond à un moment fort de la production littéraire féministe au Québec et la revue devient très tôt un véhicule privilégié de la critique féministe. Suzanne Lamy avait publié *d'elles* en 1979 et devient collaboratrice dès le début 1980. Elle sera la collaboratrice la plus étroitement liée à la critique littéraire féministe mais elle fait partie d'un groupe important de collaboratrices qui s'identifient à une approche féministe (Gail Scott, Louise Dupré, Carole David, France Théoret, Monique LaRue, Louise Cotnoir et plus tard Lori Saint-Martin et Andrée Yanacopoulo).

La revue durant les premières années se dévoue très largement aux productions des femmes et aux livres d'intérêt féministe (les chroniqueurs masculins traitent également de ces livres). Mais la question féministe devient également l'objet de dossiers et de déclarations éditoriales. *Spirale* a publié en septembre 1980 un dossier consacré aux 'femmes et la critique' (no 11) où Suzanne Lamy et quatre autres collaboratrices posent le problème de la position de la critique face aux conditions spécifiques de la production des écrits de femmes. Le problème majeur que pose la critique pour Suzanne Lamy est la question de l'évaluation. Comment la critique peut-elle tenir compte du fait que 'la femme souligne constamment le lieu d'où elle parle et à quelles conditions elle le fait' mais en même temps oser distinguer le 'témoignage' du 'texte où l'écrivain a réellement pris le risque de l'écriture?' En juin 1983, un éditorial soulève la même question d'une manière différente: 'Il y a certains propos qui se tiennent en privé et qu'il vaudrait la peine de rendre publics. Depuis un bon moment à *Spirale* des hommes ne veulent plus parler de livres de femmes. Selon eux, la majorité des productions de femmes seraient moins exigeantes, prendraient en compte les besoins de la sororité . . . Mais faudrait-il vraiment que la solidarité entre femmes prenne le pas sur la lucidité et sur la connaissance? . . . Dans ces conditions, peut-il exister une critique au féminin?'

Il faut croire que les collaboratrices ont fini par trancher puisque *Spirale* est définitivement devenue un lieu où la critique négative de productions de femmes serait possible — à l'intérieur tout de même d'une perspective fémi-niste. Ainsi, pour donner seulement quelques exemples, Andrée Yanacopoulo a reproché à Jovette Marchessault son manque de riqueur dans *Lettres de Ca-lifornie*, a critiqué la naïveté de Lise Payette dans *Le pouvoir, connaît pas* et a prié Elisabeth Badinter de cesser de prêcher les évidences du post-féminisme (no 65, nov. 86); Suzanne Lamy a dénoncé la fausse modernité et la misogynie des *Fous de Bassan* d'Anne Hébert (no 29, nov. 1982), a adressé une sévère mise en garde contre la récupération du féminisme par des écrivaines comme Erica Jong (no 17, mars 1981) et a distingué des discordances au niveau de l'écriture dans *Journal intime* de Nicole Brossard, (no 44, juin 1984).

Évidemment, il n'y a pas eu que des articles négatifs, loin de là. Mais juste-ment la spécificité du lieu de *Spirale* semble se définir par son désir de s'extraire des réseaux de complicités. (C'est un thème qui revient souvent dans les édito-riaux, indépendamment du contexte féministe). *Spirale* se distingue donc par ses efforts continus de situer les assises de sa parole de façon explicite, pour ce qui est du féminisme comme pour la critique en général. En cela la revue fait état d'un questionnement caractéristique de la pensée moderne et qu'on re-trouve autant chez Blanchot et Barthes que chez Foucault et c'est la mise en question de l'autorité de la parole non-située.

Et l'avenir?

On peut dire que le féminisme occupe dans les revues littéraires et cultu-relles québécoises un espace paradoxal: à la fois central (par les problémati-ques théoriques qu'il implique et la qualité de la production) et diffus (par l'absence de lieux exclusifs d'expression).

Associé dans le domaine littéraire à l'écriture et à la création plutôt qu'à la recherche savante (consacrée à des objets divers, tel qu'on le voit dans *Signs*, par exemple, ou dans les *Cahiers du Grif*) le féminisme littéraire québécois a trouvé dans la psychanalyse et les théories textuelles ses principaux points d'appuis théoriques (Bayard, 1983). Ces présupposés théoriques font l'objet d'un réel concensus, contrairement à la pluralité des méthodologies et des approches aux États-Unis et contrairement à la tendance thématique et expérientielle qui a longtemps caractérisé les critiques féministes de langue anglaise.

L'époque de cette belle congruence entre la critique féministe, l'écriture féministe et la modernité (qui s'exprime de façon achevée dans les textes de Suzanne Lamy) tire tout de même à sa fin.[8] S'il y a quelques années il suffisait à une revue (comme à un individu) de se déclarer féministe et moderne pour s'assurer une place dans l'avant-garde, cela n'est plus le cas. La multiplication des féminismes, comme l'épuisement de la modernité, obligent à redéfinir ces termes par rapport à un projet renouvelé. En tant qu'expressions vivantes des idées et des écritures, ce sont les revues qui exprimeront en premier les configurations à venir.

Université Concordia

Bibliographie

Andrès, Bernard, 'Institution et avant-garde: Herbes rouges versus nbj.' *L'institution littéraire*, dir. Maurice Lemire, CRELIQ/IQRC, 1986.

Bayard, Caroline, 'Qu'en est-il de la théorie depuis que les dieux sont morts?,' *Féminité, Subversion, Écriture* sous la dir. de Suzanne Lamy et Irène Pagès,Montréal, Ed. du remue-ménage, 1983.

Bertrand-Jennings, Chantal, 'La presse des mouvements de libération des femmes en France de 1971 à 1982,' *Féminité, Subversion, Écriture*, sous la dir. de S. Lamy et I. Pages, Montréal, Ed. du remue-ménage, 1983.

Boschetti, Anna, *Sartre et 'les Temps modernes,'* Paris, Minuit, 1985.

Dubois, Jacques, *L'institution de la littérature*, Bruxelles, Nathan/Labor, 1978.

---

8 Les derniers écrits de Suzanne Lamy font état de cette évolution. En particulier sa communication présentée à l'APFUCC en juin 1986, 'Des ambiguités de la fiction à la tentation du récit.'

Frémont, Gabrielle, 'Le féminisme à la NBJ: un second souffle,' dans *Voix et images*, vol. X, no 2, hiver 1985.

Gallop, Jane, 'Interviews with four feminist academics,' *New Orleans Review*, Vol. 13, no 4, hiver 1986.

Lamy, Suzanne, 'Un goût de perversion,' *Trajectoires: Littérature et institutions au Québec et en Belgique francophone*, sous la dir. de L. Gauvin et J-M Klinkenberg, Bruxelles, PUM-Labor, 1985. Les indications paginales renvoient à la parution de l'article dans le recueil de Suzanne Lamy.

Michon, Jacques, 'Les revues littéraires d'avant-garde au Québec de 1940 à 1979,' *Trajectoires: Littérature et institutions au Québec*, sous la dir. de L. Gauvin et L. Klinkenberg, Bruxelles, PUM-Labor, 1985.

Nepveu, Pierre, 'De l'empire du sens au fait divers,' *Liberté* 134, mars-avril 1981, 'L'institution littéraire québécoise.'

—, 'BJ/NBJ: difficile modernité', *Voix et images*, vol. X, no 2, hiver 1985.

Pelletier, Jacques, 'Stratégie: de l'analyse des pratiques signifiantes à la lutte idéologique,' *L'Avant-garde culturelle et littéraire des années 70 au Québec*, Montréal, UQAM, 1986, 'Cahiers du département d'études littéraires.'

Sabourin, Claude, 'Les numéros "femmes" de la BJ/NBJ: pour une transformation des pratiques discursives,' *Voix et images*, vol. X, no 2, hiver 1985.

DAVID STAINES

Canadian Journal Publishing: notes from a new editor

I am a relative newcomer on the block of journal editors. A few years ago, I was invited to take over the editorship of a small periodical, *Journal of Canadian Poetry*. After giving much thought to the *Journal* and its editorial duties, I decided that I would venture into the realm of Canadian journal publishing with certain qualifications: first, there would be an active and working editorial board that would function *as* an editorial board, reading articles, suggesting reviewers, and assuming some responsibility; second, the journal would be an annual, devoted to the year's work in Canadian poetry and poetry criticism; third, the journal would aim to publish and foster criticism, true and objective criticism of a culture, I believe, in need of criticism.

I was, I know now, an innocent, unaware of the roadblocks ahead. Some of my colleagues and friends immediately warned me of the dangers – from their perspective – of journal publishing. 'We don't need criticism,' I was told. 'We need more outlets for creative work.' 'The poets have no channel of communication any more,' one colleague informed me, and added that I might create a critical journal which would be further evidence of the absence of homes for poetry. I did some investigation, and I decided that creative writers have many – perhaps not ample, but is there ever ample? – publishing outlets for poetry. The small journals, the little magazines, began as avenues for poets rather than critics. And I did not find, in my studies, that poets have so few avenues for publication.

My second obstacle, surprisingly, was the Canada Council. 'You should not publish an annual journal,' one colleague cautioned me, 'because the Canada Council only funds journals that make at least two appearances a year.' I explained to that colleague that I was not undertaking anything revolutionary; to the contrary, all I wanted to attempt to create was an annual journal that would become an honest and informed analysis of the year's work in and on Canadian poetry. 'Well,' my colleague concluded, 'you are doomed to failure, for not only will the journal fail, but it will never qualify for funding.' I made a final protestation that I was more interested in creating a viable, practical, and needed publication than one that might conform to the standards for outside financial assistance.

As an editor, I believed that my duties would be essentially twofold. First, in the area of articles, I developed a rule, which has been observed, that all articles will be read by two or three outside referees, and at least one — usually two — of these referees will be members of the editorial board. Second, in the area of reviews — and here, I confess, is a real problem — I hoped that reviewers would bring informed honesty to their writing. Canada is a small country where writers know one another. I have tried, and not always with success, to find reviewers, both at home and abroad, who would be informed and informative, and, more importantly, candid and honest. I cannot know all the friendships, hatreds, and rivalries that exist among writers, but I wonder if I need to. I would like to trust reviewers to understand the value and function of reviewing, the value and function of criticism. I find this understanding, alas, sadly lacking.

I did not anticipate some of the responses to my invitation to review for the *Journal of Canadian Poetry*. One academic colleague wrote me, declining the invitation to review; he did not desire to review, he informed me, because promotion and tenure committees do not regard reviews as highly as they regard original articles, and therefore, he concluded, their guidelines should be followed. Writers often wrote me, applauding my hopes and urging that their books be reviewed, but sometimes declining the invitation to review. Why? Because they did not like the book, and if they could not praise the book, they frankly admitted, they were reluctant to write with honesty. This attitude, alas, I encountered with some frequency.

I often think that our literature is only as healthy and alive as the current of critical ideas that the literature fosters and is fostered by. And, therefore, my personal reflections on my position as a new editor invite some more general reflections on the state of Canadian criticism. And as my touchstone, to try and shed light on some of the problems I have encountered as an editor, I wish to summon up the ominous ghost of Matthew Arnold.

Of all the Victorian poets, Arnold had the greatest influence on his own literature and on other English literatures. And the reason for his influence was his prose, his lucid, often witty, and objective criticism, which bore little resemblance to the poetry he wrote, where he could never attain the detachment he sought as a writer. Arnold believed that his own age could not provide the materials for poetry and he therefore sought criticism in his age of expansion. He observed that his own age had not been preceded by a cerebral critical tradition which would provide the critical milieu where an artist could create and thereby convey his vision to an audience.

Arnold had a high, lofty, and unbending regard for literature. And he also had an equal respect for criticism. His own critical writing often emphasized the value of the critical mind. In 'The Function of Criticism at the Present Time' (1864), Arnold raised questions that are still relevant today:

> Is it true that criticism is really, in itself, a baneful and injurious employment; is it true that all time given to writing critiques on the works of others would be much better employed if it were given to original composition, of whatever kind that may be? . . . is it certain that Wordsworth himself was better employed in making his Ecclesiastical Sonnets than when he made his celebrated Preface so full of criticism, and criticism of the books of others?

As a critic, Arnold was the major literary figure of the later nineteenth century, perhaps of the nineteenth century, because he held criticism in such high regard, because he believed and affirmed that literature was central to the well-being of society, and because he demanded that his readers have a cosmopolitan outlook, an outlook created by the critical writing of his time. Through Arnold, twentieth-century criticism took its roots in the very tenets that were known as Arnoldian. Through Irving Babbitt, many of Arnold's beliefs were developed in the new humanism. And despite his anxiety of influence towards many of the Victorians, especially Arnold and Tennyson, T.S. Eliot acknowledged Arnold's seminal importance with the very title of his work, 'The Function of Criticism.'

In Canada, Arnold's influence, still to be adequately studied and documented, has been all-pervasive. The major critical minds of this century not only studied under Arnold's tutelage, but also wrote about him and his influence. Both E.K. Brown and Douglas Bush wrote books about Arnold. A.S.P. Woodhouse and Pelham Edgar wrote about the criticism of Arnold which shaped their own thinking, as did later critics such as Malcolm Ross. And Northrop Frye has written about Arnold, and shows, his own *Anatomy of Criticism* as many critics have pointed out, Arnold's major influence.

Somewhere between this Arnoldian influence and the present world I sketched as I confronted my new duties as a journal editor, something has happened which we need to analyze and rectify, something has happened to make criticism less a glorious depiction of the ideas of our time than the tired, bland, and often unobjective twaddle that passes as reviewing on the pages of the *New York Times* or the *New York Review of Books*. With a distinguished literature that has been growing up and flourishing before our eyes, we deserve and should demand a criticism commensurate with our literature.

In the first issue of *Canadian Literature* (1959), George Woodcock outlined his purpose in founding this distinguished journal. I quote his purpose in full because it is one further example of the Arnoldian influence:

Canadian Literature seeks to establish no clan, little or large. It will not adopt a narrowly academic approach, nor will it try to restrict its pages to any school of criticism or any class of writers. It is published by a university, but many of its present and future contributors live and work outside academic circles, and long may they continue to do so, for the independent men and women of letters are the solid core of any mature literature. Good writing, writing that says something fresh and valuable on literature in Canada is what we seek, no matter where it originates. It can be in English or in French, and it need not necessarily be by Canadians, since we intend to publish the views of writers from south of the border or east of the Atlantic, who can observe what is being produced here from an external and *detached* viewpoint.'

To study the pages of our periodicals and the books of our criticism reveals, alas, how far contemporary writing has eschewed the principles that lead to external and detached critical investigation. There has been a change in our critical activity, a change too indicative of our own culture.

In our contemporary culture, which has been so shaped by Arnoldian principles, criticism that is informed and honest, that is external and detached, is relatively absent. The new *Journal of Canadian Poetry*, a small attempt to elevate criticism, will be successful only insofar as a critical perspective is feasible in our culture. I am not certain if it is feasible, but I do know that it is necessary.

University of Ottawa

CONSTANCE ROOKE

Literary Periodicals: questions of funding and editing

The editors of literary magazines are generally sorely over worked. This state-ment is not gratuitous self-pity or self-congratulation; I do not intend here to complain or to praise my own tribe. But my assigned topic is the funding and editing of literary magazines, and more particularly the *inter-relationship* of funding and editing. And I begin with this issue of the over worked editor be-cause in my own experience it impinges closely on questions of funding. I begin with this issue also because I believe that it has far-reaching implications for the quality of our literary magazines, and for the development of writers in this country.

Because the work that editors do is underpaid or, more typically, unpaid, some other labour is nearly always required to support them. Some editors want to work at other jobs; others are obliged to do so. Either way, they end up being over worked. Consider the best case, which is arguably that of a university teacher who is granted some 'release-time' from teaching duties to compensate for editorial work. Not all editors with a university affiliation fare so well, of course; and even where release-time is offered, two problems remain. First, the magazine may have to pay the wages of the editor's part-time sessional replace-ment — and that additional strain on the magazine's budget will mean more *work* for the editor, as I shall be suggesting shortly. Second, the release-time that is carved out of the editor's teaching load is always inadequate, always much less than the time that is actually spent on editorial work.

I use the term 'editorial work' here very loosely — or broadly if you like. And that is the problem. I use it to cover all the work done by editors on behalf of their magazines. If we begin with the recognition that for economic and other reasons editors nearly always have other responsibilities that claim a sizable portion of their time, and consider next how much of their remaining available time must be spent in tasks that are not strictly speaking editorial, the problem becomes obvious. Real editing takes a great deal of time. Real editing is the work that real editors want to do; it is the indispensable work they can attend to only when other pressing operational tasks have been performed. It becomes, therefore, what it is not – dispensable.

I'm not saying it doesn't happen; I'm saying it doesn't happen enough. The heart of editorial work is finding the manuscripts and working with the writer to improve them. Finding the right manuscripts means going after them, which requires (among other things) that the editor read prodigiously, and read far more than the work submitted to his or her own magazine. But that takes time and care and the mountain of unsolicited manuscripts must somehow or other be scaled before the outlying country comes into view. Because the mountain replenishes itself, it really is fiendishly difficult to get to the top and look out.

Working on manuscripts to improve them is perhaps the most important task of all, and it is important even with manuscripts that are not ultimately published either by the editor who offers assistance or by anyone at all. This is a critical juncture in our literary institution, a test of common sense that we fail at our peril. Editing (real editing) *must* happen here, where the new writers begin. I haven't forgotten creative writing classes, writing friends, or writers-in-residence. I know that other help is available to developing writers, but I would still maintain that the editors of literary magazines need to be empowered in this way. They can supply a critical supplement in the system as a whole.

'We all begin in little magazines' – writers have been acknowledging this fact for a long time. It is important, though, to recognize that many established writers *stay* with the little magazines, and that any good writer is a 'developing' writer. A literary magazine is not just brute space or a consolation prize for writers who cannot make it into book publication. What occupies the space must be found and shaped. What pleases the writer – whether she is a beginning writer or an old hand – is the knowledge that her work is treated with respect and that it has found good company. New writers *like* to appear with a Findley or an Atwood; more seasoned writers *like* to appear with talented newcomers; any writer worthy of the name *likes* to be queried if a modifier is dangling or a paragraph is misplaced or a character is speaking out of voice.

So editing a little magazine takes large chunks of time. The picture I have tried to sketch of an editor's working life has three phases: work unrelated to the magazine that is undertaken in part because editing a literary magazine does not pay, the 'other' editorial work that must be performed if the magazine is to stay alive, and finally the real editing that must increase and improve if our magazines and our writers are to realize their full potential. The questions are: how can we make that happen, and more particularly how can the funding of literary magazines inhibit or speed up the editor's progress through to the place where real editing occurs?

My answer to those questions is the crude, predictable one. We need more money. Let me take that money through the phases, beginning with the question of payment for editorial work. I'm in favour of it. It is a good place to put some of the extra money that we need. I am not suggesting that all editors of literary magazines should be paid well enough to work on their magazines full-time. I am not suggesting this for the good and sufficient reason that many editors *want* also to write or teach or whatever; much of that work is in fact useful to them as editors. But it doesn't make sense to have gifted editors working in gift shops in order to pay their bills. Editors should be able to decide how much time they wish to devote to their magazines; they should be able to prepare budgets that provide adequate payment for themselves. Then, if they are good enough, if their magazines are good enough, they should get it. Quite apart from questions of natural justice, this would be money well spent.

Money spent on the first phase — on release-time for editors, whether they are academics or not — buys time for the second and third. But more money also needs to be injected into the second phase, to speed our editors on to the critical third phase, and for other compelling reasons as well. This is where the money we currently have gets spent, on the operation and production and distribution of our magazines. What is left over — if I may be forgiven for conceptualizing it in this way — goes to the writers, in payment for their work. Very clearly, there is not enough of that.

Like many editors, I was delighted when the Canada Council instituted its fund for payment to contributors; like others, I was devastated when that program was discontinued. It was lovely to have an additional pot of money earmarked for this purpose. We could increase our rate of payment — if not to a really commendable level, at least to something more than tokenism. So we did. And then the fund dried up. We were left with the choice of dropping our rates again or scrambling still harder in other areas of the budget. Again, I would make the point that such scrambling on the part of unpaid or underpaid editors and their helpers in not really 'free': the cost is paid in the third phase, where the indispensable editing process is undercut.

Unforgivably, I have referred to the editor's helpers very late in the day. I have seemed to assume a one-man or one-woman show. Literary magazines in this country as elsewhere have organizational structures that vary from co-operatives (in which editorial and other decisions are made by consensus, in which all the labour is shared) to the model that involves an editor making all the major decisions, and possibly doing nearly all the work. Most literary magazines, however, have an editorial board of some kind; many assign particular editorial and other tasks to particular individuals, so that we have circulation managers and poetry editors and so on. What this means is that there are other people who should be paid, and other people who might do some of that real editing in the third phase.

I am not suggesting the impossible: that literary magazines must be able to dispense with volunteer labour. I am saying that when too much of the work done on literary magazines is unpaid, too little real editing gets done. I want more money for editors, and not just editors-in-chief. I want more money for people doing non-editorial tasks, for reasons of natural justice and because at present too much of that work is being done by editors. We also need more money to meet the rising costs of production, distribution, and promotion, and to improve our performance in these areas. And — to repeat myself — we need more money for our contributors.

At present, editors use too much of their *energy* as well as time on the fight to keep their magazines alive. Increased funding from federal and provincial governments is the answer. We should not need to fight so hard either for what we have or for the additional money we require; we should be freed to concentrate our energy on improving the quality of our magazines and on helping writers.

But we should not, in my opinion, be freed from the struggle to increase the number of our subscribers, or from the pressure currently exerted by funding bodies to perform that really Herculean task. (We should, however, be *helped* to do this; thus I applaud the Canada Council's promotion fund, and would like to see it increased.) Greater success in the selling of literary magazines should help to ease an increased financial burden on government, but not by much; indeed, the cost to government of funding our promotion efforts may in the short term outweigh the revenues that are generated. (You will see that I am fully and unrepentantly aware of our need for heavy subsidies.) I would acknowledge too that the energy spent on building a subscription base is costly in relation to that third indispensable phase of an editor's working life. Nevertheless, I welcome the pressure to increase sales. We need more readers because our country needs more readers. From the perspective of my own unhidden agenda, the additional revenues gained from new subscribers are a secondary good.

It should be evident from these remarks that I am not opposed to accountability. I have suggested, for example, that editors should be paid properly if they and their magazines are good enough. I am content with the system of peer review, because as a system it is the only one that makes sense. But certain obvious difficulties arise. Among them are differing tastes and the trouble jurors will have in agreeing upon literary merit, especially since the magazines themselves *must* take risks with the writing they print. New magazines will have to compete for funding with the established ones, and juries must find ways of funding both. They will need to consider regional, ideological, and other factors in order to preserve a balanced range of literary magazines. But the issue of excellence (however vexed that may be) must remain their principal concern.

Canada Council has placed a semi-official ceiling of $20,000 on annual operating grants to anglophone literary magazines. I think only three magazines (*Descant*, *Fiddlehead*, and *The Malahat Review*) get that much. I want to protest not only the low level of that ceiling (which gives us insufficient head-space, as I have been arguing) but also the very notion of a ceiling. Given budget restraints and an increasing number of deserving applicants, it is easy to understand how the ceiling came to be installed. No doubt it is convenient as a fixed point when so much else is necessarily in flux. But it is still wrong, in my opinion – wrong in principle – and should be removed. Consider, for example, the effect of a fixed ceiling in the case of a fine magazine whose costs are going up and whose other means of support are collapsing: the magazine will deteriorate and then go under. To increase Canada Council funding by reducing or cancelling support of a mediocre magazine would seem preferable in these circumstances.

I want to turn briefly now to the matter of provincial funding, which varies dramatically. In British Columbia, all the literary magazines put together receive about $13,000 a year. In the Atlantic provinces, the situation is equally grim. The prairies are better off: in Manitoba, for instance, literary magazines get about $100,000 a year; in Ontario about $150,000. These figures are approximate, but they indicate both the need for lobbying at the provincial level (particularly in provinces like B. C.) and the widely divergent financial packages with which literary magazines can approach the Canada Council. Funding by universities and colleges also varies widely; and it can be cut at any time, most often in response to changes in provincial funding of secondary education. Literary magazines are therefore often doubly reliant upon the Canada Council to make up for provincial disparities.

In posing the topic of this conference, the organizers were concerned in part with the possible disadvantages of government funding. Any threats to the autonomy of literary magazines, and particularly any interference with editorial judgment would obviously be cause for serious concern. I know that the accountability of which I approve is regarded by a few editors in just that light. They occasionally protest against pressures to increase payment to contributors or to meet publication schedules or to increase sales or to reduce costs or to improve quality. And I acknowledge that my attitudes on this subject might be different if my own magazine had been the recipient of similar critiques, particularly if I knew that I were doing the best I could with minimal resources. All I can say is that I see the danger – and that despite the risk of injustice, accountability seems to me a necessary and salutary thing. It is not inevitably a synonym for interference.

Governments, however, must be accountable too. Funding must become more adequate to our needs, and at present it is very far from adequate. The Director of the Canada Council knows this; he has acknowledged that the periodicals program is one of the most seriously under-funded of all the Council's programs. All the people involved in allocating funds to literary magazines – jurors and readers alike – know this and deplore it. What remains is to change the situation.

I hope that happens soon. I repeat that the most serious problem by far with the funding of literary magazines in Canada is that there isn't enough of it. And I repeat that one of the most serious consequences of under-funding is that it makes real editing nearly impossible.

University of Guelph

Scholarly Publishing in Canada

I feel it wise to explain, before I launch into a set of statements that finally focuses on scholarly publishing, where my experiences of the book trade in Canada have been. Those experiences will, I hope, indicate why a historical and cultural overview is the form of commentary with which I feel comfortable at this particular time and for this conference.

I began in scholarly publishing at the University of Toronto Press in 1941, and (with three years, 1942-45, out for war service) became the press's managing editor in 1965. In 1969 I was appointed general editor of the *Dictionary of Canadian Biography* (established 1959), then Canada's major long-term commitment in scholarly publishing in English and in French, as it was in scholarship about Canada. Two years before, in 1967, I had initiated a course in Contemporary Publishing with concentration on Canada, given in the Faculty of Library Science at the University of Toronto, the first such academic course to be mounted in this country.[1] The course continued, as did my general editorship of the *DCB/DBC*, after I became professor and dean of the faculty in 1972, an association which included the stimulus of getting to know librarians, inte-

---

1 Other Canadian library schools, such as the University of British Columbia and Dalhousie University, were later to introduce a course or a unit on Canadian publishing, to offer individual lectures, sometimes to sponsor conferences. In 1984 Simon Fraser University initiated discussions about the establishment of a Canadian Centre for Studies in Publishing, whose aim would be to offer not only continuing education for those in publishing but also academic courses at the undergraduate level (leading to a minor) and at the Master's level (ultimately a specialization in publishing studies) and to facilitate research projects. The Centre was founded in 1987, and undergraduate courses were offered for the first time in the autumn of 1988. The Centre's advisory board has representatives from the university (of whom F. G. Halpenny is one), and from the publishing, bookselling, writing, editing, and library fields. Ann Cowan and Rowland Lorimer of Simon Fraser and a preliminary working committee from the book trade have been instrumental in the initiation of the Centre. Douglas Gibson became chairman of the board in 1988.

gral members of the book trade. Through the work of the course's students over twenty years and my own academic undertakings in its subject field much useful factual and contextual material became available to me for study in years when Canadian publishing was on the move, at times down rather than up it must be acknowledged, but nevertheless doing more and more with Canadian authors. Later (between 1979 and 1982) I had the good fortune to be a member and then chairman of the National Library Advisory Board and to be involved (1978-1987) as committee member and chairman in the liaison work of the Book and Periodical Development Council, founded in 1975 as the umbrella organization of the book trade. In addition to its on-going activities the Council has recently had special task forces on the feasibility of a reprography collective (completed) and of a CD-ROM Canadian master for all books published in Canada, a matter of great technical and cultural moment for this country's book trade.

For the Council I have been involved as director in two research projects: the first, using a case study approach, was issued in 1985 as *Canadian Collections in Public Libraries*[2];the second, about to be launched under the title 'From Catalogue to Reader,' is studying the process by which 150 Canadian trade books of a specific publishing season proceed from publishers' announcements to promotion and review and on to acquisition by libraries. Like many others in the trade and in universities, I have served on my share of committees investigating questions about publishing or on editorial boards or on juries of the Canada Council and the Social Sciences and Humanities Research Council. These varied experiences have been a privilege for which I am grateful. They will indicate, among other things, why I asked permission to offer, as I began my presentation to the conference, some general comment about the book trade related to the University of Alberta's project 'Towards a History of the Literary Institution in Canada.'[3]

---

2 Francess G. Halpenny, *Canadian Collections in Public Libraries*, a report of a research project carried out under the auspices of the Book and Periodical Development Council (Toronto: the Council 1985).
3 See also my chapter 'From Author to Reader' in the fourth volume of the *Literary History of Canada*, now in press. Recent studies in the United States on the sociology of publishing offer analytical background; see Lewis A. Coser, Charles Kadushin, and Walter W. Powell, *Books: The Culture and Commerce of Publishing* (New York: Basic Books 1982);Walter Powell, *Getting into Print: The Decision-Making Process in Scholarly Publishing* (Chicago: University of Chicago Press 1985); Irving Louis Horowitz, *Communicating Ideas: The Crisis of Publishing in a Post-Industrial Society* (New York: Oxford University Press 1986).

A large store of ideas and questions has been presented to this second conference on its announced theme of publishing and distribution. The needs and possibilities of the project's study of this particular context are both stimulating and daunting, as they are with other contexts. For so many of the topics introduced at this conference, and others that can be pointed out as relevant, we have perceptions, tentative hypotheses, practical experiences, but not the assemblage of detailed information, not the grasp of interactions and influences that can lead on to a sufficiently wide-ranging, persuasive interpretation. The life-history of publishing in Canada is sketchy — George L. Parker's book is the first full-length work to chart the early development of the trade on the basis of extended original research.[4] As M. Giguère has noted, there has been one slim volume for the French-language trade. The work to date of his Groupe de recherche sur l'édition littéraire au Québec at l'université de Sherbrooke and of the Institut québécois de recherche sur la culture at l'université Laval is an earnest of new knowledge.

A great deal of the accounting for the anglophone book trade so far has come in a stream of reports, position papers, background documents for commissions of inquiry — material that is time-bound and yet repetitive. Badly needed are histories and analyses, long or short, of individual publishing houses and of players in them (directors, editors, promotion planners, designers), of the authors they have presented and the lists they have developed. Literary biography, autobiography, and letters are beginning to tell us something of compulsions to authorship and the experience of publication, but we lack the careful exploration of what literary careers have meant in Canada that will take us beyond the sketchiness of interview, preface, and anecdote. This conference has demonstrated the need to look with more information and greater depth at the effect upon literary traditions and current literary expectations of where and how authors write and publishers publish. We need dispassionate, disinterested, and extensive accounts of how and why programs of public support for literature have come into being, how they have been organized, how they have interacted with one another and with the book trade.[5] The indirect support system of the

4   Reference should be made to the work of Delores Broten and Peter Birdsall in *Paper Phoenix: A History of Book Publishing In English Canada* (Victoria:CANLIT 1980). See also John Wiseman's work on the nineteenth-century dissemination of books and periodicals in Ontario, *Publishing History*, 12 (1982): 17-50.
5   In this connection see Bernard Ostry, *The Cultural Connection: An Essay on Culture and Government Policy in Canada* (Toronto: McClelland & Stewart 1978); David Helwig, ed., *Love and Money: The Politics of Culture* (Ottawa:Oberon 1980); Paul Audley, *Canada's Cultural Industries:Broadcasting, Publishing, Records and Film* (Toronto: Lorimer 1983).

CBC is often alluded to, but too many references remain allusions; we need studies. The connections of academics with literary creation, with granting bodies, with publishing initiatives, with reviewing media have come up frequently at this conference: here is a potent theme for in-depth research into cause and effect.[6]

Certain aspects of the procedures and results of writing and publishing literature in Canada have not been tackled at this conference, and I suggest to the research group that they should be taken up at some point. These aspects will show themselves if one looks at what a broader spectrum of activity related to books means. For instance, *Canadian Books in Print 1986* shows that books issued by Canadian publishers or originated in Canada by subsidiaries totalled 25,637 entries, 2,949 with a 1985 imprint; how does literature fit into this output, and what does recognizing its place there tell us about its character as an institution? To take a different approach: the 'book trade' is a continuum, which puts authors, and their agents, in the beginning slot, then moves on to publishers (with their associates: printers, binders, warehousers), takes in wholesalers, and through bookstores and libraries reaches readers; in reverse, the reactions of readers affect what appears in bookstores and libraries, what is published, and often what is written.[7] Bookstores and libraries are thus vital components in any analysis of these contexts of publishing, for literary as for other works. James Lorimer's *Book Reading in Canada*, which points up the importance of the stores as a route to readers,[8] and *Canadian Collections in Public Libraries*, which analyses not only the kinds of books collected but also the attitudes of librarians and readers, provide hard data and point the way to further research. The activities of the National Library, founded 1953,[9] in its work with legal deposit, the current national bibliography, the retrospective bibliographic record, interlibrary loan, the 'Conspectus' survey of collections in libraries across Canada,[10] and leadership with the provinces in the Decentralized Program for

6 Under the Canadian Studies Research Tools Programme of the Social Sciences and Humanities Research Council a major project for an annotated bibliography of the book trade in Canada from 1935 has been under way in the Frost Centre for Canadian Heritage and Development Studies at Trent University, with Darienne McAuley as research associate. It is taking account of monographs, articles in major and minor periodicals, and 'grey' literature such as reports and briefs.
7 For a 1980 colloquium of the Royal Society of Canada reflecting this cycle, see A. G. McKay, ed., *The Written Word/Prestige de l'écrit* (Ottawa: the Society 1981).
8 James Lorimer, *Book Reading in Canada: The Audience, the Marketplace, and the Distribution System for Trade Books in English Canada* (Toronto: Association of Canadian Publishers 1983).
9 See F. Dolores Donnelly, *The National Library of Canada: An Historical Analysis of the Forces Which Contributed to the Identification of Its Role and Responsibilities* (Ottawa: Canadian Library Association 1973).
10 See *National Library News*, October 1985, 1986.

Canadian Newspapers – all these are elements of context for the identification of a Canadian Literature and study thereof.[11] So too is the work of the Canadian Institute for Historical Microreproductions (founded 1978 with funds from the Canada Council) in creating a comprehensive library of Canadian imprints on microfiche to counter the effects of physical deterioration of library holdings and of the wide dispersal of a miscellany of collections in Canada and abroad that together hold the country's cultural heritage. CIHM completes in 1988 its program for pre-1901 monographs and embarks on another for pre-1901 periodicals (of an estimated 150,000 individual issues, less than half have survived). The role of academic libraries in building student and research collections also needs attention. Moreover, in any study of how publishing and distribution work in Canada one needs to take into adequate account the professional organizations which promote, encourage, assist, lobby for their members: the Canadian League of Poets, the Writers' Union of Canada, the Canadian Booksellers Association, the Association of Canadian Publishers, the Literary Press Group, the Canadian Book Publishers' Council, The Children's Book Centre, the Canadian Book Information Centre, the Freelance Editors Association of Canada, the Periodical Writers Association of Canada, the Canadian Periodical Publishers' Association, the Canadian Authors Association,[12] the Canadian Library Association, along with many provincial equivalents. Finally, there are the readers. Who in Canada reads what? When? How? Why? Who in Canada reads Canadian-authored literature? When? How? Why? We know too little.

Now to scholarly publishing, and first a definition. It is publishing that concerns itself with the results of scholarship. That might suggest its books and periodicals are published for scholars, but the lists of scholarly publishers are not so confined in audience. Some non-fiction titles have a trade life as well as one among scholars and teachers, though the basis of their content is still in scholarship and research. Some scholarly publishers, however, enter occasionally into poetry and fiction. Scholarly publishing (except for help from texts or occasional important trade titles) is, over-all, non-profit publishing, sustained by subsidy and grant. The University of Toronto Press, the largest of the Canadian univer-

---

11 In June 1986 the National Library offered a national colloquium on 'Availability of Publications in Canada' in order to examine the application in Canada of the international concept of Universal Availability of Publications (UAP), a program and an objective promoted by the International Federation of Library Associations and Institutions (IFLA) with support from UNESCO. The *Proceedings* of the colloquium and its recommendations were issued by the National Library in 1987, as was a *Background Document*, which discusses readership, publishing, bookstores and libraries.

12 An indication of the inquiries that need to be made into organizations, and of their potential value, is given in the chapter 'The Canadian Authors' Assocation' in Clara Thomas and John Lennox, *Arthur Deacon: A Canadian Literary Life* (Toronto: University of Toronto Press 1982). For further references, see note 2 to that chapter.

sity presses, with approximately 850 titles in print and a normal publishing year
of 80 to 100 books, receives support mainly from the Aid to Publications Program of the Humanities Research Council and the Social Sciences Research
Council (themselves funded by the Social Sciences and Humanities Research
Council) but also, for its trade titles, from the Canada Council's and Ontario
Arts Council's block-grant systems. The other university presses receive similar support, and have varying assistance from their universities.

Scholarly publishing is not, of course, confined to university presses. It has
many auspices, including government departments (for example Parks Canada,
a division of Environment Canada), research institutions, universities, and
houses that address themselves particularly to the trade (the Penguin and Oxford imprints have been cases in point; so have such a varied group as McClelland & Stewart, Macmillan, Anansi, and NeWest). The university presses have
an important role, however. A particularly North American phenome-
non[13] (paralleled in Britain by the university presses of, for example, Edinburgh
and Manchester and, in their lists, to some extent by trade houses such as Allen
& Unwin and Routledge), they have addressed the great volume of writing that
scholars in or out of universities have developed especially since the war, and
with trade houses cutting back on more specialized titles for financial reasons
in recent years, they have had to try to encompass even more. Canadian
scholarly journals in the humanities and social sciences, some 120 of them in
1978-80 when measured by an inquiry into scholarly publishing in English and
French, make a highly significant contribution by university presses, universities, or national and regional societies to the creation, criticism, and reviewing
of Canadian literature as they do in many other fields. A periodical which surveys developments in publication, *Scholarly Publishing: A Journal for Authors &
Publishers*, was begun in 1969 by University of Toronto Press, with an international advisory board.

At this point I shall turn to a more personal view of scholarly publishing in
the Canadian field as I experienced and observed its growth. When I went to
the University of Toronto Press in 1941 with a B.A. and M.A. in English literature from the University of Toronto I had been little exposed to Canadian literature.[14] In my course work I had had a few lectures in the fourth year by E.K.
Brown tacked on at the end of a parade of American literature, and my M.A.
thesis was on realistic American fiction of the late nineteenth and early twen-

---

13 See Gene R. Hawes, *To Advance Knowledge: A Handbook on American University Press
    Publishing* (New York: American University Press Services 1967).
14 For an account of the changing program at the University of Toronto see Robin A. Harris,
    English Studies at Toronto: A History (University of Toronto, 1988). In 1988-89, as part of a
    revised program, all specialist and major students in English literature are required to take
    one full course in Canadian literature.

tieth centuries. Few universities were doing any better by Canadian literature, and they were not sending out many readers interested in Canadian writing or prospective employees in Canadian publishing and reviewing media keen to develop and promote it. The training I had had in my course, particularly under E.K. Brown with his intense and sensitive analysis of the structure of individual works of poetry and fiction, was to help me immeasurably as an editor and reader of manuscripts but I had much to discover about what was going on in my own country in order to fulfill the mandate I took on.

I was set to work on the *University of Toronto Quarterly*. At that time the publishing of the press was largely distinguished by four journals in which original Canadian scholarship found a significant outlet: the *Quarterly* (founded 1931), the *Canadian Historical Review* (1920), the *Canadian Journal of Economics and Political Science* (1934), and the *University of Toronto Law Journal* (1934). The reviews and bibliographies included in the *CHR* and the *CJEPS* were essential guides to studies in Canadian history, political science, and economics which, unlike studies in Canadian literature, had been developing for a good many years with practical needs acting somewhat as a prod. But *UTQ* also had a review survey and a bibliography, 'Letters in Canada.' Of a different sort, it had been started in 1935-36 by A.S.P. Woodhouse and E.K. Brown to deal with the lack of any 'annual publication devoted to the cultural and literary life of the Dominion' or of any 'bibliography of books and articles on this subject.' Later, the survey began to include writing in French and in languages other than English and French. By working on 'Letters in Canada' especially I began to be aware of what had been and was happening in Canadian literature and in scholarly responses to it. *Queen's Quarterly* and *Dalhousie Review* were already in the field. There had been single events of great importance: for example, in 1936, from Macmillan, both the poetry anthology *New Provinces* and W.E. Collin's brilliant essays on poetry *The White Savannahs*. The Governor-General's Awards were founded in 1936 also. The CBC, established in 1932, had begun to broadcast not only poetry and short stories but also lectures. It is indicative of the scale of creative writing in 1941, however, that the bibliography I prepared for 'Letters in Canada' included individual poems appearing in *Saturday Night*; ten years later, the picture was to be greatly different in all fields of writing, and with relief the bibliographic task was relinquished in 1951 to the national bibliography *Canadiana* (taken over by the National Library on its founding in 1953). In 1943, after I had left for war service, two particularly significant events in scholarship occurred: E.K. Brown's *On Canadian Poetry* from Ryerson and A.J.M. Smith's *Book of Canadian Poetry* from Gage, which have been described by Desmond Pacey as 'the final event in the long-drawn-out campaign to make Canadian literature academically respectable.' D.G. Creighton's *Dominion of the North* 1944 from Macmillan, displayed a skill at historical narrative that carried Canadian history beyond the classroom and into the hands of general readers.

For some months before I returned to the Editorial Department of the University of Toronto Press in 1945 it had had no full-time staff member. But the activities of the press were soon to change greatly. In 1945, three senior professors, G.W. Brown (History), A.S.P. Woodhouse (English), and V.W. Bladen (Economics), all of whom had been involved closely with the UTP journals in their disciplines, made a trip to six senior university presses in the United States to examine organizational structures, financing, and editorial policies. As a result of their report the press was reorganized for a much more independent role based on its having 'all its profits at its disposal not only for maintenance and replacement, but for necessary expansion and for the support of scholarly publication.' Its specialized printing plant was to provide an important part of the profits. With Professor Brown as part-time Editor from 1946 to 1953 and with the arrival from trade and educational publishing of Eleanor Harman in 1946 and of Marsh Jeanneret as director in 1953, the press expanded its original publishing, transformed its production skills, and built up its editorial department. In the early years after the war, leaders on its list were the seminal works of R. MacG. Dawson, J.A. Corry, Alexander Brady, and S.D. Clark in Canadian history, political science, and sociology, which influenced generations of students and set a pattern for scholarly endeavour. From these disciplines came editors and contributors for two important series supported by the Social Science Research Council and the press's Publications Fund: the Canadian Government series (inaugurated 1946), and Social Credit in Alberta series (1949, completed in ten volumes on schedule in 1959). The Department of English Studies and Texts series had been founded in 1942 but really developed after the war. Of consequence for literature in ways unsuspected then were the later books of Harold Innis on communication for which I worked with him until his death. I was to become Editor of the press in 1957.

The building of a scholarly publishing program was inevitably affected of course by the conditions of scholarship in those years: no set pattern of research leaves, few funds for travel or subsistence, no microfilm or photocopy, little outside subsidy for publication. The help of the two research councils was certainly important in its encouragement to authors as well as to publication; it became an added spur when Mr. Jeanneret was able to arrange with the councils for royalties to be paid to authors from the first copies sold instead of after any subsidy had been reimbursed. The non-returnable subsidies revolving in the press's Fund along with its own contributions meant later manuscripts would benefit.[15]

15 For a fuller account of all these events see the volume published by the Press in 1961 on its diamond anniversary: *The University as Publisher*, ed. Eleanor Harman (Toronto: University of Toronto Press 1961).

On a wider scene, the early 1950s brought the inquiries and the report (1951) of the Royal Commission on National Development in the Arts, Letters and Sciences (the Massey Commission) with its stimulus to 'a vigorous and distinctive cultural life' — a study that still stands out as a lighthouse nearly forty years after the commission was established, that had practical results not only in the National Library but in the Canada Council (1957), that addressed issues of cultural destiny no less urgent today, and that has yet to have the full-length scholarly study of origin and influence it deserves in the perspective of time. Also during the 1950s a number of new literary periodicals appeared, a great many new poets joined established fellows, fiction was advancing in subtlety of subject and technique, biography took hold of scholarly and general audiences. In this atmosphere came *Canadian Literature* in 1959 from the University of British Columbia, to provide a systematic and critical account in articles and reviews of past and present. To assist those interested in conducting full scholarly examinations of Canadian Literature to date, there appeared from the University of Toronto Press in that same year R.E. Watters' *Check List*, which indicated what the body of that literature might be considered to comprise. At the same time was being planned a new effort of large-scale assessment based on the *Check List*. Conceived in 1956 by Alfred G. Bailey, Claude Bissell, Roy Daniells, Northrop Frye, and Desmond Pacey, the *Literary History of Canada* went through years of discussion and shaping among editors and contributors, often at the meetings of the Learned Societies since the project had practically no resources. Finally in 1965 appeared the first edition from UTP, presented by the editors as 'a comprehensive view of Canada and the Canadians as their literary works have expressed them over the years.'[16] It was reprinted in 1966, 1967, 1970, and 1973, and there was a second edition in three volumes in 1976 which moved the account forward. A fourth volume, with end date in the early 1980s, is now in press. Interests in criticism and attitudes to literature have changed a great deal since 1965 and voices are heard asking whether such an endeavour would make practical or critical sense in the future. At the time, the *Literary History*, like the Watters *Check List*, and in company with the *New Canadian Library* reprints (including their introductions) begun under Malcolm Ross's editorship in 1958 and published by McClelland & Stewart, made it possible to map the territory to be explored and to provide guidance through it. These undertakings met a distinctively Canadian need when they appeared. One should not forget those many expostulations then, in university circles and outside them: 'But has Canada any literature?'

---

16 For an account of the preparation and publication of the *Literary History* see Francess G. Halpenny, 'Literary History of Canada: An Essay in Co-operation,' *Papers of the Bibliographical Society of Canada*, IV (1965): 6-13.

Other scholarly material related to Canadian literature was appearing in
book form and in a growing range of periodicals. One can only be selective,
hoping to indicate the range of commentary and the publishing auspices. Desmond Pacey's path-breaking *Creative Writing in Canada* was published by Ryerson in 1952. With Malcolm Ross as editor, *Our Sense of Identity* was issued,
by Ryerson also, in 1954 and he served as editor for *The Arts in Canada* from
Macmillan in 1958. In 1957 from UTP came the first entry in the series *Our
Living Tradition* initiated at Carleton University (which also took the lead in the
Carleton Library series, published for many years by McClelland & Stewart and
now by Carleton University Press). A new university press was founded at
McGill in 1960. Ryerson in 1961 and 1962 added to its contributions A.J.M.
Smith's gatherings of essays, *Masks of Fiction* and *Masks of Poetry*, and in 1967
another by Louis Dudek and Michael Gnarowski, *The Making of Modern Poetry
in Canada*. In 1962 from UTP appeared John P. Matthews's *Tradition in Exile*.
The year 1962 was also to see Marshall McLuhan's *Gutenberg Galaxy* (UTP),
which along with *Understanding Media* (1964) was to have an extended influence
in literary studies. In 1959 the *Dictionary of Canadian Biography* had been
founded, its first volume appearing in 1966; as its volumes accumulate and
proceed past 1900 in coverage, it will be making an increasing contribution to
literary scholarship through biography.[17] The *DCB* and its French edition, *DBC*,
published by Les Presses de l'université Laval, rank as the first of the major
long-term editorial projects for which Canada has obtained an international
reputation, projects which have been publications of university presses and in
two cases were initiated by them.

In the late 1950s and 1960s occurred the massive, now almost legendary expansion in numbers of universities, of academic staff, of graduate students, and
of undergraduates. As I saw from my editorial post, academics at Canadian universities took up many new fields of teaching and research, and publication assumed greater importance in a university career. UTP was challenged to be a
national scholarly publisher with an international market, and a good deal of
my time was spent talking with academics across Canada about their theses and
books (and the difference between the two formats) and with authors and university representatives about publishing. We were attempting to build a wider-
ranging list that would reflect Canadian scholarship. The meetings of the

17 An examination of one aspect of the *DCB/DBC* contribution to literary scholarship, relating
    to nineteenth century women authors, is given in my forthcoming paper 'Problems and
    Solutions in the *DCB*, 1800-1900,' presented at the symposium on nineteenth-century women
    writers held at the University of Ottawa in the spring of 1988 and to appear in the series on
    Canadian writers entitled 'Reappraisals' (under the general editorship of Lorraine
    McMullen); this series, initiated in the 1970s and published by the University of Ottawa Press,
    has now reached fifteen titles.

Learned Societies, with more and more organizations being created and participating, became a great forum for discussion of members' work and also for publishers' awareness of what they were doing. A study of the roles of ACUTE, ACQL, CHA, the Humanities Association, the Royal Society of Canada and others in the building of a Canadian literary institution would be highly relevant. The book fair at the Learneds, which took off from a tiny display I mounted for the Royal Society when the Learneds were at the Royal Military College in 1950, has become a meeting and business place that in some ways parallels what in the trade the Canadian Booksellers Association's annual gathering does for publishers, authors, literary agents, and its own members.

In 1967 the Toronto and Laval presses became the publishers of the Canada Council's offering to the Centennial, Russell Harper's *Painting in Canada*. It was the first full-scale scholarly treatment of its subject, and a landmark in Canadian book publishing because for the first time in this country a generous number of colour illustrations requiring high fidelity in book reproduction were printed.

The year 1967 has also been otherwise marked in publishing memory because it saw the start of many of the new, smaller, often literary presses across Canada. They sprang up in all parts of the country rather than in Toronto or Montreal, and they were often the creation of editors or authors interested in a different kind of list than the older establishments'. Some of them, such as Anansi and New, were to add a few titles in criticism of Canadian literature, usually by academics, to their concentration on creative writing. New university presses also appeared: the UBC Press in 1970, followed by Alberta, Wilfrid Laurier, Calgary, Manitoba, and Carleton; McGill became McGill-Queen's. It was an important development, one welcomed by UTP. The intense growth in Canadian scholarship had been such that other university presses were needed: to share the responsibility of publication, to provide a variety of lists to prospective authors, to give them the opportunity of choice. These presses began to develop their own special interests and emphases, with Canadian subject-matter an important component. They are alike in not being parochial publishers: in common with university presses elsewhere, they give no preference to their own campus but welcome authors from across Canada, or beyond, and seek an international market for them. In 1972, this group formed the Association of Canadian University Presses. One should not forget in the period of the 1950s and 1960s the changes in production and distribution techniques which brought offset printing, illustrations on the same paper as text, and paperbacks. Through them and other innovations a wider distribution of material became possible, by which, in Canadian literature, teaching and also scholarship could develop and which put copies for knapsacks, gardens, and subway into the hands of general readers. They played their part in establishing a literary institution.[18]

The excitement of these years was palpable. Publishing of Canadian literature and criticism took off, defying summary. And yet the problems of publishing Canadian material over a huge country with a scattered and relatively small market, largely domestic, were still endemic. In the later 1970s they surfaced, and they have not gone away in the 1980s. They hit the trade publishers, large and small. They hit scholarly publication as it became clear that the years of growth in colleges and universities were an aberration of special times. One of the supports of a number of large trade houses was educational publishing — it fell into deep trouble with realignments of curriculum and of resources for other aids than books. Independent bookstores, which carry the widest range of Canadian writing, have been facing the fierce competition of the chains, interested especially in quick turnover of good sellers. The prevalence of photocopying became a threat to sales. Takeovers of Canadian firms and branch plants raised concern about what would happen to Canadian material on publishing lists. Costs of production have risen for all publishers, of books and of periodicals; that metaphor of the 'bottom line' is a potent one, inevitably. Library budgets, public and academic, have been cut continuously. In academic libraries the pressure to maintain serial subscriptions especially in the sciences has affected book purchases, with the humanities too often a victim. The budgets of the Canada Council and its companion after 1978, the Social Sciences and Humanities Research Council, have contracted and their power to aid growing numbers of writers, scholars, book publishers, journals, trade and learned societies has diminished. Governments' interest in 'strategic' research has been disquieting. The newer university presses were not able to grow as had been hoped, and in 1980 McGill-Queen's would have disappeared had not the University of Toronto Press brought forward an offer of co-operative effort until it could re-establish itself (achieved in 1987).

In this atmosphere of crisis and concern, publishing in Canada became ironically, for almost the first time, front-page news, the fate of the Ryerson imprint (that mainstay of Canadian writing and criticism in the 1930s and 1940s) being the catalyst in 1970. Lobby groups raised their voices more and more loudly,

---

18 The more recent developments in word-processing and electronic transmission — altering the preparation of a manuscript, making camera-ready copy a preferred form of submission to publishers, and speeding up production by eliminating re-keyboarding — must also be taken into account. They are of great importance in reducing the high unit-cost production typical of scholarly publishing.

and they continue their pressures today. The procession of inquiries and reports began. The first major one was Ontario's Royal Commission; Marsh Jeanneret's membership on it meant scholarly publishing would not be ignored. The *Background Papers* of the commission's report are still required reading for anyone trying to understand the characteristics of publishing in Canada. The Commission came out stoutly in support of the need for publishing that would offer adequate representation of what writers and scholars had learned of this country's people.[19] Into the debate about Canada's knowledge of itself came the Commission on Canadian Studies sponsored by the Association of Universities and Colleges of Canada, and the first two volumes of its report *To Know Ourselves* (1975). The report blew up storms in many places, especially in universities where Canadian literature was still regarded as a protesting infant and Canadian studies were deemed as undisciplined congeries often presented by lightweights. Nevertheless, after the dust settled and in retrospect, the report can be seen to have had a slowly accelerating and salutary effect in consciousness-raising and in action by many institutions, organizations, and individuals. As a part of its effect, but also because of a changing climate of opinion about Canada generally, interest in what is published by Canadians, about Canada, has markedly increased.

Scholarly publishing was also the subject of inquiry in these trying years. An inquiry was instituted in 1976 by the Canada Council (continued by the SSHRCC), which sent out questionnaires, invited submissions, made investigations of its own, and held discussions, leading to its report, finally published in 1980.[20] That report's recommendations did not call for radical new departures. What it pointed to as a continuing need was maintenance in English and in French of the mix of auspices under which scholarship in Canada has made its appearance: the university presses, the trade houses large and small, the liter-

19 Ontario, Royal Commission on Book Publishing 1971-72: *Background Papers* (Toronto: Queen's Printer 1972), *Canadian Publishers and Canadian Publishing* (Toronto: Queen's Printer 1973). Ten years later came another inquiry, under federal auspices: Federal Cultural Policy Review Committee, *Speaking of our Culture : Discussion Guide* (Ottawa: Information Services, Dept. of Communications 1981), *Summary of Briefs and Hearings* (Ottawa: Information Services, Dept. of Communications 1981), and *Report* (Ottawa: Information Services, Dept. of Communications 1982). The Department of Communications commissioned a number of studies of the book trade in the mid-1980s, only a few of which were made public.
20 Consultative Group on Scholarly Publishing, *Canadian Scholarly Publishing* (Ottawa: Social Sciences and Humanities Research Council 1980). During the time the Consultative Group was meeting, an investigation was going on in the United States; see *Scholarly Communication:The Report of the National Enquiry* (Baltimore: Johns Hopkins University Press 1979). In 1980 the Aid to Scholarly Publications Programme of the Canadian Federation for the Humanities and the Social Science Federation of Canada held a Symposium on Scholarly Communication, whose papers were published in Ottawa by the sponsors in 1981.

ary presses, the scholars' presses, the scholarly and critical journals. In recent years scholarly publishing has had to review its problems steadily: to watch over costs, to confront the question of inventory, to re-examine the focus of its lists, to seek to improve its participation with scholars as authors and readers and teachers in the spread of knowledge. It is a learner world. Grants are essential. Yet important books continue to be written and to be published. The excitement of a fine match of book or journal article to appreciative readers does not diminish. That is what keeps a scholarly publisher — any publisher — going.

As a last exercise for the topic assigned to me, I picked up a number of publishers' catalogues and looked at several checklists for a quick, browsing impression of what scholarly publishers have been doing with Canadian literature in the 1970s and 1980s. The mapping of the territory which began with the *Check List* and the *Literary History* has continued steadily. Clara Thomas's guidebook came from New Press in 1972, Elizabeth Waterston's survey from Methuen in 1973. *The Oxford Companions* of 1967 and of 1983, in which William Toye played a major role, are noteworthy contributions about works, authors and context, with Canadian literature here finding a place in the great Oxford series. ECW Press has been heading up a major effort by contributors to its two series, *The Annotated Bibliography of Canada's Major Authors* and *Canadian Writers and their Works*, and in 1986 added a recurring *Canadian Literature Index*. NC press has published John Moss's series on *The Canadian Novel*, McClelland & Stewart his *Reader's Guide* to it. Dundurn Press, under Jeffrey Heath's editorship has produced six volumes in its *Profiles in Canadian Literature* series. Publishers outside Canada have taken an interest in Canadian literature: Twayne for a number of volumes in its 'World Authors' series and Gale Research Inc. for its 'Dictionary of Literary Biography.' For literature in French, Fides has published the volumes of the *Dictionnaire des oeuvres littéraires du Québec*, headed by Maurice Lemire. It needs to be emphasized here that the activities of ECW Press, Twayne, Gale and others have an intent eye on users in colleges, universities, and senior secondary schools; the increase in study of Canadian literature in those institutions has provided an audience for such survey works. The same target was aimed for by other, related publications in the years of expansion, such as the 'Canadian Writers' series of McClelland & Stewart, 'Canadian Writers and their Works' of Forum House, 'Critical Views on Canadian Writers' of McGraw-Hill Ryerson, 'Studies in Canadian Literature' of Copp Clark. The addition of titles to these series of short paperbacks reflected the choice of writers being taught. That choice was not broad enough to sustain series like these.

Works of reference which inform many groups of people from readers to booksellers to librarians to teachers should not be forgotten in any analysis of distribution. University of Toronto Press began *Canadian Books in Print* in 1968 (there is an equivalent in French), and it has also published several editions from 1978 of the annotated *Canadian Selection: Books and Periodicals for Libraries*, sponsored by Ontario's Ministry of Citizenship and Culture; it has had several editions of *Canadian Books for Young People*. Both of these had been campaigned for as a means of building up Canadian collections in schools and libraries. Hurtig's *Canadian Encyclopedia* (1985, 1988) provides a rich store of information in general articles and entries on particular subjects or persons, much of it contributed by scholars of many places, that will reach thousands of users in the general public as well as students, teachers, librarians, and academics.

Bibliography is a continuing need.[21] It has been carried on in sections of journals such as *Canadian Poetry*, the *Journal of Canadian Fiction*, and the *Journal of Commonwealth Literature*, as well as in the ECW series, the back sections of books or beneath items in reference works. Much of it is enumerative in form. Welcome as this effort is, we badly need the analytical bibliography that can make an important contribution to histoire du livre and to knowledge of writers' careers. The aims and activities of the Bibliographical Society of Canada, evident through its published *Papers* and its colloquia as well as its encouragement to expert bibliographic activity, deserve study in the context of this paper. In 1988, significantly, the Society decided to hold its annual meeting with the Learned Societies rather than with the Canadian Library Association. Related needs concern documents. Tecumseh Press has offered two volumes edited by Douglas M. Daymond and Leslie G. Monkman, *Towards a Canadian Literature: Essays, Editorials and Manifestos* (1984) for the years 1752 to 1983. A considerable aid to scholarship is the *Canadian Archival Inventories* series being edited by J. Tener and A. Steele (University of Calgary Press), which provides guides to the university's holdings in papers of Canadian authors. NeWest press has a series of 'Western Canadian Literary Documents.'

It is worth noting that when Eli Mandel prepared his collection of critical essays, *Contexts of Canadian Criticism* (1971), he felt obliged to state in the preface: 'The history of Canadian criticism remains to be written. We possess fragments, bright and sharp though they may be.' His introduction and his selection of essays from E.K. Brown in 1943 to Dorothy Livesay in 1969 attempted to map out problems and patterns and contexts. The full bibliography in the book is in itself a suggestive way of discovering and reviewing what the record was in this significant year. Mandel's collection has a pertinent publishing story also. It belonged to a series entitled 'Patterns of Literary Criticism,' initiated by Marshall McLuhan and R.J. Schoeck, both then at St. Michael's College, in discussions with University of Toronto Press. The series was to invite distinguished scholars to draw together collections on themes from world literature; the prac-

21 See Francess G. Halpenny, 'Bibliography: The Foundation of Scholarship' in the proceedings of the Symposium on Scholarly Communication (cited in the previous note).

tical way to issue such a series was with a publisher in the United States and UTP proposed to University of Chicago Press that it initiate publication, with the Canadian market to be held by Toronto. Canadian literature and criticism, the ninth collection in the series, made an unusual entry into the world market for this time.

When one looks over catalogues and lists one is reminded strongly of the attraction of theme studies that characterized the 1970s. The variety of publishers is to be noted. One of the earliest studies was D.G. Jones's *Butterfly on Rock*, published by University of Toronto Press in 1970. Anansi was a contributor with *The Bush Garden* in 1971 (which included Frye's critiques of poetry in 'Letters in Canada' and his reverberating conclusion to the first edition of the *Literary History of Canada*) and Margaret Atwood's *Survival* in 1972. The latter year saw W.H. New's *Articulating West* from New Press, which had issued R.J. Sutherland's first full-length essay in comparative French-English study, *Second Image*, in 1971 (his *The New Hero* came from Macmillan in 1977). John Moss's work on fiction, *Patterns of Isolation* (1974) and *The Ancestral Present* (1977), had the M & S imprint. UBC Press offered Laurie Ricou's *Vertical Man/Horizontal World* in 1973 and Tom Marshall's *Harsh and Lovely Land* in 1979. Dick Harrison's *Unnamed Country* came from University of Alberta Press in 1977. David Staines's *The Canadian Imagination* had a Harvard 1977 imprint. Margot Northey's *The Haunted Wilderness* (1976) and Gaile McGregor's *Wacousta Syndrome* (1985) from UTP suggest a continuing attraction for an analogous approach.

But criticism with different interests has made its appearance also. The eclectic collections of articles from *Canadian Literature* may be cited. George Woodcock's essays spanned the decades, issued by M & S in 1970, Douglas & McIntyre in 1980. An important shift to critical analysis of texts as wholes in creation may be represented in W.K. Keith's work on Rudy Wiebe (University of Alberta Press and NeWest 1981) and his *Canadian Literature in English* from Longman's (1985) or by Janice Kulyk Keefer's 'critical reading of Maritime fiction' in *Under Eastern Eyes* from UTP (1987) or W.H. New's analysis of 'the art of the short story in Canada and New Zealand' in *Dreams of Speech and Violence* from UTP (1987). Comparative in interest also is Joseph Pivato's edition *Contrasts: Comparative Essays on Italian-Canadian Writing* (1985) from Guernica. Mosaic Press introduced a new voice in 1984 with B.W. Powe's *A Climate Charged*.

A method of criticism stemming from modes and principles influential in Europe and North America appears in the work of Sherrill Grace or Lorraine Weir published by UBC press (1982, 1983). Western Producer sponsored *Figures in a Ground* for Sheila Watson (1978, ed. Diane Bessai and David Jackel). ECW brought out E.D. Blodgett's *Configurations* in 1982. Turnstone has published Frank Davey's *Surviving the Paraphrase* (1983) and Dennis

Cooley's *The Vernacular Muse* (1987). Robert Kroetsch as conversationalist, as writer of criticism, and as the subject of criticism has been presented through *Open Letter* and NeWest Press. *Future Indicative: Literary Theory and Canadian Literature*, edited by John Moss as no. 13 in the Reappraisals series (University of Ottawa Press 1987), shows many of the current approaches in action. The world is turning. It should be noted, however, that behind the publishing decision about many a collection of critical essays or critical work, especially on an individual writer, hides recognition of the importance of the subject's interest for graduate and senior undergraduate students. It is no accident that between 1980 and 1984 Margaret Atwood was the subject of at least four studies and had a collection of her essays published.

Biography does not cease to hold the attention of a large and mixed audience. In any count of titles published in Canada or in any list of reading interests it ranks high. For present purposes I set aside the affectionate memoir, the autobiographies of politicians and celebrities, the anecdotal efforts of journalists. Standing out is the amount of biography issuing from careful research that contributes to literary understanding: D.G. Pitt and Susan Gingell on E.J. Pratt (UTP), Elspeth Cameron on Hugh MacLennan (UTP) and Irving Layton (Stoddart), Sandra Djwa on F.R. Scott (M & S), John Coldwell Adams on Charles G.D. Roberts (UTP), Clara Thomas on Anna Jameson (UTP) and, with John Lennox, on William Arthur Deacon (UTP), Claude Bissell on Vincent Massey (UTP), Lorraine McMullen on Frances Brooke (UBC), Betty Keller on Pauline Johnson and Ernest Thompson Seton (Douglas & McIntyre), Marian Fowler on Sara Jeannette Duncan (Anansi), Usher Caplan on A.M. Klein (UTP). We have not many collections of letters as yet: for Frederic Philip Grove by Desmond Pacey (UTP), for Ralph Gustafson with W.W.E. Ross (ECW), for Bliss Carman by H. Pearson Gundy (McGill-Queen's), for Susanna Moodie by Carl Ballstadt, Elizabeth Hopkins, and Michael Peterman (UTP), for Thomas Chandler Haliburton by Richard A. Davis (UTP) and for W.A. Deacon by John Lennox and Michele Lacombe (UTP forthcoming). Literary biography and letters can tell students of the institution of a literature much about literary impulses in this country, the conditions of a literary career, the experiences of publication, the reactions of reviewers, critics, and readers. The pace of their appearance is quickening.

An important need, taking several forms, has always been for texts to read and teach. The oddity of not having texts in print when Canadian literature finally had a strong entry into curricula made the New Canadian Library necessary, and its centrality is likely to continue in a revised program now being planned under David Staines. But frustrations remained. Were there not other works that should be read in order to fill out the picture of a literature? Of course there were. In the 'Literature of Canada' series edited by Douglas Lochhead and published by UTP between 1973 and 1979 (significant years for

Canadian literature) were 21 older titles — poetry, fiction, collections of essays — offered in cloth and paper in a generous format using offset from earlier editions. The results were disheartening. When I checked sales figures in April 1987 I found that only one entry — Day's *Rockbound* — had got beyond 3000 copies in paper, that the next highest were Stead's *Homesteaders* at about 2800 and Crawford's *Poems* at 2130, and that the range of the rest was from 486 to well under 2000. The series had to be discontinued, and the over-stock went to remainder tables. Perhaps the format was not well conceived. Nevertheless, the market was simply not there — in libraries, among individual scholars, with students. The problem of out-of-print, out-of-sight does not diminish with contemporary creative writing given today's financial problems. Runs are shorter, inventory cannot be held, poetry can migrate from little magazine to slim volume to anthology to collected works; many short stories will follow a similar path. Novelists who lay firm hold of public attention will find their place in trade paperback, some perhaps in mass market. Mid-list fiction and first novels have a chancier life.

One of the developments of recent years is a rising attention to the condition of the texts we read.[22] The invaluable NCL editions were, it was realized, shortened and edited on no very evident consensus about textual principles. The concern is addressed in critical editions of F.R. Scott (M & S), and of A.M. Klein and E.J. Pratt (UTP). The Centre for Canadian Poetry at the University of Western Ontario is issuing a series of editions of individual early Canadian poems with authoritative texts, critical introductions, and notes (under D.M.R. Bentley's editorship). Pioneering efforts for Canadian texts are also being made by the Centre for Editing Early Canadian Texts directed by Mary Jane Edwards (published by Carleton University Press); it also is bringing the modern methods of textual editing and descriptive bibliography to bear. These text series' at last break forth out of the hazards of publication that had beset them and in the process a great deal of valuable publication history for a country that developed its own publishing late is coming to light.

What this overview has impressed upon me to happy effect is the amount that has been accomplished in scholarly study of Canadian literature as that literature changed not only in quantity but in accomplishment and in recognition.

---

22 See *Editing Canadian Texts*, ed. Francess G. Halpenny, the proceedings of one of the Editorial problems conferences held annually at the University of Toronto (Toronto: Hakkert 1975).

The bleakness of 1940 is no more. Much yet remains to do in research and understanding of the past and the present, and for that work to make its effect the efforts of the range of publishers taking on scholarly writing in Canada will be needed.

University of Toronto Press

JACQUES PELLETIER

Une expérience d'édition universitaire: les cahiers du département d'études littéraires de l'U.Q.A.M.

Avant d'évoquer l'expérience des *Cahiers* que nous avons initiée au Département d'études littéraire de l'UQAM, je rappellerai brièvement les principaux problèmes auxquels fait face l'édition universitaire.

On sait que celle-ci se situe, pour reprendre le vocabulaire de Pierre Bourdieu, dans la sphère de production restreinte. Pour l'essentiel il s'agit d'une production très spécialisée dans laquelle des scientifiques s'adressent d'abord, sinon exclusivement, à leurs collègues: en bref d'une production de pairs pour d'autres pairs, rejoignant très rarement un large public.

Généralement, et je dirais même, par définition, les Presses universitaires n'ont pas une fonction d'abord économique: il ne s'agit pas d'entreprises visant à réaliser des profits, fonctionnant selon une logique marchande. Leur fonction est d'abord sociale: elles ont en effet pour mission de contribuer à la diffusion du savoir.

Or cette production est actuellement en crise pour diverses raisons, dont les suivantes:

Premièrement cette production est très largement soumise à l'obtention de subventions des organismes gouvernementaux ou para-gouvernementaux que l'on sait, cette obtention étant un des critères importants — si ce n'est privilégié — régissant ce qui doit être publié, indépendamment, à la limite, de la qualité des manuscrits soumis.

Deuxièmement cette condition quasi-obligée implique des délais: il faut des mois, et parfois des années avant que la réponse attendue des organismes subventionnaires n'arrive; et une fois celle-ci obtenue, d'autres délais s'ajoutent qui, cette fois, relèvent de la programmation des maisons d'édition; si bien qu'entre le moment où un manuscrit est déposé et celui où il est finalement publié, quatre ans, cinq ans, ce n'est pas rare, se sont passés: le processus est donc très long.

Troisièmement ces ouvrages coûtent cher à produire et comme ils ne rejoignent qu'un marché fort restreint, leur prix de vente est élevé (on ne trouve rien, ou presque, à moins de $20); ce facteur, par ailleurs, ne contribue pas à favoriser une diffusion plus large: on les achète donc pour des raisons professionnelles, si j'ose dire, et il faut être professeurs, ou à la rigueur étudiants gradués, pour s'offrir des produits que l'on considère de plus en plus comme de luxe.

Ces facteurs cumulatifs engendrent des frustrations, des insatisfactions à la fois chez les auteurs qui s'estiment mal servis en raison des délais de production, de la distribution fort restreinte de leurs ouvrages et chez les lecteurs qui hésitent à s'offrir ces produits de luxe que sont devenus très/trop souvent les ouvrages dits savants.

Pour ce qui concerne plus spécifiquement le département d'études littéraires de l'UQAM, nous étions quelques-uns à être insatisfaits du mode de fonctionnement des Presses universitaire en général, et en particulier de nos propres Presses de l'Université du Québec: pour ne donner qu'un exemple significatif, notre regretté collègue, André Belleau, avait été échaudé par l'abolition d'une collection *Genres et Discours*, qu'il dirigeait avec Marc Angenot, collection dans laquelle avaient été publiés quelques titres remarquables, mais malheureusement, semble-t-il, non *rentables*. D'autres collègues avaient également connu des déboires analogues.

Que faire alors pour se sortir de ces problèmes? C'est la question que nous nous sommes posée dans des réunions que nous avons tenues quelques collègues (J. Allard, A. Belleau, G. Thérien, A. Vanasse) et moi-même à l'hiver et au printemps 1983.

Au terme de ces réunions, nous en sommes venus à la conclusion que nous devions et que nous pouvions fonder une maison d'édition (ou plus modestement une collection) dont l'objectif serait de produire des ouvrages à coût modique dans des délais raisonnables, ouvrages qui, par ailleurs, ne seraient pas destinés exclusivement à nos pairs mais aussi à nos étudiants. Ce qui impliquait qu'on n'édite pas uniquement des ouvrages dits savants mais également des livres informés par des préoccupations pédagogiques.

Nous avons alors envisagé diverses formules sur le plan organisationnel: la mise sur pied d'une maison d'édition 'privée,' la création d'une coopérative, enfin un rattachement institutionnel à l'UQAM. C'est cette dernière option que nous avons retenue, en nous assurant toutefois de pouvoir conserver une marge de manoeuvre importante par rapport à l'Université et même par rapport à notre propre département.

En clair, la collection est dirigée et animée par le groupe initial des pères fondateurs, publiée comme le veut une formule consacrée sous l'égide du Département d'études littéraires de l'UQAM et diffusée par le Service des publications de l'Université — qui se trouve à être en même temps notre 'éditeur.'

En 1984, André Vanasse — qui a une certaine expérience de l'édition, prise chez H.M.H. où il anime une collection — est directeur de la collection.

Notre mise de fonds initiale est d'environ $3,000; elle provient, pour l'essentiel, d'un 'don' de notre Département. Ce n'est pas beaucoup. Ce sera suffisant pour démarrer. Après, disons-nous, on verra.

Nous prenons une décision importante que nous n'aurons pas à regretter par la suite: celle d'utiliser les nouvelles technologies en édition (et notamment l'impression au laser).

Nous demandons à un collègue, Maurice Poteet, de nous soumettre des projets de maquettes pour les pages couvertures de la collection. Nous en choisissons une — d'allure assez scolaire — qui nous semble bien convenir à l'esprit de la collection.

En 1984, nous fonctionnons de manière très artisanale avec réunions sporadiques du comité de lecture et sans véritable politique d'édition.

Nous publions deux titres: des essais de votre serviteur, *Lecture politique du roman québécois contemporain*, et une anthologie de textes destinés à nos étudiants, *Le social et le littéraire*: nos préoccupations d'ordre pédagogique trouvaient ainsi une première incarnation bien concrète.

L'année suivante, en 1985, nous publions à nouveau deux titres. Des *Travaux sémiotiques*, ouvrage en collaboration constitué exclusivement de textes d'étudiants de notre doctorat en sémiologie. En cela nous innovons, en donnant à nos étudiants la chance de trouver un lieu éditorial où ils pourront faire connaître leurs travaux (et du même coup se faire connaître). Et nous publions également des essais de Gilles Thérien consacrés aux *Sémiologies*.

À l'automne 1985, je succède à André Vanasse comme responsable de la collection. Et nous publions trois ouvrages en 1986, un de plus que les années précédentes. Deux de ces ouvrages présentent des travaux de groupes de recherche. Le premier porte sur *l'avant-garde culturelle et littéraire des années 1970 au Québec* et il réunit, à part égale, des textes de professeurs (Jules Duchastel, Esther Trépanier et moi-même) et d'étudiants (Jean-Guy Côté, Claude Lizé, Pierre Milot, Joël Pourbaix). Le second est le fruit d'une rédaction collective sur le phénomène Harlequin, sous la direction d'une professeure, Julia Bettinotti, avec la participation d'étudiant-e-s: Hélène Bédard-Cazabon, Jocelyn Gagnon, Pascale Noizet, Christiane Provost. La collection, sur ce plan présente un double intérêt: elle permet une publication et une diffusion rapide des résultats des travaux des groupes de recherche; elle founit à des assistants de recherche et à des étudiants un débouché éditorial intéressant. Enfin, nous publions un essai d'Enrico Carontini, *Faire l'image*, consacré à l'étude des énonciations visuelles, ouvrage dont la vocation est d'abord didactique. Avec cet ouvrage, nous ouvrons aussi la porte à l'édition d'auteurs n'appartenant pas à notre Département — Enrico Carontini étant professeur au Département des communications de l'UQAM—politique qui ira en s'accentuant avec les années.

Par ailleurs, sur le plan du fonctionnement, nous passons de l'artisanat à une certaine forme de professionnalisme: les manuscrits soumis—en plus grand nombre—font l'objet de lectures attentives, les réunions du comité sont plus nombreuses et les discussions serrées: certains textes sont refusés et ceux qui sont acceptés font l'objet de propositions de modifications (suppressions, ajouts, re-writing, etc.): bref, nous accomplissons un véritable travail éditorial, y compris sur le plan très concret et très technique de la correction de textes (avec toute l'attention que cela demande).

Quels sont les coûts de production? Ils comprennent trois niveaux relativement importants de dépenses: d'abord une partie 'salaire': pour l'entrée des textes sur disquettes, il faut compter environ $4 la page (ce coût comprend une première correction d'épreuves); ensuite les coûts d'impression proprement dits impliqués par ce qu'on appellait chez notre imprimeur, Logidec, la préparation du manuscrit, à quoi s'ajoute l'impression elle-même (à raison de 0.025c la page); enfin, la reliure à un coût fixe de $2,30 l'exemplaire.

En tout la production d'un cahier d'environ 175 pages nous coûte entre $2,500 et $3,000, tout compris, pour un premier tirage de 200 exemplaires, soit entre $12,00 et $15,00 par exemplaire. Les tirages subséquents nous reviennent moins cher compte tenu que nous économisons les parties 'salaire' et les frais de préparation du manuscrit. Si bien que pour certains titres, au-delà de 400 exemplaires vendus, nous atteignons presque l'autofinancement.

Nos revenus peuvent, à leur tour, être décomposés comme ceci: une première partie provient de la mise de fonds intitiale ($3,000); une seconde partie provient de subventions obtenues grâce aux programmes d'aide à la publication de l'UQAM et du fonds F.C.A.R. (environ $5,000 jusqu'à maintenant); une troisième partie est assurée par nos ventes—par courrier ou par la coopérative étudiante de l'UQAM ($24,000 environ depuis le début de l'expérience).

Au total, en date du 1er mars 1987, la collection a entraîné des dépenses de l'ordre de $29,900 et a généré des crédits de $32,100. Nous disposons donc d'une marge de manoeuvre d'un peu plus de $2,000: c'est peu, mais c'est suffisant pour que nous puissions donner suite à nos projets avec confiance pour l'année présente et pour celles qui viennent.

NOS TIRAGES ET NOS VENTES?

Cahier I:	440	400	(dont près de 300 par la poste)
Cahier II:	800	750	(dont près de 300 par la poste)
Cahier III:	170	130	(dont près de 115 par la poste)
Cahier IV:	255	215	(dont près de 150 par la poste)

Cahier V:	220	190	(dont près de 170 par la poste)
Cahier VI:	250	210	(dont près de 190 par la poste)
Cahier VII:	250	210	(dont près de 80 par la poste)

2,385   2,105

À noter: Plus de la moitié des ventes sont réalisées par commandes postales; les autres se font via la coopérative étudiante de l'UQAM.

Quel public rejoignons-nous? D'abord celui consitué par les bibliothèques (des polyvalentes, des C.E.G.E.P., des Universités) au Québec, au Canada anglais, aux États-Unis. Ensuite, à l'occasion, celui des librairies (au Québec) où pourtant nous ne déposons pas nos ouvrages. Enfin, des individus au Québec, au Canada anglais, aux États-Unis, un peu en Europe. À ce propos une constatation troublante et en même temps réjouissante d'une certaine manière: chez les individus, nous 'vendons' autant au Canada anglais et aux États-Unis qu'au Québec. Ce qui est un indice sûr, à mon avis, que nous sommes loin d'avoir fait le plein au Québec, que le marché local n'a pas été suffisamment touché jusqu'à maintenant et que nous avons donc des progrès à faire que nous sommes cependant confiants de pouvoir réaliser.

Quel est l'intérêt de ce type d'entreprise? Il me semble qu'il est de plusieurs ordres.

Premièrement, nous ne sommes pas soumis aux impératifs impliqués par les demandes de subventions aux organismes gouvernementaux et para-gouvernementaux: nous publions ce qui nous paraît intéressant, subventions ou pas;

Deuxièmement, nous écourtons de façon substantielle les délais de production grâce notamment à l'utilisation des nouvelles technologies (entre le moment où un manuscrit est accepté par le comité de lecture et celui où il est publié, il faut compter environ deux mois: c'est peu, surtout dans le secteur de l'édition universitaire);

Troisièmement, nous pouvons fixer des prix de vente de nos ouvrages qui nous paraissent tout à fait 'corrects' (entre $8,00 et $15,00) et accessibles par conséquent même au public étudiant;

Quatrièmement, grâce au recours aux nouvelles technologies (et notamment à l'impression au laser), nous ne connaissons pas de problèmes de stockage: nous imprimons au besoin, à la demande, en conservant un dépôt minimum;

Cinquièmement, nous rejoignons les premiers intéressés—professeurs, chercheurs, étudiants—directement chez eux, par l'envoi de dépliants publicitaires: à cette fin nous avons constitué une 'mailing list' assez importante grâce à des échanges avec d'autres maisons d'édition et avec des revues;

Sixièmement, nous évitons les frais reliés, premièrement, à la distribution traditionnelle qui représente, on le sait, 15% du prix de vente des livres et deuxièmement, à la diffusion en librairie qui représente, pour sa part, 40% du prix de vente (la coop de l'UQAM nous demande actuellement 20% du prix de vente); il n'est toutefois pas exclu que nous décidions d'aller un jour en librairie, mais ce sera dans quelques librairies seulement vraiment intéressées par nos publications et dans le cadre d'ententes du type de celle que nous avons réalisée avec la coop de l'UQAM;

Septièmement, cette formule nous permet de rendre accessibles rapidement les résultats des travaux des groupes de recherche et de fournir un point de chute, pour la publication des meilleurs essais de nos étudiants.

Toutes ces raisons nous incitent à poursuivre l'entreprise, à la consolider et à l'élargir.

Jusqu'ici nous avons publié essentiellement des manuscrits de professeurs et d'étudiants de l'UQAM. Cependant, durant l'année 1987, d'une part, nous publierons au moins quatre ouvrages, dont deux d'auteurs non-uquamiens: un ouvrage de Bernard Proulx consacré à ce qu'il appelle *Le roman du territoire* dans lequel celui-ci propose une interprétation nouvelle du roman de la terre au Québec et, au-delà, de toute une tradition historiographique concernant le XIXe siècle québécois véhiculée principalement par ce qu'on a convenu d'appeler l'école historique de Montréal (Brunet, Séguin etc.); un ouvrage de Jean-Jacques Nattiez, *De la sémiologie à la musique*, dont le titre est très indicatif du propos; les autres ouvrages acceptés pour publication proviennent de professeurs de l'UQAM (G. Thérien et collaborateurs, J. Allard et collaborateurs) mais des discussions ont lieu avec d'autres auteurs, tant américains qu'européens. Si bien que notre catalogue s'enrichira d'ici deux ou trois ans d'ouvrages de nouveaux collaborateurs, et non des moindres, à qui notre formule sourit.

À compter du numéro huit, une nouvelle maquette (conçue et réalisée par Louis Anaouil) donnera à nos livres une facture plus attrayante de même qu'un nouveau choix de caractères en rendra la lecture plus aisée. Bref, nos productions, en plus d'être utiles, seront 'belles.'

Enfin nous avons la ferme intention de réaliser des 'percées' sur les marchés américains et européens grâce notamment à la publication de nouveaux auteurs qui nous assureront des 'entrées' dans les réseaux qui sont leurs et que nous n'avons pas réussi à vraiment investir jusqu'ici.

En terminant, je dirai que des expériences comme celle-ci sont possibles à condition, 1) de pouvoir compter sur un certain appui institutionnel (en ce qui nous concerne, le Service des publications de l'UQAM a fourni un appui logistique important, surtout au niveau de la diffusion); 2) d'être prises en charge par des gens qui y croient, qui sont prêts à y investir du temps et de l'énergie (pour lire les manuscrits soumis, pour faire du re-writing et de la correction d'épreuves, etc.)

Quant à savoir si de telles expériences, en se multipliant, pourraient remédier aux manques des Presses universitaires, c'est là une autre question, une grande question qui reste à débattre et à laquelle, pour ma part, je n'ai pas de réponse à apporter, si ce n'est par la pratique évoquée ici.

Université du Québec à Montréal

LORRAINE WEIR

'Maps and Tales' : the progress of Canadian Literature, 1959-87

In his Editorial to the first issue of *Canadian Literature* in 1959, George Woodcock committed his new journal to the throwing of 'a concentrated light on a field that has never been illuminated systematically by any previous periodical' and he stressed that it would provide 'services . . . for writers, scholars, librarians and – by no means least – the curious reader.'[1] But, he cautioned, '*Canadian Literature* seeks to establish no clan, little or large. It will not adopt a narrowly academic approach, nor will it try to restrict its pages to any school of criticism or class of writers' (4). Rather, the journal would seek 'Good writing, writing that says something fresh and valuable on literature in Canada.'

Light, service, good writing; freshness and value *vs.* the narrowly academic, the 'clan': these are the hallmarks of Woodcock's pledge together with his populist commitment to both readers and writers, librarians and scholars. A bold endeavour in 1959 and one proudly taken up again by W.H. New when in 1977 he succeeded Woodcock as editor of the journal. 'This journal has never been bound by its academic connection,' he wrote. 'It seeks readers and writers both inside and outside university circles' (74 [Autumn 1977]:3) and renews its commitment to its subject – in Woodcock's words, 'Canadian writers and their work and setting, without further limitations' (1:4; 74:4).

As Roderick Haig-Brown's essay, 'The Writer in Isolation' – the first essay in Woodcock's first issue – indicates, being a writer in Canada was limitation enough. Haig-Brown's vigorous rejection of the notion that good writing can be accomplished in isolation is grounded in his definition of a writer as 'a man

---

1 Editorial 1 (Summer 1959):3. Subsequent references to *Canadian Literature* will be in parentheses within the text. Although on occasion Associate Editors Donald Stephens, Ronald Sutherland, Herbert Rosengarten, and Laurie Ricou have contributed editorials, only those of George Woodcock and W.H. New have been considered in this study.

sensitive to influences; he may reject them or accept them, search for them or flee from them, but he cannot be neutral or unfeeling about all of them' (1 [Summer 1959]:5). Situating himself within a tradition, the writer is a point of social and cultural confluence. Like Woodcock's critic, Haig-Brown's writer is a man of the world and his capacity to engage actively with the world is at least a partial index of his success as a writer. Thus Victorian 'muscular Christianity' meets late-Modern *'engagement'* in its populist form.

My study, however, is less concerned with history than with rhetoric and having indicated some of the major semantic elements present at the birth and rebirth of *Canadian Literature,* I want to move now from overture to more detailed consideration of the logical system within which these and similar elements have power and meaning and from which they derive their status in single editorials like the two already quoted. I am considering, in other words, some of the entailments which are the logical consequences of the ideological circumstances of production of *Canadian Literature* from 1959 to the present and considering also some of the variations introduced in the journal's second phase under W.H. New's editorial guidance.

We have already observed one of the root metaphors crucial within the *Canadian Literature*-system, that of service. Service entails accessibility to the designated clientele and since that clientele includes the 'curious reader,' the librarian, the writer, and the scholar, a linguistic register appropriate to all four categories must be selected. Following Aristotle, rhetoricians refer to this process of category selection and accommodation as 'ethos,' which is permeated here not only by the prescribed service function of the journal but also by the anti-exclusionary bias of that selection. A level of readerly competence is being set, in other words, which assumes the 'curious reader' as the norm (neither a professional like the librarian and the scholar nor a full participant in the generation of texts like the writer or the reader who is also a writer). Since, unlike academics and those otherwise professionally invested in reading even when 'good writing' isn't much in evidence, curious readers require that what they read say 'something fresh and valuable' (1 [Summer 1959]:4), writing which is perceived as 'good' must exhibit 'freshness' in order to have 'value.' But we need more information about 'value' before the ethos of *Canadian Literature* can be adequately described.

One of Woodcock's clearest statements on the value and values of the critic, his editorial in the Summer 1971 issue takes as subject Northrop Frye's concept of the 'public critic.' He quotes Frye's *Anatomy of Criticism* as follows:

> It is the task of the public critic to exemplify how a man of taste uses and evaluates literature and thus show how literature is to be absorbed into society.... He has picked up his ideas from a pragmatic study of literature and does not create or enter into a literary structure. (49 [Summer 1971]:3)

'... I would ask for no better description of the course which I myself have followed,' writes Woodcock, putting himself in the company of V.S. Pritchett and Edmund Wilson. Unlike Frye with his conference papers on abstract topics ('tribal exercises,' Woodcock calls them), Woodcock prefers, he says, 'to search out my diamonds at muddier levels, nearer to life or, for that matter, nearer to literature as a direct and particular experience.' There follows our editor's parable of the field naturalist versus the natural historian: the former sees 'birds in real flight'; the latter, 'specimens superbly stuffed and classified, arranged in attractive displays and fitted into families and genuses.' The former 'follows literature as it appears, ... [and] submits himself to the biographical heresy and the intentional heresy and the aesthetic heresy and by all these and any other means seeks to stimulate his empathetic understanding of the work' (5).

Meantime, the latter, 'the Mandarin,... the academic critic,... the structuralist with his beautiful webs and mind-made palaces' is consigned to the dusty museum of Academia while 'our humble servant, the public critic' (5) goes about his exhilarating work on the wing.

Service, again. And Frye is saved from the museum only by his inconsistency, by the disparity which Woodcock perceives between the 'Angkor Wat' of the *Anatomy of Criticism* — 'a great and intricate edifice of theory and myth whose true purpose is its own existence' (4) — and the genial public criticism of *The Bush Garden*. Rewarded for not neglecting 'the literature of his own country,' Frye has fulfilled his service function at last and, like *Canadian Literature* itself according to Woodcock's fifty-fifth editorial, serves the cause of Canadian survival (55 [Winter 1973]:6). In this he is evidently the exceptional academic for, as Woodcock wrote three issues later, professors who have 'found the zenith of their political activities in the conclaves of the Modern Languages [sic] Association' are foolish followers of 'the old Marxist illusion that by seizing the institutions of power and prestige the rebel can transform them, whereas in fact it is the rebel who is transformed, like a figure in a fairy tale, when he enters such enchanted portals' (58 [Autumn 1973]:6).

But if Northrop Frye is only a part-time frog prince, the rest of us, stuffed specimens and taxidermists alike, are entrammelled by a greater evil, that of 'specialization' which 'breeds privilege, privilege generates more specialization[;] both isolate teachers from the concern of students and, often, of the society generally'(7).[2] Better, like Woodcock, to choose the living tradition of criticism that has long flourished outside the universities. As he says himself, using his editorial 'we,' 'perhaps we had an advantage in that we did not have to inflate the importance of our fields of studies to meet the demands of thesis-oriented research programmes'(6). Partial salvation — or is it partial servitude — is possible, however, in Woodcock's eschatology and a 'writer-who-

2　Woodcock here quotes Ellen Cantarow, *The Politics of Liberation.*

teaches' like Frank Davey preserves the literary element in criticism and will therefore survive while mere 'teachers-who-write' like Clara Thomas and Elizabeth Waterston have only their academic skills and their works will accordingly be consigned to the memory hole (64 [Spring 1975]:4). The fact that the particular critics selected inevitably predetermine the logic of the assertion is of no consequence to Woodcock; we are dealing here, I think, not with logic but with a secular theology.

'Real people' are a core component of it (36 [Spring 1968]:3): real people in novels and biographies, real people who read such books and real people who write them. Mr. Justice Thomas Boyle, author of *Justice Through Power*, is, for example, able to rise above the humdrum level of Stanley Knowles and H. Scott Gordon because 'he not only presents an idea, which we can accept or reject; he also projects the temperamental image of a man who holds that idea with a great deal of feeling because he has reached it through thought tempered by much experience' (10 [Autumn 1961]:5). Though Woodcock hastens to admit that Boyle is of the family but not the literary quality of Thomas More, William Morris, *et al.*, he does argue that 'the best political prose writer is as conscious as a novelist that he is dealing with people in a real and tangible world' and that he must keep before his 'mental eyes the image of life going on in a believable landscape' rather than falling 'into the trap of relying solely on the abstractions of political theory, of thinking of Man instead of men' (6).

Twenty-six issues later, however, abstraction began to seem more congenial to Woodcock, though, like his unsung source, William Blake, he would make an absolute distinction between abstraction and imagination. Thus, in dealing with the autobiographical and biographical emphases in Canadian literature, Woodcock writes that in moving 'frequently into the lives of real people,' 'Canadian literature frequently goes to more of reality... than do other literatures' (36 [Spring 1968]:3). A sign of a 'rather misplaced Canadian consciousness,' this tendency results in a diminished 'capacity for the vision and dependence on the imagined world and its primacy over the real that will lift Canadian literature to greater international status' (4). For Woodcock as for the great Romantics, imagination is an agent of freedom, a vehicle of triumph over social conditioning and 'environmental determinism,' a means to the creation of 'memorable' characters (4). Remaining true to literature itself, to the demands of *writing*, to the unfettered pursuit of ideas, the public critic serves his public best when he defends the fundamental freedoms of language and thought at the heart of a democratic society. Reminding his readers again and again of their responsibility to speak out on government funding of the arts, legislation to ban pornography and other violations of the freedom of the individual to speak according to his conscience, Woodcock is at his Orwellian best with the master's great essay, 'Politics and the English Language,'[3] always in view.

Curiously, T.S. Eliot occupies a similar station in Woodcock's undeclared pantheon. His memorial tribute to Eliot provides the clearest instance of this indebtedness and of its terms of reference as Woodcock writes of Eliot in the context of a Canadian reassertion of 'continuity with the common Anglo-Saxon tradition' (24 [Spring1965]:3). Surprisingly, however, it is to Eliot's later works of social critique with their High Church cast that Woodcock apparently turns. In his understanding of community, language, and the function of the writer, Woodcock the anarchist comes closest to Eliot's early modern sense of the need to capture the immediacy of experience and transmute it through language, his sense of the restructuring of the canon that takes place almost imperceptibly each time a new work enters it, and his sense of tradition within which each text means. Despite Woodcock's general disclaimer about 'how carefully we must avoid being influenced by a writer's opinions when we set out to judge him as a literary artist,' and his specific one about the poet's 'religious and political conservatism' (4), Eliot's 'Classicism' is evident, for example, in Woodcock's emphases upon the need to develop 'maturity' in both literature and criticism, upon the 'long testing in the minds of readers and writers by which a book is finally crowned with the laurels that do not wither' (4 [Spring 1960]:6), upon literary 'simplicity and directness,' which are the product of 'a high degree of sophistication and on the establishment of a tradition of experience that comes from the long living into an environment' (5 [Summer 1960]:3). Seen in this conservative context, Woodcock's resistance to literary 'experimentation,' resorted to 'only when it can further the purposes of... [a] novel, and never for its own sake' (47 [Winter 1971]:7), becomes more understandable as does his repeated denunciation of 'specialization' which 'has narrowed down literary criticism to a technique of analysis' (11 [Winter 1962]:4). Style — like the critic — is the servant of higher things and must never draw attention to itself without a serious reason. And 'specialization' robs the humble 'public critic' of his role as minister of community values, champion of freedom and lived experience.

But these terms demand an exploration that goes beyond mere public invocation, a philosophical or — in Eliot's case — a theological foundation which imparts meaning to this series of associated terms. Yet, for all his attempts through

---

3   George Orwell, 'Politics and the English Language,' in Orwell, *Collected Essays* (London: Secker & Warburg, 1961):337-51. See also Woodcock's *The Crystal Spirit — A Study of George Orwell* (Boston: Little, Brown and Co., 1966), in which Orwell is said to have written 'the purest English of his time' (5).

reiteration to create an innocence, a transparency which might envelope this lexical chain and remove it beyond the reach of the academic taxidermist, Woodcock's terms remain bounded by their own incompleteness and lack of definition and bounded also by the parochial spirit of anti-intellectualism and the simplistic, uncritically empirical bias which, as we have already seen, are fundamental components of his editorial stance. As we turn to the second phase of *Canadian Literature*'s existence, it is disturbing to see Woodcock's biases and touchstones taken up, polished off, and sent out again into rhetorical battle.

Surviving for much of his career as a freelance journalist outside the academy, Woodcock saw himself as a writer addressing readers and other writers as a man among men, one is inclined to say. An Anglo-Saxon male, of course; one who persisted in the use of the editorial 'we' until near the end of his tenure as editor of the journal, and who never failed to see Canadian writing in the context of 'Anglosaxony' (49 [Summer 1971]:3) and of British colonialism. It is particularly ironic, then, to find Woodcock's successor, W.H. New, using the lexicon of exploration, discovery, charting, mapping, and 'the frontier' in his editorial celebration of *Canadian Literature*'s hundredth issue. A magazine is like an 'explorer's record book' (100 [Spring 1984]:8), he writes, and the 'writers and critics' who have 'shared its pages' now 'range widely across subjects and forms, seeking self, seeking shape in the worlds they see and dream—they are map-makers all, reporting home on the territories of the mind, the memoirs of possibility, the miracles of language,' seeking 'new ways to send home maps and tales' (9-10).

Oddly, given this lush vocabulary and syntax, which seldom tempted Woodcock, New's stance is that of critic rather than 'writer,' and, of course, that of academic working within the establishment. For him, *Canadian Literature*, published by the University of British Columbia, is a 'tangible expression of [... the University's] concern for [... its] role in community education' (10). And the journal has in any case 'never been bound by its academic connection,' he writes, for 'it seeks readers and writers both inside and outside university circles' (74 [Autumn 1977]: 3). In fact, it is a shared vehicle of the 'members of the literary community' (86 [Autumn 1980]: 204) and takes upon itself the 'traditional role of artists,' which is, in the familiar cliché which has the status of article of faith in this system, 'to elucidate the human condition' (88 [Spring 1981]:4).

Light, again. Neo-Orwellian freedom isn't far behind. In an editorial appropriately entitled 'Nearing 1984,' New invokes the familiar connection with language. 'Freedoms,' he writes, 'are not lost because others take us over; freedoms are lost when we passively give them up. And we give them up the moment we lose our facility with language, our desire to know more, our willingness to question, challenge, doubt. . . . And we resist *through language*: by valuing literacy and asserting the importance of education' (99 [Winter 1983]:3). '[O]ur speech,' he maintains, 'still gives us the freedom to be who we are'(4), a point pursued five editorials later where New's brand of linguistic determinism is more fully articulated. 'To be a people,' he declares, 'is to be more than a numerical system. It is to be an embodiment of shared values' (104 [Spring 1985]:5), values which language conserves and which literature, as we already know from Woodcock, preserves in a state of freshness and vitality.

To 'be a people,' in fact, seems little different from, so to speak, being a literature: in New's system both are embodiments of shared values. 'Literature,' he writes, 'does serve human ends. It can be a radical force when doing so, radical even in reclaiming the existence of commonsense community values' (103 [Winter 1984]:6). And as he develops his concept of the people, New's Boy Scout idealism at last succeeds Woodcock's populist utopia. It is a crucial transition.

> People can be misinformed, sometimes even deliberately misled. They are sometimes naïve, and often cynical—reactions which can get in the way of honest expectation. But they are also fundamentally committed to the value of truth and they have a great store of common sense. (103 [Winter 1984]:3)

But, alas, they suffer the twin blight of machines — especially computers — and bureaucracy. Of these two, the second is clearly the worse, seeming, in 1981 at least, to be the more pervasive. Consider New's thoughts about the Governor-General's fiction finalists for 1980 and the committee system which they represent:

> Perhaps the taste for crude violence and the rejection of the intellectual subtleties of wit and argument alike reject the principle of difference and celebrate the mediocre and the extremes of human weakness as though they constituted heights of value. To follow these directions is to follow restrictions by another name, to elevate reductive, private systems into 'normal' public 'order.' From this to the next step—elevating 'order' into mandatory pattern, the loss of options, the restriction of choices—takes very little time, and does not necessarily require the machinations of an evil genius. Bureaucracy can make it happen all by itself; all that is needed is passivity, which by inertia surrenders to the purveyors of order the validity and general authority they invariably claim. (89 [Summer 1981]: 3)

This is, on one level, a classic assertion of the fundamental principle that Custom — or, in other words, community standards — is a major source and measure of law in British jurisprudence. On another, it is an expression of disdain toward individual rights and freedoms as distinguished from community norms and, in particular, disdain toward the conflict between what New refers to as the 'arrogance of the average' (3) and the will of the community.

Thus, as hyperboles of the 'average,' bureaucracies are opposed by public values insofar as they coincide with New's definition of literature, which entails, as we have already seen in Woodcock as well, a 'literary vision' that sustains vitality and, through the agency of the imagination, imparts strength. Further, lit-

erature is grounded in faith in what New terms 'public values' and 'the persistence of human aspiration,' which includes a 'passion for moral conscience and
the possibility of individual choice.' Where bureaucracy represents the triumph
of reductive, private systems canonized as order, literature, through the agency
of 'style,' shapes vision into meaning and gives that vision concrete form. Pas-
sivity motivates bureaucracy; faith motivates literature, which is to say the literary community or that group which, when he speaks approvingly, New
ordinarily designates simply as 'people' and with whom he associates 'reality.'

Woodcock's academy is New's bureaucracy; Woodcock's phantom structuralist in his 'mind-made web' is New's figure of abstraction and order, torn out
of the context of the nourishing community by his own arrogance and drive
toward power. 'Says who?' says the title of New's seventeenth editorial (90
[Autumn 1981]: 2). Suspicion, like two of New's other causes, French immer-
sion classes and quality children's literature, reinforces the norms of desirable
behaviour on the part of those admitted to his ideal, literary community, Like
Woodcock's suspicion of experimental writing, New's aversion toward forms of
behaviour—including textual 'behaviour'—which deviate from community
standards is grounded in assertions of freedom bounded by maps of known territory and of explorers' notebooks which communicate only insofar as readers
share their values and can recognize their experiences. One must never go too
far from home. As New says of the question of whether a 'taboo' language can
be effectively incorporated into a literary text, 'a reader must actually be able
to recognize what's going on, to distinguish between the verbal signs themselves
and the social significance that readers give them' (105 [Summer 1985]: 4). Or,
in the case, say, of *Robinson Crusoe* written in the language of *Finnegan's Wake*,
readers must be able to map the tale, experience situation and character, or the
journey will be for nought and the text inadmissable to literature, that long con-
versation which a community has with itself. Thinking about Eli Mandel's reflections on landscape and readership, New writes that in 'sharing the fiction,
[...] we reach back for ourselves into regions we scarcely know, and actively listen
for the voices we recognize as our own' (77 [Summer 1978]: 3). But what if we
don't recognize them? What if they are not our own voices?

Fearing abstraction, New fears difference; privileging a thin version of that
concept of community which the hermeneutic tradition sustains through reference to Talmud and Torah, to Gospels and generations of interpretation, New
writes (this time about computers but the reference goes, I think, much further)
'who writes it? who controls it? who reads it? and who judges it? [...] If under a
single control, who makes the decisions and who makes the profit?' (87 [Winter
1980]: 3) As self-selected spokesman for the community which constitutes his
norm—'we, and other members of the literary community,' as he puts it at one
point (86 [Autumn 1980]: 4)—New redistributes the 'profit' across the system.
That profit is apparently *Canadian Literature* with its assertion of the ambigu-

ity and plurality of language and of those 'puns, metaphors, and contextual distinctions' which, taken altogether, are analogous to 'a style of life [which] depends on circumstances, moral understandings, custom, ceremony and other non-exclusive claims upon a complex heritage' (87 [Winter 1980]:4).

But the 'complex heritage' studied in the pages of *Canadian Literature* since its inception has been, for the most part, the patriarchal heritage of Anglo-Canada with its subtle, gender-biased assumptions about 'moral understandings, custom, ceremony' and other tag phrases of a group long enough in power that the lexicon of their own comfort and status seems innocent. The Yeatsian overtones of New's grouping of morality with custom, and custom with heritage[4] also call to mind all too clearly the aristocratic heritage of the Anglo-Irish aristocracy and their attempts to gentrify an ancient civilization reduced to poverty and despair after centuries of oppression at the hands of its English 'owners.' The analogy could be developed in much more detail than is warranted in this paper but let me conclude by citing some statistics relevant to one sign of *Canadian Literature*'s editorial position with respect to an easy target group: women.

Given the almost universally acknowledged position of a number of women writers in the Canadian canon, one would expect their works to be well represented as subjects of articles published in the journal. And one would expect to find not only that works by female authors are regularly reviewed but also that female authors of articles and reviews are in evidence much of the time if not as frequently as male authors because of the statistical dominance of men in tenured positions at Assistant Professor level and above in university English departments in Canada. Such expectations prove, however, to have little to do with statistical reality. A glance at the graphs which form an Appendix to this paper will reveal the situation quickly, and provide comparative data about changes in journal policy between the Woodcock years (1959-77), or the first phase, and the New years (1977-87), or the second phase surveyed for this study.

Graphs 1 and 2 provide information about the sex of the authors of articles published in *Canadian Literature*. Here, male authors of articles published during the first phase account for 79.81% while those by females account for only 20.19%. During the second phase, articles by male authors decrease to 67.71% and those by females increase to 32.29%. Graph 3 focusses on the number of studies published by *Canadian Literature* of texts by female authors. During the first phase, the average is 17.44%; during the second, 26.38%. (Articles classified as having non-gender-specific subjects account for 28.95% during the first phase and 16.75% during the second.) The conclusion that stu-

---

4 Cf. 'A prayer for My Daughter': 'How but in custom and ceremony / Are innocence and beauty born? / Ceremony's a name for the rich horn, / And custom for the spreading laurel tree' (*Collected Poems* 2nd ed. [London: Macmillan, 1955]: 214).

dies of texts written by male authors are dominant — in fact, 53.16% during the first phase and 56.87% in the second — is inevitable. Finally, Graphs 4 through 8 inclusive provide data relevant to the sex of reviewers and the sex of the author of the works being reviewed. In the first phase, male reviewers constitute 80.94% of the total and female reviewers only 19.06%, while in the second phase, male reviewers decline to 62.64% and female reviewers increase to 37.36%. When reviews are classified according to the sex of authors of works reviewed, however, the pattern shifts and in the first phase we find 78.61% of texts by males and only 21.39% of texts by females while in the second phase we find 64.29% of texts reviewed are by male authors and 35.17% are by female authors.

The customs and ceremonies perpetuated here are very familiar ones although it is true, of course, that there are signs of improvement in the second phase of operations, chiefly in the increase in the number of female reviewers at work for the journal, and in the number of reviews published of books by women. However, figures like 32.29% (articles by women), 37.36% (female reviewers), and 26.38% (articles on texts written by women) indicate that, even in the improved, second phase of the journal's existence, there is much to be done. But, as editorial eighty-seven suggests, we are not 'in the land of either/or' (87[Winter 1980]: 2), and the inclusion of many marginalized groups (women, the indigenous peoples of Canada, those from minority groups outside the English- and French-speaking so-called 'founding peoples,' the literature of those who are not included in the 'main stream' because of class, sexual choice, race, religion, and so on) will not in itself solve the problems occasioned by the ideological conditions of production of *Canadian Literature*, whether past or present. An exclusionary bias which justifies itself in terms of notions of the 'average' cannot be undone by headcount.

Nor are numbers the point in themselves: adjusting statistical averages and institutionalizing 'norms' will not *de facto* change the 'maps and tales' which govern this editorial 'exploration.' As Canada moves beyond the Susanna Moodie topos, beyond the either/or double bind of knowing the language or declaring the place empty, neither the classical stance of the man speaking to men nor the post-Lacanian echo of the father's no will any longer suffice to contain the manifold writings of all of those whose place this is.

University of British Columbia

Appendix

I am indebted to my research assistants, Andrew Chesterman and Cynthia Flanders, for the collection of statistical data presented here, and to Ms Flanders for the graphs. In tabular form, the data are as follows:

	Woodcock as Editor	New as Editor
Articles		
By men:	79.81%	67.71%
By women:	20.19%	32.90%
On texts by men:	53.61%	56.87%
On texts by women:	17.44%	26.38%
On non-gender-specific subjects:	28.95%	16.75%
Reviews		
By men:	80.94%	62.64%
By women:	19.06%	37.36%
Of texts by men:	78.61%	62.49%
Of texts by women:	21.39%	35.71%

Much more extensive statistical studies would, of course, have to be undertaken in order to demonstrate how *Canadian Literature* fares in comparison with other Canadian literary journals. Based on an unpublished study of *Essays on Canadian Writing* done by Suzanne James, I would think *Canadian Literature*'s situation not an unusual one with respect to the categories considered above. James's study shows *ECW* as having published 68 articles and 47 reviews by women out of a total of 524 contributions made to the journal over twelve years (Winter 1974 - Fall 1986). In other words, only 22.72% of journal entries were written by women. (The number of texts written by female authors and reviewed or discussed in the pages of *ECW* for this period was not considered in Ms James's paper, 'An Analytical Study of *Essays on Canadian Writing*,' M.A. Graduating Essay, Dept. of English, Univ. of B.C., April 1987.)

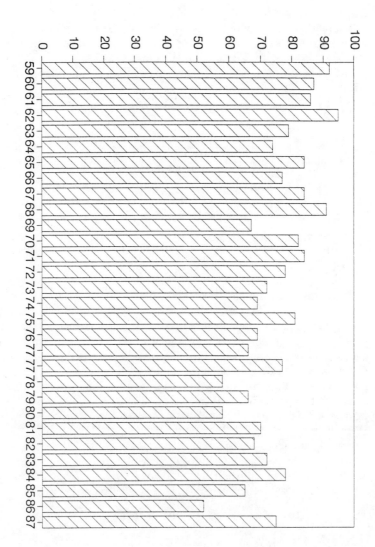

1. *Canadian Literature Articles*

By Male Authors

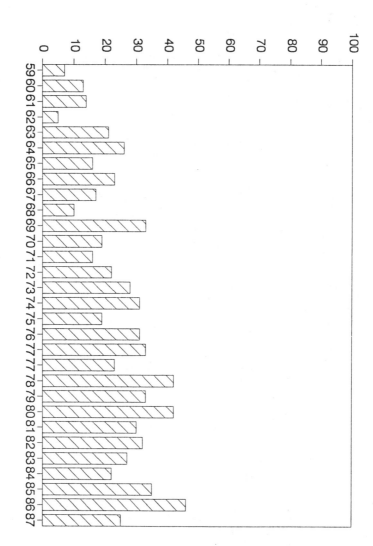

2. *Canadian Literature* Articles

By Female Authors

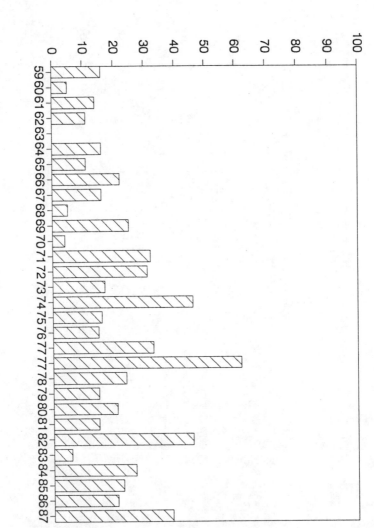

3. *Canadian Literature* Articles on Texts

By Female Authors

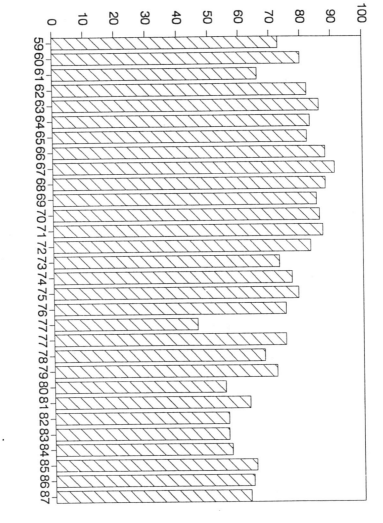

4. *Canadian Literature* Male Reviewers

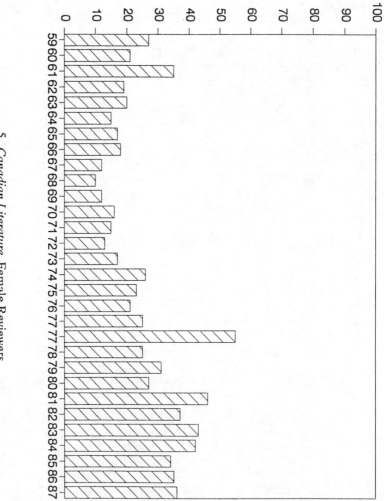

5. *Canadian Literature* Female Reviewers

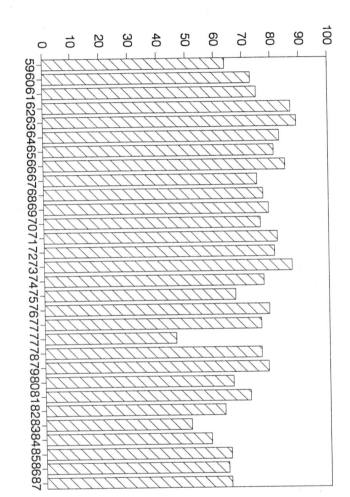

6. *Canadian Literature* Reviews of Texts

By Male Authors

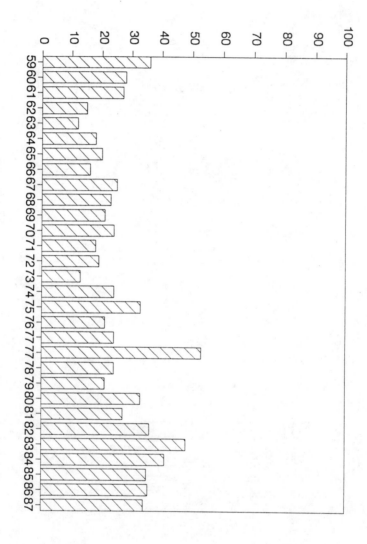

7. *Canadian Literature* Reviews of Texts

By Female Authors

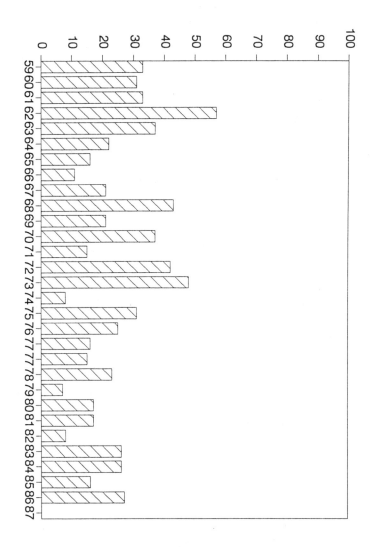

8. *Canadian Literature* Articles
on Non-Gender-Specific Subjects

CLAUDINE POTVIN

Postface

En présentant les Actes du deuxième colloque organisé par l'Institut de recherches en littérature comparée et centré sur les "Questions d'édition et de diffusion," l'équipe de chercheurs qui travaillent au projet de rédaction d'une histoire de l'institution littéraire au Canada entendait ainsi ouvrir la discussion sur un pôle auquel les travaux du premier colloque renvoyaient déjà. Certaine circularité de l'appareil institutionnel qui rend évident le lien entre les modes de réception et les modes de production du texte.[1]

Récemment, de nombreuses études ont montré comment les différentes lectures opérées par des agents multiples à divers niveaux (critique universitaire ou journalistique, presse, revues, médias, école, salons du livre, publicités, concours gouvernementaux, etc.) agissent directement sur les choix des éditeurs, les décisions des agences gouvernementales ou des jurés de sélection. Les instances de production sont en fait fortement marquées par les (et rarement autonomes face aux) instances de consécration ou de légitimation, surtout quand l'éditeur est lui-même un intellectuel ou un écrivain comme on l'a souvent signalé.

E. D. Blodgett remarque dans sa conclusion à l'édition des Actes du premier colloque qu'il était certes justifié de s'intéresser dans un premier temps aux problèmes de réception littéraire. "Inasmuch, écrivait-il, as our object is a history — indeed, histories — of a certain literary institution, it is no more than appropriate

---

1 Au sujet de la circularité éditoriale, voir Robert Giroux, "Le statut (fictif) de l'écrivain," *L'institution littéraire*, Ed. Maurice Lemire, Institut québécois de recherche sur la culture et Centre de recherche en littérature québécoise, 1986, 191-204.

to begin with the problem of reception, which as Felix Vodicka observes, is one of the principal tasks of the historian."[2] Blodgett propose de s'intéresser à un processus métacommunicationnel ou, pour le formuler dans les termes de Jacques Dubois, "éviter de partir d'une définition figée des institutions et, pour cela, préférer voir comment elles fonctionnent dans la structure sociale, quelle place elles y occupent, comment elles s'y articulent à d'autres ensembles."[3]

La première démarche de ce projet, d'où les différents colloques, consiste précisément à désigner des lieux, cerner des objets et des mouvements, élaborer des éléments de "définitions," répertorier des informations, nommer des catégories, bref, saisir le fonctionnement du/des code(s) littéraire(s) et culturel(s) canadien et québécois afin de jeter les bases d'une "certaine" histoire de l'institution littéraire canadienne. Ce deuxième recueil constitue donc une autre étape dans l'évolution du projet: les réflexions qui s'y trouvent portent sur un ensemble de questions fondamentales dans les secteurs de l'édition, de la diffusion et du financement des gouvernements. Elles éclairent une dimension importante de l'appareil institutionnel et montrent jusqu'à un certain point que les unités du système sont liées les unes aux autres et ne peuvent être analysées qu'en inter-relation.

Le thème de cette conférence situait d'emblée la littérature comme appareil et l'envisageait dans sa première phase, la production. Le producteur, c'est l'éditeur, remarque Robert Escarpit soit "l'entrepreneur qui prend la décision, responsable de fabriquer et de mettre en valeur le livre."[4] Jacques Michon et Richard Giguère considèrent le monde de l'édition comme "un lieu privilégié d'observation des stratégies, des rites, des règles qui président à l'instauration du littéraire."[5] Tout choix suppose une stratégie, une position esthétique ou idéologique situable dans une lutte du pouvoir et pour le pouvoir. L'éditeur joue un rôle d'autant plus important qu'il intègre, souvent simultanément, le discours de la censure transmis par la tradition (l'enfance, la famille, l'école, le

---

2 E. D. Blodgett, "Afterword," *Problems of literary reception/Problèmes de réception littéraire*, ed. E. D. Blodgett et A. G. Purdy, Edmonton, Institut de recherches en littérature comparée, Université de l'Alberta, 1988, p. 173.

3 Jacques Dubois, *L'institution de la littérature*, Bruxelles, Fernand Nathan/Editions Labor, 1978, p. 32.

4 Robert Escarpit, *Le littéraire et le social*, Paris, Flammarion, 1970, p. 32.

5 Voir l'article de J. Michon et R. Giguère dans cette collection, "Pour une histoire de l'édition littéraire moderne au Québec," p. 27.

groupe social, le milieu, le travail), formation scolaire et sociale[6] — l'effet répressif —, et l'attente — l'effet avant-garde — d'un sujet littéraire lui-même marqué par l'*habitus*. Pour reprendre à nouveau les termes de Michon, ajoutons que:

> L'éditeur en tant qu'acteur du jeu institutionnel se trouve donc au carrefour de plusieurs lieux de détermination. Diachroniquement, il est tributaire d'une tradition de lecture et d'un fonds littéraire. Synchroniquement, il s'interpose entre les intérêts des auteurs et ceux des lecteurs pour les ajuster les uns aux autres et en tirer des bénéfices. On ne peut cerner la spécificité de son rôle qu'en le situant à l'intersection de ces deux axes de légitimation.[7]

Il s'agit donc d'en tirer aussi des bénéfices, bien sûr. Tout éditeur cherche à établir son pouvoir et assurer une certaine stabilité financière: réussite monétaire, ne serait-ce que pour pouvoir continuer de publier, rentabilité de l'entreprise, prestige, reconnaissance, contrôle des marchés, distribution efficace, ventes, etc.

Mais comment vendre s'il n'y a pas de lecteurs? André Vanasse, Byrna Barclay et Ken Norris ont signalé ici l'ampleur du problème au Québec et dans le reste du Canada. Plusieurs des textes recueillis dans ce volume s'attardent à l'aspect économique du marché du livre. André Vanasse, par exemple, a dressé un tableau assez sombre de la situation au Québec, tentant d'établir un rapport entre le social, l'historique, l'économique et le fait littéraire. Frank Davey pour sa part s'est penché sur l'histoire de l'édition canadienne-anglaise vue à travers ce qu'il nomme le "petty commodity mode."

Toutefois, ce qui ressort de toutes ces considérations d'ordre économique, c'est l'importance du rôle de l'Etat dans la production et la diffusion des oeuvres littéraires. Plusieurs participants (Byrna Barclay, Ray Ellenwood, Constance Rooke, Francess G. Halpenny, Jacques Pelletier) s'y sont intéressé. Dans la majorité des cas, les intervenants s'accordent pour proclamer la nécessité des subventions gouvernementales tout en lamentant le manque d'autonomie qu'elles présupposent parfois ou les interférences indésirables de l'Etat au niveau administratif par exemple. Jacques Pelletier, par contre, témoignant d'une expérience d'édition universitaire, remarque qu'il est possible et avantageux pour l'édition savante de s'autonomiser et de créer alors son propre mode de fonctionnement.

6 Voir Joseph Melançon, Clément Moisan et Max Roy, *Le discours d'une didactique. La formation littéraire dans l'enseignement classique au Québec (1852-1967)*, Québec, Centre de recherche en littérature québécoise, 1988.

7 Jacques Michon, "L'édition littéraire pour grand public de 1940 à 1960," *L'institution littéraire, op.cit.*, p. 167.

Selon Ray Ellenwood, l'impact que l'aide gouvernementale a eu sur le développement de la traduction littéraire au Canada révèle les dangers d'une industrie qui opérerait essentiellement grâce à l'aide des fonds publics. Constance Rooke, au contraire, proclame que les petites revues ne sont pas suffisamment subventionnées au Canada alors qui Silvie Bernier qui a traité de la fonction de l'illustration dans la légitimation de la littérature, fait état de la distance, en termes de qualité du produit fini, qui sépare souvent les ouvrages subventionnés des autres.

D'un autre côté, les petites maisons d'éditions, après avoir publié le nombre de livres possible selon les argents qui leur ont été distribués, ne sont plus en mesure d'en assurer la distribution ou la diffusion. Autre facette du problème: les nombreux comités de sélection constitués pour otorguer des bourses aux écrivain(e)s, aux maisons d'édition, aux revues savantes, aux petites revues de création, aux projets de recherches, à la publication de thèses ou d'ouvrages spécialisés, etc., sont composés des mêmes membres qui demandent ces subventions (écrivain(e)s et/ou enseignant(e)s le plus souvent universitaires). Dans l'institution littéraire à laquelle nous nous referons, nous nous jugeons les uns les autres et nous nous accordons de l'argent les uns aux autres, plus ou moins aimablement selon la position, le statut, que nous occupons dans le système. En d'autres mots, "Le marché restreint, voilà ce que nous, littéraires, de nos universités, de nos chroniques, de nos revues, appelons littérature, voilà ce que nous instituons littérature."[8]

Si Denis St-Jacques nous propose de continuer d'étudier le champ de production restreinte "et le sort des habitus qui le déterminent," il nous recommande de nous intéresser également à l'institution de la littérature de grande diffusion. Dans un cas comme dans l'autre, il faut s'interroger encore sur qui lit quoi?, quand et pourquoi des lecteurs, des lectrices donnés lisent tel ou tel livre? comme le suggère Francess G. Halpenny:

> This conference has demonstrated the need to look with more information and greater depth at the effect upon literary traditions and current literary expectations of where and how authors write and publishers publish. We need dispassionate, disinterested, and extensive accounts of how and why programs of public support for literature have been organized, how they have interacted with one another and with the book trade.[9]

Bien qu'il reste beaucoup à faire, ce colloque, parmi d'autres à venir, a certainement aidé à placer ces questions dans un cadre plus précis, celui d'une certaine histoire d'une certaine institution littéraire. Quoique la réflexion

---

8　Denis St-Jacques, "L'envers de l'institution," *L'institution littéraire, op. cit.*, p. 42.
9　Voir ici Francess G. Halpenny, "Scholarly Publishing in Canada," p. 115.

théorique et pratique amorcée au Québec semble nettement plus élaborée (et je renvoie aux enquêtes détaillées réalisées à l'intérieur des groupes de recherches bien établis - CRELIQ, GRELQ, IQRC -), il n'en reste pas moins que la participation et la collaboration des chercheurs québécois et anglophones à nos colloques permettront d'élargir la compréhension du phénomène de l'institution littéraire canadienne dans son ensemble ou des multiples institutions qui s'y greffent et la composent. L'enthousiasme avec lequel les critiques et historiens ont répondu permet d'envisager des échanges productifs et dynamiques lors des prochaines rencontres.

Les futurs colloques prévus par l'Institut sont les suivants:

3. Préfaces et manifestes littéraires. (Image du public dans le texte et définition du texte à l'intention du public.)

4. Les littératures de moindre diffusion. (Évolution des *autres* littératures canadiennes.)

5. Les genres littéraires. (Importance relative des genres, styles, modes, etc., selon les époques.)

6. La littérature au féminin. (Mécanismes de distribution; rôle des presses, revues, magazines, etc.; influence des théories féministes américaine et française; rôle des programmes de promotion de la femme, colloques, sociétés, etc.)

7. Traditions orales indigènes. (Conservation et diffusion; influence des traditions orales sur le folklore et la littérature des colons et sur les écrivains canadiens.)

8. La traduction littéraire. (Rôle de la traduction dans l'évolution de la littérature au Canada; réception et distribution de textes traduits venant de l'étranger.)

9. La paralittérature. (Littérature pour la jeunesse, science-fiction, romans policiers, romans Harlequin, etc.)

10. La canonisation. (Mécanismes de sélection, de valorisation et de consécration des oeuvres littéraires.)

Ces colloques tendent à révéler que l'ensemble des recherches présentement en cours sur l'histoire et l'institution littéraires québécoise et canadienne combinent les analyses de type socio-critique et l'approche polysystémique du champ littéraire.

La théorie du polysystème représente l'hypothèse générale de travail adop-
tée par le groupe. Dans sa brève introduction suivie d'une bibliographie sur la
notion de polysystème, Milan V. Dimic et Marguerite K. Garstin insistent sur
le caractère ouvert de la théorie et sur le fait que "this theory promises to be
particulary useful in studying the totality of a multilingual literature such as Canada's."[10]
Théorie d'abord formulée par Itamar Even-Zohar et, à sa suite, par ses collègues et disciples de l'Institut de Poétique et de Sémiotique Porter, de l'Université de Tel-Aviv, elle pose le système littéraire comme un ensemble de
relations ou d'éléments interdépendants, entendus dans un rapport opposition-
nel de sous-systèmes primaires et secondaires, constamment en mouvance, tra-
vaillés sans cesse les uns par les autres. Even-Zohar écrit à ce propos:

> The idea that semiotic phenomena, i.e., sign-governed human patterns of communication
> (e.g., culture, language, literature, society) should be regarded as systems rather than con-
> glomerates of disparate elements, has become one of the leading ideas of our time in most
> sciences of man. Thus, the positivistic collection of data, ..., has been replaced by a
> *functional* approach based on the analysis of *relations*. Viewed as systems, it became
> possible to describe and explain how the various semiotic aggregates *operate*.[11]

Par conséquent, le texte ne pourrait plus se définir ou s'analyser à partir d'un
modèle figé, d'une norme statique, situés dans un champ historique ou autre;
il faudrait plutôt chercher "for the shifts in models in terms of *relations* within
the period, and also *relational* shifts outside the individual historical period."[12]
La notion même de littérature qui a longtemps reposé sur l'existence d'*un* canon, apparemment unique, doit composer avec des éléments oppositionnels,
doubles ou multiples: texte canonisé/ texte non-canonisé, "haute" ou bonne lit-
térature/ "basse" ou mauvaise littérature, monopole-centre/ région-périphérie-
marge, culture savante, officielle/ culture populaire, vulgaire, contestataire,
texte créateur/ texte dérivé, etc. Il faut entendre l' exclamation de Lucie Robert
qui se refusait à admettre que l'étude de la littérature fasse abstraction des oeu-

---

10 Milan V. Dimic et Marguerite K. Garstin, *The polysystem theory: a brief introduction, with
   bibliography*, Edmonton, Research Institute for Comparative Literature, Université de
   l'Alberta, 1988, p. 6. Egalement paru en "Appendice" dans les Actes du premier colloque
   de l'Institut de recherches en littérature comparée, *Problems of literary
   reception/Problèmes de réception littéraire*, ed. E. D. Blodgett et A. G. Purdy, *op. cit.*,
   177-196.
11 Itamar Even-Zohar, "Polysystem theory," *Poetics Today*, 1: 1-2(1979), p. 288.
12 Milan V. Dimic et Marguerite K. Garstin, *op. cit.*, p. 3.

vres ratées dans ce contexte: "La frontière du littéraire est ailleurs que dans les critères de qualité," écrivait-elle à ce propos.[13]

Le polysystème renvoie donc à un principe d'interrelation entre les éléments qui le composent et de circulation, non plus seulement en diachronie ou en synchronie, mais en multiples échanges à plusieurs niveaux, échanges dynamiques entre les sous-systèmes agissant les uns sur (et avec ou contre) les autres. En inscrivant nos recherches sur l'histoire de l'institution littéraire dans le cadre de la théorie du polysystème, nous espérons rendre compte du "jeu" par lequel l'appareil signifie et se signifie (ses règles, ses codes, ses fonctions) ainsi que des différents discours qui parlent le texte et qui parlent en lui, voire aussi faire entendre la polyphonie des voix et des langages d'un territoire.

Université de l'Alberta

13 Lucie Robert, "Institutions, formes institutionnelles et droit," *L'institution littéraire*, op. cit., p. 18.